Nuclear Armed Regional Conflicts:
South Asia in Transition

NUCLEAR ARMED REGIONAL CONFLICTS

South Asia in Transition

Kwang Ho CHUN

CHONBUK NATIONAL UNIVERSITY PRESS

CONTENTS

PREFACE

"The advertisement for Cadbury's Temptations was issued entirely in good faith, with no intentions whatsoever to offend the sentiments of the public that may have been offended."

The above statement was released by an official from Cadbury's India Limited in response to an advertisement for a new confectionary product. The advertisement depicted a map of Jammu and Kashmir along with the caption: *'I'm good, I'm tempting, I'm too good to share. What am I? Cadbury's Temptation or Kashmir?'* The advert was, quite rightly, viewed by politicians in both India and Pakistan as abhorrent. It trivialised the most sensitive international relations dilemma between the two states. A dispute that has caused the deaths of millions of people and, as many commentators have written, tensions over the territory of Jammu and Kashmir is symbolic of the animosity between India and Pakistan. However, the Cadbury debacle did allude to the misunderstanding between two intractable foes and, perhaps unwittingly, hit upon the notion of Lord Palmerston's famous aphorism, uttered in the House of Commons in 1848: 'states have no permanent friends or permanent enemies, merely permanent interests'.

After seven decades of war the relationship between India and Pakistan is at a crossroads. The states have a choice: continue the stalemate, with both governments poised for nuclear exchange, or, take advantage of the numerous opportunities for cooperation and prosperity that positive bilateral relationships can offer. However, the choice is not easy given the emotion that the world's most enduring conflict has generated. Moreover, it is the UNs longest standing peace keeping mission, having commenced in January 1949. The casualty statistics since the partition on 14 August 1947 are morose: millions have died and millions more have been displaced from their homes. The violence that ensued from the division alone caused between '100,000 and one million deaths and approximately 15 million people were forced to leave their homes to re-settle in the new states'. More sobering is the fact that since the 1947-48 First Indo-Pakistan War, millions more have died in the following conflicts: the Second War of 1965, the Bangladesh War of 1971, and the Kargil War of 1999. Furthermore, there have been a number of armed conflicts that stopped just short of all-out war: the 'Punjab War Scare (1951), Runn of Kutch (1965), the Brasstacks Crisis (1987), the Kashmir Nuclear Crisis (1990), the India-Pakistan Nuclear Test Crisis (1998), the New Delhi Parliament attack crisis, (2001), the Kaluchack attack crisis (2002), and the Mumbai terrorist attacks (2008).' These crises constitute a legacy of inhumane treatment of belligerents, not to mention innocent civilians.

Given their history of conflict, what hope is there for India and Pakistan to resolve their long-standing dispute? Especially, the situation in South Asia has been totally changed after the possession of nuclear warheads by both states. Nowadays, South Asian conflict is a one of the utmost dangerous conflict in the world since they are ready to use nuclear if necessary.

Perhaps the noticeable transformations that have taken place since partition will provide an answer. Once considered as a 'minor-power' confrontation based on ideological divergences, the Indo-Pakistan conflict now has serious implications for the entire international system. The ramifications of terrorist networks in Pakistan and Kashmir has demanded that leading world powers focus on the Indo-Pak dialogue. Furthermore, where realist perceptions appear to have once predominated the thoughts of the opponents in this dyadic confrontation; the pure *realpolitik* pursuits have been altered by both sides' possession of nuclear weapons. Another international relations conundrum that is worthy of consideration in the South Asian context concerns the need to identify whether realist assumptions have had the effect of stabilising the region or promoting further conflict. Furthermore, has colonial association with the European 'Westphalian' state system failed to adequately consider important socio - political aspects of these South - Asian states?

Emerging from this transformation are a number of core issues that constitute the crux of the enduring Indo - Pakistan confrontation. Some of these are intractable, however, some are opportunities for peace. This book will identify the core obstacles impeding peace and determine whether these obstacles can be successfully removed or transformed. In doing so the primary question concerning the prospect of further conflict between India and Pakistan can be answered.

This book will begin by looking at the historical context of South Asia as a region, a region of conflict, and a region of nuclearisation. Then the Indo - Pakistan war and analyse whether the causes of the conflict contain enduring issues for the future. Where necessary this book will make use various approaches applicable to each chapters' different angles. But mostly Waltz's three levels of analysis for causes of war: the State, the Individual and the International System, in order to distil the origins of the enduring conflict. The aim of the book is to demonstrate that the issues concerning the territory of Kashmir constitute the main cause of friction between India and Pakistan. Additionally, the historical analysis will show that the two states failed to acknowledge the need to adequately consider Kashmiri, socio - religious elements of friction, and instead pursued realist principles that threw the opponents into a perpetual cycle of conflict.

In the subsequent chapter, additional causal factors, mostly nuclear issues in the region that have emerged since 1970s will be identified and ascribed to their effect on the Indo - Pakistan relationship, including a brief examination of the effect of globalisation in the South Asian context.

Given the underlying causes of tension, the aim of this book will be to reviewing whether potential for peace within South Asia exists through the people - centric benefits of cross - Line of Control interactions framed within any peace - building model. Furthermore, could such outcomes 'spill - over' and assuage the regional level, peace - inhibiting conflict causes outlined in the initial sections of this book.

Some of chapters in this book are fully revised and updated from previous monograph and journal publications such as Korea International Institute for Economic Policy, 2016, *The Journal of Peace Studies*, Vol. 17, No. 6, 2016, *The Korean Journal of Area Studies*, Vol. 35, No. 3, 2017 and *Crisisonomy*, Vol. 14, No. 4, 2018;

Just like my other books *Democratic Peace Building and Security in East Asia: A Post - Cold War Analysis, Africa: A Region of Never Ending Conflict, and Complexity in Crisis: Deconstructing Conflict in the Middle East*, this is a series of my academic efforts for primary researches of "Conflicts in the World". I personally hope that any academic approaches could make a just small corner stone for broader world peace by an academic studying consistently the subject of peace and war.

I

GEOPOLITICS OF KASHMIR:
Keeping India and Pakistan Apart

> "Only chaos followed the partition of [British] India, neither the Hindus nor the Muslims have benefited from the partition...instead [the countries have] suffered economically, internationally and...[are without] prestige or power... the partition gave [rise to] the Kashmir problem (Chitkara 2002, xvii)."

1. INTRODUCTION

The dispute over Kashmir has kept India and Pakistan apart since the creation of the two separate countries on the partition of British India in 1947. The relations between Pakistan and India have led to three major wars and a number of skirmishes, with the incident at Kargil in 1999 being the most recent. At the time of partition it was thought by many that the two successor states would work in collaboration. The creation of Pakistan was thought at the time to have been sufficient to satisfy Muslim aspirations thereby allowing the essentials of the unity of the sub - continent to be retained (Lamb 1992, 1).

History has since shown that the reality has been very different from those early assumptions about the future of the two new countries. The dispute over Kashmir has plagued India and Pakistan, driving their domestic and foreign policy security agendas at the expense of other, perhaps more fundamental and pressing needs, including the respective state infrastructures, as well as the economic, welfare and educational needs of the people. Resolving the Kashmir issue has been stated by many commentators as the major key to realising most of these objectives. In this paper I contend however, that the conflict between the two countries has endured for a number of reasons and not least because domestically it suited the needs of each country. The Kashmir dispute has enjoyed differing levels of interest from the international community. This interest has varied depending on the levels of conflict between the two protagonists; the superpower alignments during the cold war; and the changing order of the current international environment.

The 11 September 2001 bombings in New York and the events of 7 July 2005 in London brought further international focus on the disputed Kashmir region. Although denied by Pakistan, India has long claimed that Pakistan provided support to Kashmiri separatists and insurgents in the disputed region of Kashmir.[1] W John asserts that such groups have been able to use the Kashmir dispute as the basis for their actions and as a way of exploiting the terrorist networks within Pakistan to further a more global campaign of terror (John 2005). This has resulted in the Kashmir issue being elevated in the national and international arenas. Pakistan denies the allegations by India, asserting instead that it only provided moral support to the Kashmiri struggle for self-determination (Beach 2003). The severity of the situation was evidenced by the level and intensity of the international mediation attempts, particularly by the United States and China.

In order to analyse the key issues that have kept India and Pakistan apart, this paper will first place the India-Pakistan relationship vis-à-vis Kashmir in historical context. The paper will then look at the impact of domestic issues, and the differing perspectives of both countries. The paper will then move on to consider the enduring nature of the conflict, including alignments with the superpowers. The paper then considers the more recent events and the changing climate for negotiations. The paper will show that the dispute has been intractable not only because it is a 'paired minority conflict (Cohen 2003)' or as T V Paul and others define it 'an enduring rivalry (Paul 2005)', but also because of leadership weaknesses. Although necessary to set the historical context in which the two countries have been in conflict, this paper moves away from looking at the Kashmir dispute from purely an historical perspective.

---

1 The term Kashmir in this paper will include the states of Jammu and Kashmir.

Instead the paper argues that the conflict between the two countries has become entrenched, due to mistrust and nationalism embedded in the differing perspectives over the Kashmir sovereignty Plebiscite and accession decision. Different from other work in this area, this paper asserts that the dispute has been deliberately used by successive Indian and Pakistani leaders to gain economic and military development aid from alliances and partners. At odds with other commentators this paper asserts that the current international environment and economic imperatives are too significant for either country to ignore. Notwithstanding the continuing domestic and nationalist considerations, India's economic rise can bring development benefits to Pakistan. As such this paper argues against the realist held position that the two countries will continue to build their respective military forces at the expense of all other pressing requirements (Waltz 1959). Instead this paper argues that the emphasis will now shift away from the two countries being conflict prone to one of limited economic interdependence. This coupled with commitment from each countries leadership and international pressure has significantly increased the prospect for long term meaningful peace (Friedman 1999).

2. THE CONFLICT IN CONTEXT

The Kashmir dispute is anchored in the partition of India and Pakistan in 1947 and perhaps as early as 1940, when aware of the eventual pull back of the British Empire, the Muslim League proclaimed a post-war plan for the future of the Northern provinces of the sub-continent. The plan proposed that those provinces with Muslim majorities should be brought together to form a country for the Muslims. R Johnson states that the dispute has 'been distorted by more recent issues (Johnson 2005).' S Widmalm concurs with this view, asserting that it would be a mistake to see the conflict from simply a Western, Pakistani, or Indian perspective and then to propose solutions to the issues. In more recent times the West has viewed the conflict as a part of the Islamization of Asia or the spread of global ethnic conflict. Widmalm claims that:

> The latter description goes with a view of ethnic identity as something different in kind from other denominators such as class, and is therefore uniquely capable of inflaming political competition (Wildmalm 2002, 2).

The arguments in much of the literature about the Kashmir conflict resulting from cultural, ethnic, or socioeconomic factors are contested in this paper. Wildmalm supports this position, asserting that it has been political variables and a lack of institutions which have caused the troubles. It is therefore not feasible to accept the commonly asserted view that the recent conflicts during the 1980s and 1990s in Kashmir were the result of cultural, religious and economic differences alone (Wildmalm 2002). The India - Pakistan conflict has been described by T V Paul as an 'enduring rivalry' in which the military stalemate is only one part of the story. Paul sees the India - Pakistan conflict as simultaneously being over territory, national identity, and power positioning within the region (Paul 2005, 8). In order to better understand the Kashmir dispute, there has to be an appreciation of the situation as it existed at the time of the partition. This understanding is crucial today as it was then because as Lamb puts it:

> The language of the Kashmir dispute...has evolved over the decades; and, to add to the confusion, considerations which were totally absent in 1947 are now advanced as if they have always been of fundamental importance (Lamb 1992, 2).

2.1 Same River: Different Streams

The two divergent views over Kashmir, one from the Pakistani and the other from the Indian camps, stem from the circumstances leading up to and including the delayed decision made by the Maharaja of Jammu and Kashmir in October 1947 to accede to India. S Cohen sees Kashmir as both 'a cause and the consequence of the India - Pakistan conundrum.' Accepting the complexities of the strategic and territorial dimensions, Cohen claims that the dispute is essentially about justice and people (Cohen 2003). The issues over Kashmir are so intractable that it is not easy to define between domestic politics and foreign policy. Both Cohen and Lamb thus assert that the Kashmir conflict is not only about territory, resources and people but that it also includes the clash between the different identities and self imagination. It is from these different self images that stem the divergent strategies, histories, and policies.

From Pakistan's point of view, India is at fault for not allowing the Kashmiri people their right to justice, through the denial of the free will to either join Pakistan or India. Of similar significance to Pakistan is the non acceptance by India of its legitimate existence. The Pakistanis tend to claim the moral and legal ground and with some justification (Hussain 2004, 14 - 20). The accession of Kashmir to India is seen, (especially by Pakistan and the UN), as in violation of the very concept which was put in place for the sub - continent to be partitioned. Indeed R Johnson notes that as far back as 1916, Mohammed Ali Jinnah, at the time a lawyer in the Muslim League,[2] signed the Lucknow Pact with the Indian National Congress, (led by Mohandas Gandhi and Jawaharlal Nehru), offering support to the Congress in return for the recognition of separate Muslim electorates. Despite initially accepting the proposals for separate Muslim electorates in 1916, the Indian Congress Party rejected the idea in the constitutional proposal it made in 1928. Although he resigned from the Congress due to its lack of support for Muslim interests, Jinnah continued to press for an independent Muslim state, (as first put forward by the poet Muhammad Iqbal in 1930). In March 1940, Jinnah, got the support from the Muslim League for a separate Pakistan in what became known as the Lahore Resolution (Paul 2005, 6). With the gap between the Congress and the League already wide, the failure of the May 1944 Gandhi and Jinnah talks and the June 1945 Simla conference only added to the deadlock.

India on the other hand asserts its position over Kashmir based on the instrument of accession as carried out by the Maharajah of Kashmir at the time of partition, (against the wishes of the majority, the Pakistanis

2 The Muslim League Party was actually formed in December 1906. The Leagues' claims for separate electorates was accepted by the British in the Government of India Act of 1909, because it was seen as helping to weaken the nationalist movement. Over time, however, this policy helped unify the Muslim community and helped foster the ides of the creation of Pakistan.

would argue). India also contests that Pakistan is a state 'defined and driven by its religion and is given to its irredentist aspirations in Kashmir because it is unwilling to accept the fact of a secular India (Cohen 2003).' Therefore from an Indian perspective, (arguably nominally secular in nature), the fact that Kashmir happens to be a region with a Muslim majority does not and should not determine its fate with a Muslim nation. Thus the presence of this minority within India belies the need for Pakistan to exist. In essence, having declared itself a multi ethnic secular state at the time of partition, India argues that religion alone does not make a nation. This is, however, at odds with what Jinnah espoused when he called for a religious based partition of British India. It is from this basic assumption that elements from within the Indian ruling elites make assertion about the idea of Pakistan re-uniting with India. And it is from this same basis that the Pakistanis assert that India has yet to reconcile itself to the existence of Pakistan (Cohen 2003).

After the Second World War the relations between Hindus and Muslims deteriorated considerably. Under the circumstances the transfer of power was brought forward from 1 July 1948, to independence for India and Pakistan on the 15 August 1947 (Johnson 2005). The announcement for independence was accompanied by the acceptance by the British that the partition would take place along Muslim and non-Muslim lines. A Boundary Commission was established in order to orchestrate the demarcation (Lamb 1992, 103).

The partition resulted in Pakistan gaining the majority of the British-administered areas in the North West and Bengal and the remainder of British India became India. The fate of the princely states was less definite and did not fall under the same jurisdiction, allowing them the option to join either India or Pakistan. Although the large majority of the princely states joined either India or Pakistan, three remained independent of both. Theses included Jammu and Kashmir in the north, Hyderabad in the south and Junagadh in the west. Both Hyderabad and Junagadh had Muslim rulers over Hindu majority populations and over time both acceded to India by way of 'internal revolt and or Indian police actions (Paul 2005).' With a Hindu ruler over a Muslim majority, Kashmir emerged the most contentious. The partition was not without atrocities. Partition resulted in the migration of over six million people from either side. It is claimed that rioting, massacres and sustained fighting accounted for in the region of 500, 000 lives (Johnson 2005). A period which would not be easily eradicated from the psyche of both nations people. It was during this period that the Maharaja of Kashmir, Hari Sing, delayed the decision to join either Pakistan or India. His decision to first remain independent and then to eventually accede to India does not sit easily with Pakistan. The discontent was further fuelled by the fact that the boundary awards were not seen as entirely impartial by Pakistan, especially when around seven majority Muslim districts were apportioned to India, with no non - Muslim regions being assigned to Pakistan.

Pakistan saw Mountbatten as being partial towards India and believed that he had unduly influenced the Boundary Commission set up by Sir Cyril Radcliffe. Although denied for decades by India, these earlier suspicions by Pakistan were made apparent in 1992 after the publications in the UK of the documents concerning the Transfer of Power, where 'evidence points to British manipulation in order to provide India with a border with Kashmir (Beaumont 1992).' Although weak, it can be argued, that this does not translate into an endorsement for accession. Nonetheless the doubts in Pakistan had been planted. This makes it even more crucial that the period between partition and Kashmiri accession to India is studied and understood. In doing so it should allow us to shed light on the Pakistani assertions concerning the Kashmir sovereignty plebiscite; the political circumstances under which accession decisions were made and the role played by India during this violent but crucial period.

3. THE PARTITION OF KASHMIR

3.1 Rise of Nationalism

Unlike the other Princely States of the British Raj, Kashmir was not going to be easily absorbed in to either of the two independent states of

British India. Kashmir was strategically located and for many decades had been used by the British to provide security on the northern frontier (Wildmalm 2002; Lamb 1992). The British achieved this without hostility, allowing the Princely State to operate independently in return for providing mountain defences for British India from possible Russian threats. As such Hari Singh had good grounds for believing he could retain Kashmir as an independent state without absorption in to India or Pakistan. In the case of India and Pakistan, however, 'Kashmir became a trial of national will and a question of territorial sovereignty (Johnson 2005, 95).'

In order to retain independence from both, Hari Singh sought a Stand Still Agreement. Pakistan became a signatory to the 'stand still agreement' whereas India did not (Schofield 2000, 40 - 42). Despite political negotiations within Kashmir at the time, (in October 1947), the situation on the ground deteriorated with ethnic clashes, the clamp down by the Maharajah's mainly Sikh and Hindu forces and a growing revolt by Muslims in Kashmir (Schofield 2000). So began a bloody and violent period which quickly and significantly created the link with religion. The uprising in 1947 was not only about possible Indian rule over Kashmir; it was concerned more with the notion of Kashmir being self governed. Kashmiri's, Sheik Abdullah wanted self rule and autonomy from both Pakistan and India (Stoke 2006, 7). The Muslim revolt within Kashmir was supported by 'Pushtun Afridi' tribesmen, who came across the Pakistani border. As these forces advanced on the capital, Srinagar, it is not difficult to see why Hari Singh would have been eager to secure the support from India in order to retain power over Kashmir. Johnson claims that Hari Singh appealed directly to the newly formed Indian government for military assistance. It was Mountbatten who accepted Singh's plea but on the condition that the Kashmiri people were offered a referendum to decide their future. Thus Pakistan's claims to the right of the Kashmiri people to a plebiscite over its future, is not without foundation. It could be argued that military support by India, (through Nehru), would have been conditional on the Maharajah acceding Kashmir to India. The Maharajah, having agreed to a 'stand still agreement,' should not have approached India and the accession, (according to Pakistan), should not have taken place against the wishes of the Muslim majority. Pakistan therefore asserts that the accession to India, by the Maharaja, was without legal foundation. India has countered this assertion stating that the uprising was instigated and supported by Pakistan and therefore any claims of illegitimacy are firmly placed at Pakistan's door (Schofield 2000, 71). These claims by India are disputed according to accounts by Schofield and other prominent commentators such as Lamb.

3.2 Mistrust Established

The Stand Still Agreement was not joined by India because India wanted to 'examine its implications and therefore left the state alone.' Yet India did sign the Stand Still Agreement with the state of Hyderabad, thus adding to the mounting suspicion Pakistan had over Indian designs for the future of Kashmir (Sultan 2000, 165). Very serious doubts remain over the timing of the accession agreement. India claims it had the legitimate right to send Indian troops in to Kashmir because at that time the Maharajah had acceded to India and therefore Kashmir formed part of India. Yet according to Schofield the sequence of events, concerning the signing of the accession agreement and the deployment of the Indian troops, do not corroborate this claim. Instead, notes Lamb, it is interesting that 'the Indian government found it necessary to maintain in official accounts, (of the journeys of its key official at the time, V P Menon), in order to support their argument that the Maharaja acceded to India before Indian troops were sent to Srinagar (Schofield 2000, 58).' As such it has been argued that accession before intervention, gave India the legal right to be in Kashmir. This by implication also allowed it to control the holding of a plebiscite and not to have to concede to any proposals by Pakistan (Schofield 2000, 58). During this unclear and complex time there were various significant political parties at work. Sultan claims that the Kashmir Muslim Conference, which was a significant political voice in Jammu and Kashmir, passed a resolution calling for accession to Pakistan. At the same time the National Conference, led by Sheik Abdullah and the Indian National Congress, were courting each other with a view to Abdullah becoming the leader in Kashmir and thus being favourable towards India (Sultan 2000, 165). Furthermore the accession was meant to have been temporary. Mountbatten, aware of the need for legal formalities to be in place, required accession to be a temporary measure, prior to either a referendum, a plebiscite, elections, or at the very least representative public meetings (Sultan 2000, 52). Schofield points out however, that according to Nehru's biographer, Sarvepallie Gopal, neither Nehru nor Patel attached much importance to these statements by Mountbatten. Pakistani suspicions over the role of the Governor General are therefore further deepened because had Mountbatten not insisted on an accession, the Indian presence in Kashmir would, for legal reasons, have had to have been temporary and some form of referendum for Kashmir would have been more of a reality.

The revolt started by the people of Poonch against the Maharaja of Kashmir spread to Mirpur and parts of Jammu and developed in to a full scale rebellion. Indian troops were deployed at the request of the Maharaja, but he also became a victim of the full scale incursion by the Indian forces. The Maharaja was forced into exile and abdication. Pakistan was unwilling to allow India to suppress what it saw as a popular uprising in a state it took as belonging to Pakistan. It deployed troops in support of the Muslim Kashmiris, against the Indian forces and so began the first of the Pakistan - Indian wars. As the situation worsened, ironically it was India who took the case to the United Nations Security Council (United Nations 1948, 166). For Pakistan, Kashmir not only became an issue of national identity and self - determination, Kashmir became symbolic of Pakistan's struggle for survival against a giant neighbor (Johnson 2005, 96).

This first war was concluded in 1948, with neither side making any significant gains or bringing the dispute to a conclusive point. The United Nations brokered cease - fire of Jan 1949 established the Line of Control. Pakistan was to formally control what became Azad Kashmir, which was approximately one third of the state and India was to control the Jammu and Kashmir state. The proclamation by the United Nations

Commission for India and Pakistan (UNCIP), stated that the future of Kashmir shall be determined by the will of the people and that both governments were to facilitate fair and equitable conditions, thereby allowing such will to be expressed. It is beyond argument that such conditions have never been facilitated by either India or Pakistan. From this very early period the course for domestic issues was set within narrow confines.

4. DOMESTIC FACTORS

Following independence and the violent clashes and events during 1947 - 48, the relationship between India and Pakistan has been characterised by misperceptions and the Kashmir dispute has acted as the major inhibitor of a more agreeable relationship between the two countries. These entrenched positions of the opposing sides have had a negative impact on the political and economic dynamics of each country with successive leaders on both sides having failed to get beyond the impasse.

4.1 Mirror Images

Both Hindu and Islamic religious traditions are embedded within peaceful methods of compromising and ameliorating conflict. Conversely each also has strands which firmly link it to a war mentality. Each side is therefore able to site in the others 'tradition' as 'proof' that the other tends to conquer and or dominate (Cohen 2003, 36).

India also views Pakistan as an example of neo - imperialism due to its alliance with various powerful world actors. As such, India views Pakistan as having compromised its domestic and foreign policies. The effect of such alliances, especially with the US, has resulted in the militarisation of Pakistani internal politics and foreign policy agenda. As such it has worked against India coming to an accommodation with Pakistan over the issue of Kashmir. India also accuses the Americans, through their provision of advanced weapons, of encouraging Pakistan to challenge

India as the regional power (Cohen 2003). India considered itself surrounded by an alliance of hostile states and continues to emphasise and point towards the extremist Islamic forces led by Pakistan and silently supported by China. Sectors of the Indian strategic community, having made such claims themselves, welcomed Samuel Huntington's proposition of 'a grand alliance between Islamic and Confucian civilization', claiming it as supporting their case (Cohen 2003, 37). However, Shirleen Hunter specifically counters this argument stating that the rise in Islamic fundamentalism is not a civilizational issue. Rather fundamentalism is caused by the same economic and social factors that have resulted in the fundamentalist movements in the West (Hunter 1998; Fox 2003, 27 - 46). Nationalism is considered a significant motivating factor within the Islamic civilization. Ironically this has tended to inspire many internal rather than external clashes, where it has often resulted in far better relations with non - Islamic states (Fox 2003, 30).

For an outsider it may appear unclear why India should feel threatened by Pakistan. Cohen asserts that the Indians see the very nature of the Pakistani state as a threat to their secular state. Many Indian academics and diplomats see Pakistan as having many shortcomings. (Bajpai 1983, 70 - 71; Cohen 2003) These shortcomings according to Bajpai include:

> Pakistan's limited cultural and civilisational inheritance, its military dictatorship, its theocratic identity, its unworkable unitary system of government (as apposed to federalism)...Islamabad's support of reactionary regimes in West Asia, its dependency on foreign aid, and the failure to develop a strong economic base (Bajpai 1983).

This Indian perspective of Pakistan took on an altogether more pronounced position since Pakistan began to openly support the separatist and insurgent movements within the Indian - administered Kashmir. Paul subscribes to the notions that Indians do hold negative stereotypical images of Pakistanis. The anti - Pakistan and anti - Muslim forces within India have been gathering strength since the rise of Hindu fundamentalism in the 1980s (Paul 2005). India fears Pakistan because some of Pakistan's elites are seen as 'harbouring revanchist notions towards India's Muslim population, which if allowed to manifest would be a threat against the unity and integrity of India itself. The basing of Islamic Jihadists in Pakistan, who are resigned to not only liberate Kashmir, but would wish to instigate the liberation of all of India's Muslims, (whether they would wish to be liberated or not), is seen as a significant threat to the secular make up of India (Cohen 2003).

For India there is the fear that any concession over Kashmir could lead to additional separatist movements within India. Notwithstanding the above, the Indians, see partition as having been completed in 1947. If the accession to India was not enough then the subsequent elections held in both 1957 and 1962 legitimised Jammu and Kashmir as being part of India. India therefore does not see that further concessions to Pakistan are feasible, notes Paul. However, Schofield counters this, stating that 'the elections were manipulated to the extent that it is not really possible to determine what the reality of popular opinion in the state is (Schofield 2000, 204). On the contrary, extreme right wingers within India, based around the Bharatiya Janata Party (BJP), would wish to see Kashmir forcefully integrated with India and would readily see Azad Kashmir, (held by Pakistan), to be part of this forced integration (Paul 2005). There are of course moderates amongst the Indian political groups who also would like to see the integration of Kashmir with India but essentially through a peaceful process. Harish Khare therefore asserts that the maximum concession that can be expected from even the moderates within India is the restoration of the pre - 1953 autonomous status for Kashmir (Khare 2004; Paul 2005).[3]

Pakistan's view of India is almost a mirror image of how India sees Pakistan. Pakistan, especially the military, sees itself under considerable threat from a more powerful India. Pakistan's leaders have a profound distrust of New Delhi and therefore any overtures of reassurance from India are viewed with suspicion (Cohen 2003). However, Cohen points

3 Assuming the pre - 1953 autonomous status for Kashmir was implemented the Delhi Government would limit its jurisdiction in Kashmir to defence, foreign affairs, communications, and currency. The authority of the Indian Election Commission and Supreme Court will still be maintained over the state.

out that there are those within Pakistan who believe that Pakistan is better able to meet the threat than the larger India. Pakistan views the threat emanating from an increasingly Hindu and extremist India, seeking religious revenge and dominance over its neighbouring areas. There are parallels to be drawn between the creation and existence of Israel and that of Pakistan. Each state was created for a persecuted minority, and both remain under threat from a powerful enemy. Both Pakistan and Israel have sought entangling alliances with various outside powers. Both have ultimately concluded that they cannot rely on an outside power at a time of crisis and therefore must be self sufficient in defending their own sovereign territory. As a result of the 1971 defeat by India, the Pakistani army, which has held power for half of Pakistan's existence, has become institutionally distrustful of India. As such India will find it hard to convince both the Pakistani public and the rulers, who invariably come from the military, of its intentions to create normal relationships with Pakistan. These conflicting and hostile views of each other act as significant impediments to a peaceful settlement. Similarly, both Pakistani and Indian domestic politics represent equally challenging obstacles to furthering any mediation proposals (Beach 2003).

4.2 Domestic Politics: Heart and Soul

In the period immediately following partition both the Indian and Pakistani leadership elevated the issue of Kashmir as part of their respective national identities (Cohen 2003). To the Pakistanis, Kashmir epitomised the core of the very reason for the partition in the first place, that of allowing majority Muslim areas to become part of Pakistan and to be ruled under the umbrella of the Muslim state. To the Indians, however, the inclusion of such areas as part of India demonstrated the very heart and soul of the new secular state. The official stance by India over Kashmir is that 'it is an integral part of India and that its future status needs to be addressed as a domestic problem. This is to be achieved within the framework of the Indian constitution and that any talks with Pakistan should occur in a strictly bilateral basis (Sultan 2000, 175).' The Pakistani perspective is that talks should take place under international mediation and or third party involvement, using the UN resolutions as the basis for any such negotiations (Sultan 2000, 176).[4]

Kashmir also became a useful diversion and tool, especially for Pakistan, against the massive task of nation building. In a number of major cities in Pakistan there are many Kashmiri dominated constituencies. There is also the issue of self-determination by the Kashmiri Muslims. This serge in the movement became more prominent in the late 1980s. India claims that Pakistan has been instrumental in supporting such a movement, yet there is evidence to suggest that this movement was fuelled by a period of bad Indian governance in the region (Cohen 2003, 47).

4.3 Credit through Conflict

Cohen points out however, that from an Indian perspective, the Pakistanis need India as a threat to maintain internal unity and to have a deflection from internal domestic issues such as social inequality and a lack of progress in reform within the society (Cohen 2003). There is an element of truth to this claim. Pakistan for the most part of its existence has been under military rule. From a domestic level, Paul claims that a compromise is difficult because the 'societal dominance of the Pakistani army has been built primarily on gaining back Kashmir from India (Paul 2005, 11).' Any compromise therefore could lead to a reduction in the standing of the army within the eyes of the Pakistani community and along with it the considerable corporate interests built around it. Not surprisingly some commentators argue that Pakistan's armed involvement in Kashmir, and the fact that it has a head of state who is military by background, acts as a barrier to a peaceful settlement of the dispute (Singh 1999).

4 The UN resolutions over the Kashmir issue also form part of the legacy of the Kashmir dispute. Past resolutions passed by the UN upheld the requirement for a plebiscite for the Kashmiri people as a means to resolve the conflict. The more recent UN Security Council resolution 1172 of 14 1998, urges India and Pakistan to resume dialogue to address all issues and to find mutually acceptable solutions to address the root causes of the tensions, including Kashmir. An indicator that for the UN Kashmir remains the key problem to resolve between Pakistan and India.

India has its own specific domestic constraints which prevent it from making any territorial concessions. These constraints stem from the ideas associated with democratic states not giving in territorially to non - democratic states, especially as a result of threats of violence. It is a well known fact that any politician or political party which makes such concessions is highly unlikely to be voted back in to power. Despite India holding this position for so long and the Indian part of Kashmir being more prosperous than the Pakistani side, India has not been able to win over the Kashmiri population in order to legitimize its control. India's own policy of maintaining a separate identity and autonomy of Kashmir has also conspired against Kashmiri integration with India (Paul 2005, 11).

According to Bose, what the Kashmiris, the Pakistanis and the Indians want in terms of a resolution to the Kashmir dispute varies considerably (Bose 2003, 165). The Kashmiris aspire to an independent Kashmir; the Pakistanis talk of the right to self - determination, (which would in their eyes lead to a Kashmir unified with Pakistan), and the Indians do not see much beyond a degree of autonomy for Kashmir, (but which would remain under the legislative control of India). Therein lays the challenge to any form of resolution: how to meet the aspirations of the three differing positions simultaneously (Paul 2005). Furthermore the fact that the territory in question, held by India, is linked to 'national identity,' where Pakistan will attempt to gain it, whilst India will be predisposed to resist such challenges for fear of giving up its own identity as a secular state, further compounds the problem. Part of the domestic equation is the economic considerations of both countries, which hitherto have been overshadowed by state centric, realist military power aspirations.

4.4 Economic Factors: Overshadowed by Military Accretion

Despite being strategically positioned between India and Pakistan and having boarders with China and Afghanistan, economic prosperity in Kashmir has not taken a foothold. This is primarily due to political problems and violent conflict. Security is a precondition of development. Conflict overshadows fundamental freedoms and human rights and places minorities under threat. Extremism, terrorism and the conditions for state failure are never too far away in an area of conflict such as Kashmir. The non resolution of the conflict in Kashmir has prevented both India and Pakistan from taking forward economic opportunities. Instead they have remained relatively underdeveloped. Within Kashmir investment and tourism is deterred, preventing normal economic activity. Thus it is an area that has been stuck in a cycle of conflict, insecurity and poverty. More recently both India and Pakistan have looked outwards in terms of their foreign policy and have moved forward on free market reforms, making some economic progress. Nonetheless, this has not led to substantial foreign investment and the continued dispute over Kashmir does not aid either side. Instead both India and Pakistan are spending significant amounts of their GDP on their respective militaries. If not checked this could ultimately lead to breaking the struggling Pakistani economy and at the very least hamper India's strive for speedy economic growth (Woollacott 2004). The recent sanctions imposed by the international community on both countries, as a result of their nuclear weapons development programmes and tests, did not help in the development of their economic bases. Instead it has led to incidence of further unrest in both countries. This essay concurs with Weiss who points out that although conflict is a major hindrance to development, conflict need not first cease altogether before reconstruction and development commences (Weiss 1995). Therefore leaders of both countries should pursue joint economic goals, whilst at the same time try and resolve their disputes.

In the case of Jammu and Kashmir, the past fifty years has seen it receive special status and degrees of autonomy from India. Regardless of the long period of special status and subsidies, the people of Kashmir have not been won over. Instead there remains disenchantment with the ruling Indian elite (Chitkara 2002, xxxi). Had Kashmir received an economic and industrial base, and educational institutes, instead of subsidies it may have resulted in a different outcome. With recent favourable talks between India and Pakistan, the opportunity now exists to take this approach, rather than stick to the status quo.

India's economic reforms of 1991 have produced a significant growth in its economy, far outstripping that of Pakistan (Paul 2005, 17). From a realist perspective, India with its substantial labour force, manufacturing capacity, focus on technological advancement, and open market strategy, will become a major economic power in the world. As such, realists such Waltz would assert that it is inevitable that India will also pursue major power status militarily within the region. The realist view fits well the threat perceptions held by both India and Pakistan, in that for a state to survive, it must seek security through the accretion of military power, regardless of its domestic, cultural or political complexions. As put by Waltz, eventually the systemic constraints placed on the state will force it to pursue both political and military hegemony (Waltz 1993, 44 - 79). Supported by Ganguly, I would argue that neither war nor attempted negotiations have resulted in a meaningful resolution (Ganguly 2006, 45 - 56). Commenting on the need for India and Pakistan to negotiate a settlement over the Kashmir dispute, Farooq states, 'we have seen the results of our fight on the political, diplomatic and military fronts, which have not achieved anything other than creating more graveyards.'[5] Yet hitherto both countries had tried to maintain military advantage over the other. During the Cold War India's policy of non - alignment allowed it to reap benefits from both the East and West, especially after its defeat against China in 1962 (Johnson 2005). Pakistan had kept the Indian conventional force superiority in check through acquiring advanced weapons, feeling decidedly disadvantage when in 1974 India detonated a nuclear device, albeit without having a means to deliver such a weapon. As argued by Lavoy, Pakistan was to counter Indian developments in nuclear capability, even if it meant the country going hungry (Lavoy 2002, 28). The Indian position argues that its nuclear capability was aimed at countering the Chinese expansion, rather than any expression of threat towards Pakistan. In 1998 both countries carried out nuclear tests, resulting in condemnation and economic sanctions from the

5 Mirwaiz Umer Farooq is the Chairman of the All Parties Hurriyat Conference, in Indian Administered Kashmir. His comments were in support of President Musharaf's four point peace agenda in resolving the disputes with India. Comments covered in a Pakistan editorial which urges India to take concrete action in resolving the Kashmir issue. The editorial was sourced through World News Connections 21 Jan 07.

international community. Both therefore became mindful of the need to maintain good relations with their respective powerful supporters in order to continue to gain economic and military aid (Wirsing 1998, 92). Ultimately which direction a country is taken economically or in pursuit of war or peace, is a function of leadership.

4.5 Leadership Short Comings

In the case of Pakistan and India, leadership has been lacking in bringing the sixty year old dispute to a conclusion. Other than the first generation of leaders who were focussed on developing and building their respective independent nations, those who have followed have been very narrowly focussed, often consumed by their own importance rather than serving the nation (Chitkara 2002). At the time of partition it was only Gandhi who had the vision to see that partition would lead to conflict. The leadership in India, including Patel and Nehru believed that Pakistan would not be able to function as an independent state and it was only a matter of time before it would collapse. Mohammed Ali Jinnah, the leader of Pakistan at the time, believed that post independence there was no reason why the two countries could not have good relations. After partition, he changed the emphasis in his speeches from Hindu and Muslims constituting two nations, to two nations having a tolerant approach to religion where both were multi - religious (Cohen 2003). Other than forging several agreements concerning trade and transit treaties, communication links and a number of confidence - building measures, the second and subsequent generation of leaders have not been able to deal with the complex and deep rooted conflict following partition (Cohen 2003).

Over time the approach by Pakistan concerning the issue of Kashmir has varied very little, regardless of whether the leadership has been civilian or of military stock. The tendency for both types of leadership has been to use Kashmir as a means of getting the public opinion in Pakistan on side, through engendering a sense of injustice over accession and manipulating the real empathy felt by the population with their Muslim kinsmen in Kashmir (Beach 2003, 7).

The Indian position over Kashmir on the other hand has hardened over time. There has been a clear departure from the reassurance of a plebiscite by Nehru, reinforced by various UN resolutions, following the partition. Firstly India delayed holding a plebiscite, and then gave Kashmir special status in 1951, resulting in Kashmir becoming an integral part of Indian. This made it very difficult for subsequent Indian leaders to honour the declared pledge to hold a plebiscite because this would now be against the Indian constitution (Hussain 2004, 15). To a large extent this position is a reflection of the public disenchantment over a Kashmir that has become increasingly violent. As Wirsing points out, this lends itself as an explanation for the rise of the Hindu Nationalist Bharatiya Janata Party (BJP), in India over the past two decades. The BJP's position until recently has been very hard line to the extent that it expressed views which saw the whole of the Kashmir princely state as belonging to India (Wirsing 1998).

Cohen argues that leaders entrapped in paired minority conflicts tend not to compromise even when they temporarily have the advantage for fear of being seen weak, both domestically and by the other side. The level of mistrust is considerable, and the opportunity to take advantage over the rival will always outweigh any compromise. Attempts at gaining the advantage include the buildup of military forces and the forming of alliances. Others such as V P Malik would support the assertion being made in this essay that strong leadership, (against domestic pressure), could overcome these differences (Nath 2003). The fact that neither side has been able to make nor force a settlement with the other is down to what Paul calls the 'power asymmetry (Paul 2005, 12).' As such the conflict becomes enduring in nature.

5. THE ENDURING NATURE OF THE CONFLICT

5.1 The International Dimension

The enduring nature of the conflict between India and Pakistan is characterised by what Paul refers to as 'truncated asymmetry'. That is to say despite India being many times larger than Pakistan in terms of population and geography, Pakistan has been able to balance this power difference through buying in military capabilities and through forging alliances. Scholars such as J S Levy argue therefore that equal capabilities only tempt aggressors whereas preponderance reinforces deterrence and stability (Levy 1997). The international environment after the Partition was marked by the conclusion of the Second World War. Not only were both India and Pakistan seeking alliance, they were to become allies to opposing sides of the Cold War power struggle. The key supporter for Pakistan was the US but also included China, North Korea and a number of Arab States. India, wanting to display its credentials of non-alignment, was more reluctant to forge alliances, but was nonetheless very much supported by the Soviet Union. These various permutations in the relationship have fluctuated and impacted on the capabilities and the relationship between Pakistan and India. Although the US was an ally to Pakistan, it was reluctant to be drawn in to direct conflict with India in support of Pakistan. Its main purpose in providing support to Pakistan was to create a counter balance against a Soviet Union supported India. China's support to Pakistan on the other hand was less retrained. China viewed its support to Pakistan as providing a counter to the Soviet Union and enabling Pakistan to resist better the pressure from India. Over the years, however, there has been a distinct moderation in the overt support from China to Pakistan and steps have been taken in an attempt at normalising its relationship with India.

From an Indian perspective it viewed as very important its relationship with the Soviet Union. However, the Soviets were providing this assistance to India for their own self interests, aimed at countering China (Cohen 2003). As noted by Stokes, whilst the support from the superpowers provided India and Pakistan with considerable military capability, the powers of veto exercised by either sides supporters actually contrived against the UN finding a solution to the issue of Kashmir. In Kashmir neither side has a preponderance of force to utilise against the other. Therefore claims Paul, there exists a 'near-parity' in the Kashmir theatre in terms of conventional military forces (Paul 2005, 13). In shorter wars Pakistan has the advantage over India because it can use guerrilla tactics, and its more advanced weaponry has allowed it to halt any Indian action during the initial stages of a conflict. India due to its size has the advantage if the conflict became protracted, but the intervention by external powers has in the past prevented the various conflicts from developing beyond a limited war (Paul 2005, 13).

The major powers' involvement has helped to maintain the enduring nature of the rivalry between India and Pakistan. Until recently external powers such as the UK, US and China aided Pakistan with the aim of maintaining a balance against its rival India. Both US and China were pro - Pakistan and anti - Indian during and after the Cold War because it suited their strategic interests. Kapur claims that it is the strategic interests of these external powers and not democratic values that have shaped the Anglo – US - Pakistani and Chinese coalition against the USSR and India. Without significant external assistance to Pakistan, it is argued that the rivalry between the two countries would not have been so prolonged. Academic work on the subject supports the idea that third parties can help resolve conflicts. However, resolution of the India – Pakistan conflict was not the primary motive of the involvement of the external powers in the region. Until the 1990s the aim had been to contain India and to 'maintain a situation of manageable instability (Wirsing 2003, 133).' Therefore the Indian - Pakistani rivalry does not rest on the Kashmir territorial dispute alone. It is also based on other issues such as nationhood and religion, but it has been prolonged, despite attempts at resolution, because of the involvement of the great powers.

5.2 The Key Conflicts: Attempts at Resolution

The involvement by China in the Kashmir issue became more significant when it had its own direct dispute with India along the northern boarders of Kashmir. Prior to 1959 Tibet acted as an insulator between China and India. This insulator was taken away when the Chinese People's Army entered Tibet in order to 'peacefully liberate' it. China and India were now sharing a disputed boarder and the relationship deteriorated to such a degree that it resulted in a short but decisive boarder war in 1962, with India coming off as the clear loser.

From this point onwards the nature of the Kashmir dispute changed both in political and geographic terms (Beach 2003, 10). China was the beneficiary of the border conflict with India, taking the Aksai Chin region of Kashmir from India. Even though India is not able to challenge China militarily, it continues to view the region as disputed. Despite America's agreement with Pakistan, it resulted in America coming to the aid of India with emergency supplies of arms and ammunition (Beach 2003). Mindful of America's changing association with India, Pakistan lent closer towards China for support and counter balance. This closer relationship with China resulted in Boarder Agreements and extensive Chinese aid to the Pakistani military and defence industries, as well as diplomatic support during the wars with India in 1965 and in 1974 (Beach 2003, 11). During this period there were many hawks in the Pakistani camp who advocated a military confrontation with India to regain Indian held Kashmir. The US advised against such action, whilst at odds with the wishes of many domestically, General Ayub Khan the Pakistan leader at the time heeded, but only to fall foul of the domestic pressure three years later when the 1965 War was initiated by Pakistan (Hussain 2004, 17).

5.3 The 1965 War and the Tashkent Accord

Despite the initial success and gains by the Pakistani - initiated offensive in to the Indian held Kashmir, Pakistan was left surprised by the Indian decision to take the offensive into the Pakistani mainland threatening Lahore and Sialkot. After seventeen days of fighting, nothing tangible was achieved by either side from the war. There was no conclusive outcome. The UN brokered ceasefire led to the Tashkent Accord and in the following year both sides returned to their pre - conflict positions. Pakistan had drawn further closer to China for military support and was alienated by the US from further military aid for having initiated a war against India (Hussain 2004). Although there was pressure internationally to bring about a resolution, and the efforts by the Soviet Union saw it viewed as a regional peacemaker, the UN failed to secure a lasting and conclusive solution to the Kashmir dispute. India saw its position strengthened as a result of the 1965 war. It had been successful in threatening mainland

Pakistan, and the wording in the Tashkent Accord did not make any reference for a plebiscite to be held in Kashmir (Beach 2003, 15). The Tashkent Peace Accord did not however, prevent the 1971 War between the two nations (Johnson 2005, 99).

5.4 The 1971 War and the Simla Agreement

The Kashmir dispute was not the cause of the 1970 - 71 War. Following elections in Pakistan, a separatist party gained overall controlled in East Pakistan leading to a civil war. The actions by the Pakistan authorities in East Pakistan led many to flee to India and so allowed India an opportunity to intervene. The direct intervention by India in East Pakistan found Pakistan lacking in preparation to react effectively. The two week conflict resulted in the decisive defeat of Pakistan and the secession of East Pakistan or as is now known Bangladesh. Although there was limited fighting in the Kashmir region, Indian success in the major conflict gave it an upper hand during the peace negotiations that followed between Zulfiqar Ali Bhutto and Mrs Gandhi at Simla in India (Ganguly 2006). The Simla Agreement was much more favourable to India for a number of reasons. Firstly it signified a bilateral agreement without the involvement of the UN or any other third party. Secondly although the agreement did not rule out mediation or multilateral diplomacy, according to Indian points of view the agreement was to work directly with each other over disputes without additional regional diplomacy. Thirdly for India the Simla Agreement supplanted the previous UN resolutions as a starting point for resolving the dispute. Pakistan on the other hand viewed the Simla Agreement as a supplement and not as a replacement of the UN resolutions on Kashmir (Cohen 2003). The Simla Agreement only allowed for the territories over the international boarder to be returned. Any territories over the ceasefire line were held by the respective parties. As such the previously established ceasefire line of 1949 was replaced by the Line of Control. As part of the agreement Chamb became part of Azad Kashmir and Kargil heights were retained by India. From 1972 to 1989 Kashmir did not feature highly in either nation agendas. There then followed a period of increased tension as an indigenous insurgency erupted in Jammu and Kashmir supported by Pakistan. This period also saw the removal of the USSR from Afghanistan and so the Jehadi fighters previously supported by Pakistan, USA, and Saudi Arabia were now available for action in Kashmir. The international community was becoming unsettled by the activities within Pakistan and started to view it as a failing state. My assertion that both nations resort to conflict in order to deflect attention from domestic vulnerabilities is born out by Pakistan's incursion in to Kargil.

5.5 The Kargil Incursion

The basis for the Pakistani incursion in to the Kargil region in 1999 remains unclear but nearly led to a nuclear conflict claims Hussain (Hussain 2004, 19). This paper counters this claim and instead argue that, having nuclear weapons, Pakistan assessed that it could probably take such action without the conflict escalating to an all out war with India. As Ganguly points out the intent was to 'refocus international attention on Kashmir (Ganguly 2006).' India though initially taken by surprise held a significant military advantage and was able to inflict defeat on Pakistan. More damaging to Pakistan was the stance taken by the international community in favour of India. The international community also castigated Pakistan for its actions, especially now that both countries were armed with nuclear weapons. It could be deduced that historically Pakistan has relied on external support to provide it with security and for its political viability. Therefore Pakistan resorted to taking such a risk to ensure it was able to off set its economic fragility. Any involvement from external powers in the provision of guarantees of security for Pakistan would be welcome. It could allow a reduction in the military and nuclear arms build up and for fundamental political and economic change inside Pakistan (Chitkara 2002, 155). The terrorist events of 11 September 2001, coupled with economic dynamics, have brought about significant changes in the international and regional environment.

6. RECENT EVENTS AND NEW IMPERATIVES

Following the 1998 nuclear tests and then the 1999 Kargil conflict, Pakistan found itself in a very difficult economic situation as the internationally imposed sanctions took effect. Its foreign debt amounted to about $38 billion (Hadar 2002). Pakistani involvement in the training of Mujahideen fighters in Afghanistan, linked it to the Taliban regime and therefore by implication to Al Quaeda. Following the 11 September events, India took advantage of the situation by both building up military pressure whilst at the same time resorting to sustained diplomatic offensive to get the US to apply pressure on Pakistan over the Kashmir issue (Haider 2002, 5). India's aim was to draw direct parallels between Islamabad's support for Jihadi fighters in Afghanistan and the support being provided to the Kashmiri militants. Had Pakistan not reacted so quickly and decisively on the side of America's declaration of the War on Terrorism, it would certainly have been isolated in the international community and worse it may have been subjected to military action from the US. President Musharraf quickly distanced himself from the Afghan regime which had been supported by Pakistan (Beach 2003, 20).' Despite considerable financial assistance and the rescheduling of Pakistan's debt, domestically, Musharraf has been walking a tight rope. Since the suicide attack on the Indian Parliament in December 2001, and the Kashmir elections of September 2002, which were marked by violence and controversy, significant steps have been taken by both sides towards a peace process.

6.1 Resumption of the Peace Process

There has been growing confidence over the prospects for peace between India and Pakistan since 2004. The initial talks in 2001 led to very little progress over Kashmir. The terrorist acts by Muslim militants against the Indian Parliament not only brought the two countries to the brink of war, but also led to a three year suspension of the peace process. In January 2004 however, India and Pakistan agreed to talks to settle the Kashmir dispute. The breakthrough came after a short meeting between India's prime minister Atal Bihari Vajpayee and Pakistan's president

Pervez Musharraf when both sides compromised on their own positions in order to take account of each others concerns. President Musharraf declared that he would not permit any territory under Pakistan's control to be used to support terrorism in any manner. Mr Vajpayee noted the need to continue with the dialogue, despite setbacks, and stated that he believed that a peaceful settlement of the Kashmir issue was possible to the satisfaction of both sides (Ramesh 2004). The significance of these meetings is clear from the discussions that have taken place not only over Kashmir, but also the establishment of road and rail links, and confidence building measures over the nuclear issue. The final accord issued at the New Delhi Summit in April 2005, placed the markers domestically and internationally for low - key but progressive movement towards rapprochement. There are a number of factors which could work against the current inter - governmental atmosphere. The domestic pressure on the leaders, and the influence of extremist in both countries could bring a halt to the peace process as has happened in the past. The extremists on both sides, the ultra - nationalist in India and the theocracy in Pakistan, are having to be placated through occasional recourse to hostile rhetoric. In Pakistan there is the constant threat of terrorism, requiring a balancing act between rapprochement and extremists by the government. The government in India needs to balance both factional political interests and a wide range of opinions for the peace process to succeed (Cloughley 2005). Yet this alone will not be enough to sustain the peace process. Both governments will have to realise that with several disputes affecting the relationship, the process will be protracted and difficult to complete.

As pressing to both sides are the water disputes. Both countries are dependent on water sources for their respective agricultural sectors and with the added pressures of economic growth this has taken a greater significance. There are three water flow disputes which have come about in the 1990s as a result of dams being constructed which go against the Indus Water Treaty brokered by the World Bank in 1960. India requires the hydro - electricity projects due to the rapidly rising electricity consumption rate. Pakistan is concerned about the impact the restricted river flow may have on its irrigation system. A mutually acceptable resolution has not been found and this dispute will be the subject of an independent mediation (Cloughley 2005). As M Klare would argue, access to dwindling energy resources becomes a critical national interest over time and therefore brings in to question the Democratic Peace Theory, where democracies are viewed as not likely to fight other democracies, let alone dictatorships. The likelihood of conflict, over resources, between India and Pakistan, cannot entirely be mitigated, but as Gray points out if economic interdependence is relevant, it must be seen to work and provide benefits to all to prevent war (Davis 2007).

6.2 Driving Factors

What has changed for both countries and is driving the peace process and co-operation are three key issues, economic imperatives, leadership buy-in and positive international involvement. Much value has been placed on trade and the benefit it can bring to both nations. In the past economic prosperity was not on the horizon. Now many of the middle classes and below see the opportunities that a stable region can offer. Both countries' defence programmes are impediments to economic development. As concluded by the Planning for Peace editors, 'the primary agent of placing the human species in jeopardy is war, and the usurper of the resources which might address its causes is war. (PfP Committee 2005)' Pakistan's fragile economy would not take much pressure to break. India could withstand much more pressure but would nonetheless be hampered in its economic growth. Within Indian political circles there has been a shift towards prosperity rather than Hindu identity. Pakistan's prosperity is inextricably linked to continued development in India. More broadly there are ongoing talks about a gas pipe line from Iran through Pakistan to India, and Pakistan being granted most favoured nation status. These moves are seen as mutually beneficial and further indicators of a developing relationship. The stakes have also mounted for the leadership of both countries but particularly so for Pakistan.

The leadership in both countries now have a stake in each others future. This is a critical point because this situation has never occurred in the past. The peace process, with all its obstacles, has become personalised to the two countries leaders. They have both taken a personal and political risk in pursuing the course of peace, as evidenced by the assassination attempts on President Musharraf in late 2004. Since 'war is made in the minds of leaders (Williams and Lee 2003, 209)' and used as a political force, perhaps it is incumbent on these same leaders to take such risk. As argued earlier in the paper, leaders of both countries have taken their nations to war through linking functions and circumstances primarily to suit their personal ambitions and not because the county was under imminent threat.[6] It is only through strong national leadership and international support can the two countries stay on the path to peace.

International support to both India and Pakistan has taken a positive turn since 2001. In particular the US has vastly improved political and military relations with both nations. The US wants co-operation from India and Pakistan in order that it can pursue it war on terrorism. The US requires the two nations to stabilise their relations, a stance never previously taken. Similar urges have come from China and the European countries, thus forcing compromise from both sides.

7. CONCLUSION

Although many writers remain highly sceptical about a peaceful resolution to the Kashmir dispute, I am convinced otherwise. This paper has shown that the conflict between India and Pakistan is territorial in origin, but has also been driven by misperception, mistrust, nationalism, religion, and public perceptions, even to the point where the larger more powerful party perceives itself as being weaker and under threat. Over the years Pakistan was able to bring parity to the greater military power of India through the accretion of more advanced weapons from other supportive powers. As a result the conflict became enduring in nature. However, this was not the only reason for the protracted nature of the

6 The Preparing for Peace book contains a number of papers written by experts and is a must read for further detail on leaders and war, but much more importantly it advocates that war is a redundant and obsolete institution and should be discarded.

conflict. The entrenched position taken by both sides over the issue of Kashmir has over shadowed all other considerations. The Pakistani position has remained fixated to the questionable manner in which partition and the accession of Kashmir took place. India remains at fault because it has denied the right to a plebiscite to the people of Kashmir. However, India has countered this assertion, claiming instead that the accession was legal and that this was subsequently born out by the various elections held within Jammu and Kashmir, the results of which make any requirement for a plebiscite redundant. India also is unwilling to accept that the Kashmir insurgency could conceivably be 'nationalist' in nature because this would give it legitimacy (Jackson 2006, 20). Instead it has placed the blame for such separatist movements entirely on Pakistan.

Evidence has shown that Pakistan had good justification for claiming the moral high ground over the Kashmir issue. However, despite Pakistan's initial strong position over the dispute the subsequent conflicts and the various peace agreements that followed diluted this position. The Simla agreement in particular gave India the upper hand and very much rendered Pakistan's legal argument ineffective. Despite involvement by the UN, the international community has not been able to find a resolution to the conflict. India sees advantage in any dialogue and resolution taking place without third party involvement, where as Pakistan, because of the plebiscite issue, sees a resolution being found through internationalising the dispute to its advantage (Wirsing 2003, 15). As such international efforts in the past have been hampered. Additionally any concessions or changes in priorities such as putting development in front of Kashmir, by either side, have tended to be exploited by extremists in the respective camps (Cohen 2003). Similarly domestic politics have proved a significant constraint and influencing factor in how each country has handled the conflict.

Notwithstanding the above, this paper has also argued that external powers involvement has helped to maintain the enduring nature of the rivalry between India and Pakistan. Until recently external powers such as the UK, US and China aided Pakistan with the aim of maintaining a balance against its rival India. Without significant external assistance to Pakistan, it has been argued that the rivalry between the two countries would not have been so prolonged. Resolution of the India – Pakistan conflict was not the primary motive for the involvement of the external powers in the region. Involvement suited their strategic interests. Domestic strategies tended to be interwoven with perceived threats. Both sides have been unwilling to compromise for fear of loosing domestic support, mistrust, and being perceived as weak. Instead the leadership of both countries have used the dispute over Kashmir for selfish interests, primarily to stay in power and to self aggrandise through the strengths and employment of their respective militaries.

Historically economic considerations have been subordinate to the desires of the realist camps in both countries, where military accretion has consumed a large percentage of the GDP. The instability created within the region also deterred outside investment and therefore economic growth has in the past been hindered.

Accepting the complexity and the historical nature of the conflict, with many obstacles remaining, this paper has argued that the new imperatives will make the possibility of a peace settlement more likely than ever before. For both countries what has changed and is driving the peace process and co - operation are three key issues, economic opportunities, leadership buy - in and positive international involvement. The changed environment is forcing compromise between India and Pakistan. Contrary to positions taken by many writers on the subject, this paper has argued for and concludes that the benefits of long term peace between India and Pakistan now outweigh any possible gains through continued conflict over the Kashmir issue. As such it is firmly believe that the Indian sub - continent without war is no longer just an idea, it is near enough a reality (PfP Committee 2005).

REFERENCES

Bajpai, U. S., ed. 1983. *India's Security: The Politico-Strategic Environment.* New Delhi: Lancers Publishers.

Beaumont, C. 1992. "How Mountbatten Bent the Rules and the Indian Border." Interview by Simon Scott Plummer. *The Daily Telegraph*, February 24, 1992.

Bose, S. 2003. *Kashmir: Roots of Conflict, Paths to Peace.* Cambridge: Harvard University Press.

Chitkara, M. G. 2002. *Kashmir: A Tale of Partition.* New Delhi: APH Publishing Corporation.

Cloughley, B. 2005. "De'tente for India and Pakistan?" Regional Security Issues, *Jane's Intelligence Review.*

Cohen, Stephen P. 2003. "India, Pakistan and Kashmir." In *India as an Emerging Power*, edited by S. Ganguly, 30-57. London: Frank Cass Publishers.

Fox, J. 2003. "Do Muslims Engage in More Domestic Conflict than Other Religious Groups?" *Civil Wars* 6 (1): 27-46.

Friedman, Thomas L. 1999. *The Lexus and the Olive Tree.* New York: Farrar, Straus and Giroux.

Ganguly, S. 2006. "Will Kashmir Stop India's Rise?" *Foreign Affairs* 85 (4): 45-56.

Hadar, L. T. 2002. "Pakistan in America's War against Terrorism: Strategic Ally or Unreliable Client?" *Policy Analysis*, no.436.

Haider, E. 2002. "Dramatic Reversal." *The World Today* 58 (2): 4-6.

Hunter, S. T. 1998. *The Future of Islam and the West: Clash of Civilizations or Peaceful Co-existence?* Westport, C. T.: Praeger; with the Centre for Strategic and International Studies, Washington, D. C.

Hussain, J. 2004. "Is a Kashmir Solution in the Offing: A Politico-Military Overview." *Defence Journal* 7 (9): 14-20.

Jackson, A. 2006. "British Counter-insurgency in History: A Useful Precedent?" *British Army Review*, no. 139 (Spring): 12-22.

John, W. 2005. "Lashkar-e-Toiba: New Threats Posed by an Old Organization." *Terrorism Monitor* 3 (4).

Johnson, R. 2005. *A Region in Turmoil: South Asian Conflicts Since 1947.*

London: Reaktion Books.
Khare, H. 2004. "Kashmir: New Roadmap Taking Shape." *The Hindu*, November 18, 2004.
Lamb, A. 1992. *Kashmir: A Disputed Legacy, 1846 - 1990.* Karachi: Oxford University Press.
Lavoy, P. R. 2002. "Fighting Terrorism, Avoiding War: The Indo - Pakistani Situation." *Joint Forces Quarterly* (Autumn): 27 - 34.
Levy, J. S. 1997. *War in the Post - Cold War era, Global Politics, Conflict and Anarchy.* Deakin: Deakin University.
Nath, R., ed. 2003. *Musharraf's War.* New Delhi: Lancer's Books.
Paul, T. V., ed. 2005. *The India - Pakistan Conflict: An Enduring Rivalry.* Cambridge: Cambridge University Press.
PfP Committee. 2005. *Preparing for Peace: by asking the experts to analyse war.* London: Westmoreland General Meeting.
Ramesh, R. 2004. "Kashmir Edges a Step Closer to Peace." *The Guardian*, January 7, 2004. https://www.theguardian.com/world/2004/jan/07/pakistan.india1.
Schofield, V. 2000. *Kashmir in Conflict: India, Pakistan and the Unending War.* London: I. B. Tauris.
Singh, J. 1999. *Kargil 1999: Pakistan's Fourth War for Kashmir.* New Delhi: Knowledge World.
Sultan, M. 2000. "Globalisation, Media and the Kashmir Dispute." *Institute of Strategic Studies.*
United Nations. 1948. United Nations Security Council Official Records, no. S/628. January 1, 1948.
Waltz, K. N. 1959. *Man, the State, and War: A Theoretical Analysis.* New York: Columbia University Press.
Waltz, K. N. 1993. "The Emerging Structure of the International Politics." *International Security* 18 (2): 44 - 79.
Weiss, Thomas G., ed. 1995. *The United Nations and Civil Wars.* Boulder, CO: Lynne Rienner Publishers.
Wildmalm, S. 2002. *Kashmir in Comparative Perspective: Democracy and Violent Separatism in India.* London: Routledge Curzon.
Williams, C. and Y - J. Lee. 2003. "The Minds of Leaders: De - Linking War and Violence." Preparing for Peace project. London: Westmoreland General Meeting.

Wirsing, R. G. 1998. *India, Pakistan, and the Kashmir Dispute: On Regional Conflict and its Resolution.* London: Palgrave Macmillan.

Wirsing, R. G. 2003. *Kashmir in the Shadow of War: Regional Rivalries in a Nuclear Age.* New York: M. E. Sharpe.

Woollacott, M. 2004. "After Half a Century, a Moment of Optimism: India and Pakistan Have Seized the Initiative from Extremists." *Guardian, January* 9, 2004.

II

STRUCTURAL VIOLENCE IN SOUTH ASIA WITH NUCLEARISATION

1. INTRODUCTION

Asia, inhabited by one fifth of humanity, has become a regional milieu of varying degrees of conflict and tension between and within the constituent states. In recent years, the region has earned the ominous distinction as one of the key flashpoints in the world where the dangers of nuclear conflict among its strongest neighbours is considered to be as real as the implosion of states from insurgencies within its borders. The two principal actors in the region, India and Pakistan, have fought three wars, yet without resolving the core issue of Jammu and Kashmir which is the major bone of contention between the two states. The nuclear tests in May 1998 by both the key adversarial states evoked global concerns, turning Kashmir as a potential "nuclear flash point (Naik 2003, 449)." Apart from these, there are other equally volatile and explosive conflicts in South Asia, both at the interstate and intra state level. Bilateral issues that have their roots in history, geo - political imperatives and economic necessities, have taken on characters of intractable conflicts with deep rooted mistrust and suspicions. And if one considers the numerous wars, ethnic and secessionist conflicts, not to mention the nuclear stand - offs and foreign military interventions of the last five decades, the description of the region as 'intrinsically unstable' comes across as an understatement (Shah 2004, 195). In South Asia, a combustible mix of colonial legacy, imperial ambitions, mis - governance and religious extremism ensures that the whole region inhabited by about 23 percent of the world population, is never far from Armageddon (Shah 2004, 195).

South Asia, due to its inherent nature of imbalances in terms of territory, population and natural resources, portrays a dismal picture of a region mired with regional disharmony and internal conflicts. At the interstate level, the structure of conflicts instigated by the asymmetrical power balance in the region has induced them to take on characteristics of intractable conflicts, thus making it difficult to establish a viable and enduring peace building process in the region. The establishment of South Asian Association of Regional Cooperation (SAARC) as a regional organization kindled a lot of expectations among the people of South Asia that they could finally overcome regional disharmony and look ahead towards a better future of regional cooperation and economic prosperity through this forum. Yet, in retrospect, SAARC has been a dismal failure as far as the attainment of regional harmony and cooperation is concerned and the region remains as divided as ever. Despite its more than two decades of existence, the achievements of SAARC as a regional organization can hardly be put in the same categories as that of other regional counterparts such as the European Union (EU) or the one closer to home; the Association of South East Asian Nations (ASEAN). Viewed from this perspective it begs the question as to why SAARC could not succeed when other regional organizations were reaching new heights? What went wrong and who were at fault? These are some pertinent questions, from the South Asian perspective, that need to be answered as the subcontinent enters a new millennium.

All these ominous indicators in the nature of conflicts in the subcontinent necessitate a broad analysis and understanding on the structure of conflicts in the region so as to enable an understanding of the interactions among various factors that generate conflict and violence both within and among the nations in the region. The imperative to understand the conflict dynamics in South Asia has increased due to the overt introduction of the nuclear dimension in the regional conflict between the two key antagonists in the region, i.e. India and Pakistan. Given the nature of their antagonism, the probability of a nuclear showdown between the two states has become a world wide concern. US President Bill Clinton's remark about Kashmir being 'the most dangerous place on earth' during his visit to the region in March 2000, was based not on an evaluation of day - to - day security threats faced by civilians in Kashmir, but on the concern of the potential nuclear exchange that would have far-reaching effects (Hunt 2000). The relevance of a study of the conflict dynamics in the region is also highlighted due to the imminent and volatile nature of the intrastate conflicts in South Asia; where past experience has shown that such internal conflicts may have spill over effects across the region, particularly when it involves cross-border movement of people, sharing of natural resources, or dealing with ecological problems.

In this context, the paper will examine the structure of conflict in South Asia and assess the extent to which these conflict dynamics have made it difficult to establish a viable and sustainable peace building process in the region. It will not attempt to conduct a comprehensive probe into all the sources of conflicts in the region; but will essentially focus upon two main key issues that are largely responsible for sustaining the environment of discord in the region; namely the asymmetrical power structure in the region and the nexus between security and governance. These two factors will be analysed vis-à-vis their association with the conflict dynamics in the region at the inter-state and intrastate levels.

The paper will begin with a cursory insight into the regional perspective of South Asia, the types of conflict that are prevalent in the region; and the state of peace building process in the region. The paper will take into account the conflicts involved within and among the seven initial members of SAARC only; and exclude Afghanistan which has only recently joined SAARC. In the third chapter, the paper will analyze the dynamics of conflicts at the interstate level and draw inferences there from. In the fourth chapter, the paper will focus upon the intrastate conflicts and analyze how the inability of the governance factor to understand the unique nature of each problem has led to a failure in dealing with internal crisis. This chapter will also look at the inter-state dimension that comes into play in intrastate conflicts as it can be argued that, to a large extent, intrastate conflicts are manifestations of inter-state conflicts. The fifth chapter looks at SAARC and draws analysis on how the conflict dynamics of the region have hindered the functioning of the organization. It will not dwell upon all the issues related with SAARC but will focus mainly upon the nature of the genesis of the organization.

The paper will argue that the conflict dynamics in South Asia have indeed made it difficult to establish a sustainable peace building process in the region. It will conclude that at the interstate level, the asymmetrical balance of power, manifest with India's predominance, is responsible for sustaining the environment of discord in the region. The preponderance of the hegemon - subsidiary relation vis - à - vis India's relationship with its other smaller neighbours, has resulted in generating a vicious cycle of mistrust between the aspirant hegemon, wishing to fulfil its regional dominance; and the secondary powers who come up with knee jerk reactions in their attempt to resist the influence of the aspiring hegemon; thus fuelling an environment of conflict in the region. The paper will further argue that at intrastate level, the governance or rather the mis - governance factor is responsible for sustaining the environment of conflict in the region. Since state responses to internal conflicts in South Asia are largely influenced by the predominant role of the state machinery looking for quick fix solutions that often constitute use of hard power instead of soft power, they fall short of addressing the root causes of the conflict and paradoxically end up fuelling the environment of discord in the region. Lastly, the paper will focus on the genesis of SAARC and highlight the strategic circumstances that were prevalent at the time of its formation. Since the genesis of SAARC was based in a particular context when the smaller countries of South Asia came together to resist the potential hegemonic behaviour of India, the organization essentially set out from the start in an environment mired with mistrust and apprehension between its member states. As a result, the organization was unable to develop a sound structure and an effective decision making process that could address key underlying regional and bilateral issues; and was unable to foster better relationship among constituent states to improve regional harmony.

The research methodology used in the preparation of this paper has been mainly text based, drawing mainly from secondary sources such as published materials on the topic from the library. Hence, published materials on the topic have been extensively useful for the research work, including reference to relevant internet websites.

2. SOUTH ASIA: A Regional Perspective

The concept of South Asia as a region is comparatively recent. The region found its first formal expression as a regional entity in the shape of the South Asian Association for Regional Cooperation (SAARC) in 1985. As the name implies, the South Asian subcontinent, is the southern region of the Asian continent. It is comprised mainly of the sub - Himalayan countries and, also includes the adjoining countries on both sides. From west to east clockwise, it is surrounded by Western Asia, Central Asia, Eastern Asia, South Eastern Asia and the Indian Ocean.

According to the UN sub region definition, South Asia is the most populous and densest region in the world. Almost 1.4 billion live in South Asia (Chaudhury 2006, xiii), and population growth rate is among the highest in the world. Within the region, the countries share rivers, mountain systems, oceans and ecological cycles, such as the life - sustaining monsoon rains. Due to the sheer geographic and demographic size of South Asia, there is intraregional diversity of continental proportions in the region. Every country and state, regardless of its size, has an unshared uniqueness and mystique of its own. The South Asian nations are linguistically and culturally diverse and all major religions of the world have followers in this region, making the region multiethnic, multilingual and multicultural (Dahal et al. 2003, 3). Despite being rich in culture and history, it is indeed sobering that South Asia ranks among the poorest, the most illiterate, and most malnourished region in the world. It is expected that the number of people mired in poverty and backwardness in this region will shortly touch a billion (Baral 2001, 198).

As a regional entity, South Asia constitutes a special category of 'backward region' in which the constituent nations have little or no control over their borders and attaining this ability seems a distant prospect. The region is home to insurgencies, militancy, desperation, conflicts and growing violence thus making it one of the most volatile regions in the world. The perception of the region as a Shangri-La to an outsider with its postcard-like façade of mist-clad hills, lush green forests, smooth and serene valleys, bewildering range of its languages, and rich colour mix of people, exotic locales and smiling friendly faces, in essence, is just that – a façade, as underneath lies a different truth manifested in deeper emotions such as grief, hunger and terror (Rizal and Yokota 2006, 33). For decades, this region has seethed with unrest, rebellions and violence. The region has been a battleground for generations of national identities confronting insensitive nation states and their bureaucracies as well as internecine strife (Rizal and Yokota 2006, 34).

South Asia as a region displays two important characteristics (Muni 1980, 39). First it is largely Indo-centric in character, as India is central to it both geographically and in terms of socio-cultural continuities and economic infrastructure. India shares common land borders with Pakistan, Nepal, Bhutan and Bangladesh and maritime borders with Sri Lanka and Maldives. These other countries have, individually and separately, more in common with India than with each other. The second characteristic of the region is its asymmetric and hierarchical power structure. India enjoys a dominant status in the region, not only due to its sheer size and population, but also in terms of natural resources, technological know-how, and economic and military strength, thus making it far superior to any one of its neighbours, or even to all of them put together (Muni 1980).

2.1 Conflicts in South Asia

The list of conflicts in South Asia can be broadly categorized into four types:

Interstate conflict Such conflicts dominate the political environment in South Asia and are responsible for retarding the prospect of greater cooperation in the region, thus undermining the cohesion of the SAARC alliance and depriving the region from benefiting from the alliance. The territorial dispute between India and Pakistan over Kashmir, Wuler Barrage, Siachen Glacier and Sir Creek stands out prominently. This is underlined by political and military competition between the two neighbours. This has resulted in a number of showdowns between these two countries, which in turn, on many occasions have inadvertently led the region to the brink of a nuclear confrontation, as both the belligerent nations are nuclear capable. Similarly, the differences between India and its other smaller neighbours over many issues have also contributed significantly to the heightened tension in the region at different times and it is indeed a worrying notion that some of the contentious issues remain unresolved.

Governance and Authority conflict The concern about the distribution of power and authority in society has generated conflict over governance issues where demands for democracy and political participation have led to high expectations among the populace which has not gone down quite well with the ruling elites. Even though South Asia was also caught in Huntington's famous 'third wave (Huntington 1991)'[1] with greater democratisation in the region, the region has also witnessed a significant *'spill - back'* with some countries going back to authoritarian rule. It is said that while South Asia has achieved the trappings of an electoral democracy, it has yet to achieve the goals of liberal democracy with the norms that are needed to sustain the democratic process. Hence, the failure of centralized structures to share political power and give effective representation to all strata of society has led to growing militarisation and use of coercive state power to quell resurgent nationalism (Chari 2001, 11).

Ideological conflicts Although class based conflicts with the goals to bring some form of social revolutions have experienced serious set - backs globally, its presence is strongly felt in South Asia. The Maoist movement, which gained unprecedented success in Nepal, was largely

1 The catch-phrase "the third wave" refers to the democratic transitions and democratization throughout much of the developing world , Europe, Latin America, Asia, and Africa.

based on the pattern of the *Sendero Luminoso* (Shining Path)[2] of Peru and allegedly operated with external support from Revolutionary International Movement (RIM) and operated under the Coordination Committee of Maoists Parties and Organization of South Asia (CCOMPOSA). The growing impact of class-based conflict is strongly felt in various states of India with the expansion of Naxalite[3] activities that are very similar to the Maoist insurgency. Only the sheer size of India and its military prowess has enabled the Indian government to ward off the growing influence of the Naxalite activities. The degree of threat emanating from this burgeoning conflict was succinctly described by the then Indian Prime Minister Manmohan Singh when he said, "Naxalite problem poses the single-largest threat to the internal security of the country (Ramana 2006, 64)."

Identity conflict The growing polarisation of society along ethnic, linguistic and religious lines, and an undermining of social values through which diverse communities hitherto had lived together in a pluralistic society (Chari 2001, 11) have resulted in a crisis in the region. Identity conflict is the most pervasive and violent form of conflict in the region since most ethnic, minority, or religious conflicts are characterized by international or trans-national linkages that help to sustain them in one form or another. The politicisation of ethnicity or religion is a long process, and governments often offer solutions when it is too late. Even then the solutions offered may be inadequate for resolving the problems. The diversity of cultures, peoples and religion in South Asia make it a potential hotbed for social and political conflicts, many of which have already taken its toll in the region. India's experience in the Northeast and Sri Lanka's with its ethnic Tamils show how difficult it is to redress the problem.

2 Sendero Luminoso is considered to be among the world's most ruthless guerrilla organizations. Formed in the late 1960s by then university professor Abimael Guzman, it aimed at destroying existing Peruvian institutions and replacing them with peasant revolutionary regime. (See http://www.ict.org.il).

3 Naxalite or Naxalism is an informal name given to communist groups in India. Ideologically they belong to various trends of Maoism. The CPI (Maoist) and some other Naxal factions are now considered terrorists by the Government of India. (See http://en.wikipedia.org/wiki/Naxalite).

2.2 Peace Building Process

Peace building measures in South Asia have achieved dubious results both at the inter - state and intrastate level. Building trust and confidence between hostile groups or nations has always been an uphill task. Since decades of suspicion and ill - will have institutionalized the process of conflict formation, it has made it difficult for the region to take the much needed leap from confrontation to cooperation. Even after SAARC was born, which generated a lot of expectations among the South Asia nations that they would be able leave behind their past and plan for a new prosperous future, it is disheartening that the prospect of regional harmony and cooperation in South Asia still seems distant. After more than twenty years of SAARC's existence, South Asia remains as divided as ever and the underlying issues of conflict remain extant.

Bringing in a third party to address contentious bilateral issues in South Asia has been only marginally successful. Compared to other regions of the world, there are only a number of cases in South Asia where inter - state conflicts have been resolved by third party intervention. The most significant was the Indus Water treaty of 1960 between India and Pakistan, which was achieved with the help of the World Bank. The Tashkent Agreement in 1965, that was carried out under the auspices of the former USSR, ended the war between India and Pakistan, but did not in essence resolve the issues that gave rise to the conflict. Some of these issues were later worked out in 1968 under the Rann of Kutch boundary deal by a three - member commission in Geneva but to no significant avail. External intervention in South Asia has been useful in defusing potential military crises (primarily between India and Pakistan), but not in resolving the root causes of the problems which often exacerbate and inflame them.

The record of resolution of intrastate conflicts in South Asia is even less encouraging. India's achievement in resolving multiple insurgencies has been mixed. In its Northeast, Mizoram is the only state where militancy has been resolved, while Manipur and Assam continue to remain the most violent states and Tripura and Nagaland are also rife with violence, albeit in a lesser degree. Punjab is another area where militancy has been brought under control, but the insurgency in Kashmir, particularly after the involvement of the Jihads from across the border in Pakistan since the early 1990s, continues to make it an intractable conflict. Pakistan's own case in the first instance to prop up the military regime under General Zia-ul Haq and to create Afghan *Jihad* against the Soviet occupation of Afghanistan rapidly created militant religious organizations that often competed with one another through violent means. Now, with some of these groups openly embracing Osama bin Laden's brand of terrorism, even concerted international efforts to deal with the threat have been difficult. Nepal is finally coming out of its decade long Maoist insurgency and the overthrow of the monarchy has seen the Maoists coming into mainstream politics. Although the Maoist party is supposedly at the helm of the nation building process after the landslide victory the party enjoyed in the recently held constituent assembly election, the Maoists have not been able to garner consensus among other competing political parties over many issues. This factor has been compounded by the emergence of several other ethnic movements in virtually all parts of the country which has put the country into total disarray with no sight of reprieve in the immediate future. The unresolved issue of over 100,000 refugees of Bhutanese origin in Nepal has the potential of destabilizing peace and stability in both Bhutan and Nepal. Elsewhere, Sri Lanka has gone through blood shed and instability for a considerable period of time due to the long, unresolved separatist struggle in the country. Despite the remarkable recent military success of the Sri Lankan government against the hitherto seemingly invincible Tamil insurgents, the Liberation Tigers of Tamil Eelam (LTTE), it is yet to be seen whether this will be enough to quell the five decades-long secessionist movement. In Bangladesh, the insurgency in Chittagong Hill Tracts (CHT) tends to flare up at regular intervals, affecting peace and stability in the region.

3. INTERSTATE RELATIONS IN SOUTH ASIA

The interstate relations in South Asia are interspersed with varying degrees of conflict and cooperation between and among the constituent states. Central to this fluctuating pattern of conflict and cooperation has been the role of India, quite evidently the dominant power in the region filled with hegemonic aspirations. It can be argued that Indian tendency to behave like a 'big brother' has reinforced its perception as a hegemonic power (Panda 1984, 71) and further alienated the lesser powers of the region and aggravated the tension.

Crises, sometimes bordering on military conflict, have occurred between India and nearly all of its neighbours in South Asia. The two key antagonists in the region, India and Pakistan, were again poised on the precipice of another major war over the Kashmir issue in 1990, after three previous major wars. The on and off military conflict between India and Pakistan over the Siachen glacier has not yet been resolved and these issues remain a major bilateral irritants between the two states. The hostility and suspicion which characterizes relations between India and Pakistan is also replicated, albeit to a much lesser degree, between India and its other neighbours. The Indian military intervention in Sri Lanka to deal with the Tamil separatist movement there increased the tensions in Indo - Sri Lankan relations. The Indian decisions to seal off all but two of landlocked Nepal's trade routes through India in 1989 produced a new low in Indo - Nepalese relations. Indo - Bangladesh differences persist over a variety of issues including the sharing of the Ganges river waters, flood control and refugees. The Indian military intervention in the Maldives in 1988 and the acquisition of a nuclear - powered submarine raised new concerns among its smaller neighbours (Paranjpe and Thomas 1991, 161). In other words, the troubles in the region of South Asia, its endemic tensions, mutual mistrusts and occasional hostilities are largely products of the opposing view of India's security perception compared with that of the rest of the countries of the region. It is interesting to note that India's neighbours perceive a threat to their security coming primarily from India, which for its part, considers its neighbours as an integral part of its own security system. The South Asian region has seen that the Indian hegemonic aspirations have involved the integration of the erstwhile princely states; the forcible absorption of Hyderabad, Kashmir, and Goa, and the annexation of Sikkim, an imposed protectorate over Bhutan, a dominant presence in Nepal and Bangladesh; and finally the humbling of Pakistan (Ziring 1978, 198).

3.1 Implications of Asymmetrical Power Balance

The region, as it emerged after 1947, reflected the indigenous imbalance of power following the withdrawal of Britain when India ceremoniously replaced Britain by assuming the 'responsibility' for the security and integrity of the smaller powers, albeit thwarted subsequently by Pakistani policies and the intervention of the extra - regional powers (Paranjpe and Thomas 1991, 167). The Indian ruling elite inherited the perception that, like British India, independent India was also destined to play a major role in Asian and world affairs commensurate with its geographical placement, historical experience and power potential (Muni 1980, 47). Consequently, Indian strategic thinking in South Asia was conditioned by the following assumptions:

1. India's desired objective is to maintain the territorial status quo in the region based on the principle of peaceful coexistence. India should be perceived as a benevolent giant with a role similar to that of the United States in the American hemisphere.
2. The smaller powers of South Asia should accept the Indian perspective and the subsidiary roles implicitly assigned to them by the aspiring hegemon. Non - acceptance of this assigned secondary role would be perceived as "obstacles" to be overcome by diplomacy or even military pressure.
3. The aspiring hegemon must seek to limit or offset the potential political and military interventionist policies of the external powers in the South Asian region through international diplomacy and, if necessary, by purchasing arms from one or more of the great powers (Paranjpe and Thomas 1991, 168).

Thus, after the departure of the British from India in the late 1940s, interstate relations in South Asia have been conditioned by two trends that reflect the power asymmetry in the region. Firstly, it reflects in the Indian preponderance in the region as India, by virtue of its size and location and its economic and military strength, occupies a central position in the region. Due to its centrality, India aspires for leadership in the region, which arguably has place the country in the role of a regional hegemon.

The second trend is reflected in the policies of India's neighbouring states which are often, though not always, can be amounted to a reflex reaction to the country's assertion of a dominant role in the region. Among them, Pakistan is the 'primary bargainer', which has the potential to check India hegemonic aspirations. It has already fought three major wars with India and has frequently engaged in low intensity conflict along the disputed borders in divided Kashmir. The development of nuclear weapons by Pakistan in 1998 gave the country greater deterrence capability against the threat from India, but still falls short of achieving parity with India due to its own economic and geographic limitation. The other powers in the region – Bangladesh, Bhutan, Nepal and Sri Lanka may be considered small powers in South Asia that pose no direct military threat to India and have limited bargaining capacity vis-à-vis their larger neighbour. However, at different times, these countries have attempted to offset the influence of the hegemonic power in a number of ways. These include: expanding their contact with the outside world through both bilateral and multilateral channels; relying on the external powers to provide a counterweight to the Indian influence in the region; and where possible to internationalize contentious issues so as to reduce the influence of the dominating power to exercise its authority arbitrarily in the region.

Hence, the volatility in the region can, in large part, be attributed to the tendency of the regional powers to challenge the Indian perception of their subsidiary status, which India has not always been able to address adequately to their or its own satisfaction. As theorists of hegemony suggest, a successful hegemonic power is one that engages in not only rule-making and rule-enforcement, but is also able to acquire deference of secondary states to its leadership (Myers 1991, 1-26). Since coercion alone will not gain the respect of other states, "the hegemon may have to invest resources in institutions in order to ensure that its preferred rules will guide the behaviours of other countries" by fostering cooperation, which needs to work in tandem with hegemonic policies (Keohane 1984, 32 - 46). The past half a century of interstate relations in South Asia suggests that, despite India's predominant status in the region, it has not been able to gain the much needed understanding from among its neighbours nor establish a structure of cooperation that others would see as mutually beneficial to the parties concerned.

3.2 India as a Regional Hegemon: Legacy Raj Syndrome

The shadow of the colonial rule arguably left behind a bitter after-taste for the new rulers of South Asia after de - colonisation to the effect that the ideas and institutions of this region were not free from the colonial hangover. In fact, the ideas and institutions that the South Asians have today, are, by and large, the offshoots of the colonial legacy and fragmented freedom (Chaudhury 2006, 126).

Jawaharlal Nehru, the first post independence prime minister of India, along with his generation of Indians, claimed the moral leadership of the Third World, with a projection of moral opposition to the Western powers, which were seen as tainted by colonialism and slavery. Ironically, India has also mimicked and consolidated the British colonial worldview and practices in South Asia. Even as they chased the British out of the subcontinent, Nehru and others sought to have India recognised as the rightful successor to the British Raj in the region. This aspiration towards the inheritance of the colonial legacy is aptly described as Legacy Raj Syndrome by Saubhagya Shah, a prominent scholar in South Asian scenario. He attributes Legacy Raj Syndrome, to a regional milieu in South Asia characterized by a high level of inter - state depredation and bad faith, and lying at the heart of the sub continental maelstrom (Shah 2004, 195). According to Shah, the core tensions of the Legacy Raj are sustained by the polymorphous character of the post - independence power elites, whose conception of self and mission oscillates between that of anti - colonial heroes on the one hand and heirs to the British Raj on the other (Shah 2004, 195). He argues that it is this contradictory impulse that generates the cycles of destabilization outward into the regional system in the form of economic pressures, political subversion, proxy wars and military adventures. In this context, it can be argued that independence, after the end of the colonial rule left the Indian Republic with a split personality (Shah 2004, 196).

Shah further explains that the dual nature of Indian regional policies was apparent from the outset of the post-colonial independence period. While India's representation of itself as the 'largest democracy', its anti-colonial legacy and its Gandhian profile offer a certain moral high ground on the world stage, New Delhi's ability to shake things up in the immediate neighbourhood provided the masters of the Legacy Raj with experiential proof of their imperial inheritance and a direct measure of their self-worth (Shah 2004, 196). The chasm between India's international persona and its regional practices has led some to the 'sobering thought that colonial powers such as Britain, France and USA should display greater respect for UN principles than democratic India (Datta-Ray 1984, 60).' Because the history of empires in recent centuries has been largely dominated by white Euro-American expansion and hegemony, even the most astute observers have failed to recognize the derivative imperial practices of black and brown sahibs, even when their impact is no less consequential for millions (Shah 2004, 196).

Taking the Legacy Raj Syndrome to another level, independent India came to nurture great power ambitions, in such a way that it was not satisfied with merely maintaining the level of influence the British had exercised in the region. In the case of the Himalayan states of Nepal, Bhutan and the erstwhile state of Sikkim, it can be argued that while the British had largely limited themselves to defining foreign policy options, India sought to control their domestic politics as well. Reiterating the need for security and stability of all neighbourhood countries, India has on more than one occasion delved into other state's domestic matters.

In the Nepalese context, it can be argued that the overall thrust of New Delhi's policies towards Nepal has been inspired by narrow national interests and not universal values, even if concerns about democracy, human rights and progress are occasionally raised to legitimise aggressive pursuits. India largely resorts to the argument of its security concerns vis - à - vis the strategic importance of Nepal as the 'Himalayan barrier' between itself and China; to justify its various overt and covert manipulative acts inside Nepal. For example, speaking in the Indian parliament during the visit of the then king of Nepal, Prime Minister Nehru stated that, "much as we stand for the independence of Nepal, we cannot allow anything to go wrong in Nepal or permit the barrier [the Himalayas] to be weakened.... because that would be a risk to our own security (Paranjpe and Thomas 1991, 176)." However, the fallacy of this notion was clearly evident when in 1962 during the Indo - China war, in China pushed across the long and disputed border with India, and had no need to detour through Nepal's mountainous terrain to get to India. Saubhagya Shah describes this perceived Indian security concerns vis - à - vis Nepal as a 'Himalayan Red Herring' as he argues that the much hyped up Indian concern of the Himalayan barrier, in essence is nothing but a pretext for India's meddling in the Himalayan country's internal matters (Shah 2004). For the people of Nepal and for many in South Asia, it is indeed a daunting prospect that despite the Chinese fiasco, which proved Nehru's concerns about the security of Nepal's northern frontier to be largely unfounded, the legacy still lives on with successive generations of Indian leaders and bureaucrats continuing to use the issue of Himalayan security as a pretext to place conditions on Nepal.

'Strategic coercion' refers to the 'deliberate and purposive' use of threats to 'influence another's strategic choices' in inter - state relations (Freedman 1998, 15). It can be argued that, in its quest for regional dominance, India has resorted to measures which can be compared to coercive diplomacy or strategic coercion over other regional states. In the eastern Himalayas, a treaty concluded in 1950 turned Sikkim into an Indian 'protectorate'. As it turned out, the danger to Sikkim did not come from any adversary, but from the protector itself: as twenty five years after Sikkim signed the treaty of friendship, India annexed it through a two - stage process of destabilization and military occupation. A similar treaty concluded with Bhutan obliged the latter to be 'guided' by India on foreign affairs and defence (Shah 2004, 198).

Hence, it can be argued that such inner contradictions of Indian regional aspirations have contributed to making South Asia one of the world's most volatile and violent regions.

3.3 Factors Responsible for Sustaining the Environment of Discord in the Region

At the interstate level, a number of factors can be deduced which are responsible for sustaining the environment of discord in the region:

3.3.1 Suspicion of India's Motives

Thanks to the hegemonic aspirations of India, there is a strong tendency in the region to read almost every major Indian policy move as a wicked design, a notion that India has not been able to dispel to the satisfaction of its neighbours. To begin with, foremost in the Pakistani mind has been the fear that India has not been able to reconcile to Pakistan's existence as an independent state. The frequent irredentist claims from Indian leaders in the past and the methods in which some of the major disputes were handled, such as the long-drawn-out negotiation over the sharing of the financial assets in the post-independence phase and the sharing of the waters of the Indus and the Ganges rivers, have reinforced this suspicion. Kashmir remains the central contentious issue between the two countries, for which Pakistan has blamed India for ignoring the call of the international community for a plebiscite to determine the fate of the disputed territory.

Bangladesh's relations with India started on a strong footing after the Indo-Pakistani War of 1971 led to the liberation of the country. The ties between the two countries remained strong during the lifetime of Sheikh Mujibur Rahman, but changed perceptibly after his assassination in 1975 when subsequent military and quasi-military governments sought to decrease the Indian influence by diversifying its contacts with other powers like United States, China and Pakistan. Although recognizing the geopolitical fact of India's strategic interests in the region and India's contribution to the country's liberation struggle, the same conditions have made Bangladesh nurture a growing suspicion and fear of Indian domination and control in the future. Consequently, Bangladesh sought to reinforce its separate identity and newly acquired nationhood by resisting various Indian overtures (Paranjpe and Thomas 1991, 179).

Although the dispute over sharing the waters of river Ganges was solved through a treaty signed on December 12, 1996, many festering problems remain between the two countries; which Bangladeshis attribute to Indian intransigence. These include the 1974

border agreement, which Bangladesh has ratified and India is yet to do. The issue of Bangladeshi migrants to India has also made bilateral relations bitter. Bangladesh is suspicious of India's desire to establish a transit route to the seven isolated Northeast states which Bangladesh sees as detrimental to its security interests. There is also a feeling in the country that India's allegations that insurgents from the Northeast have as many as 195 training camps in Bangladesh is being used as a ruse to target the country (Dahal and Pandey 2005, 91 - 100).

Nepal's perception of India often changes with the system of government in the country, but there is a general consensus among all the political forces that Nepal needs to be on guard so that it does not capitulate to the Indian interest. A primary bone of contention is the 1950 Peace and Friendship Treaty, which New Delhi sees as the framework of its relations with Nepal, but which Kathmandu considers as already having outlived its utility (Khatri 1998, 5 - 24). The treaty provides India significant say in security and economic matters, which

was used as the basis for imposing blockade in 1989 after Nepal acquired arms from China and introduced work permits in some districts of the then Kingdom. During the time of the Narsimha Rao and Inder Kumar Gujral governments, India agreed to set up a joint commission at the Foreign Secretarial level to re - examine the Treaty, but the talks stalled only after a few rounds of negotiations. The Nepalese are also suspicious of India's intentions of using the trade and transit treaties that have to be renewed frequently as leverage on landlocked Nepal.

Given historical memories about the Indian invasion of Sri Lanka, there is a heightened threat perception which Sri Lankan political leaders have often come to reflect. Leaders like John Kotelawala were most vocal in this regard and expressed fear that Nehru's ambition was dominating the smaller countries in the region. Both SWRD Bandaranaike and his wife Sirimavo Bandarnaike repudiated Sri Lanka's fear of Indian aggression, but remained ever vigilant of the Indian factor in the Island's security (Banerjee 1998, 167 - 170). J R Jayawardene took a more practical approach towards India, and despite the unauthorized airdrop of supplies to the Tamils in 1987, he welcomed the Indian Peace Keeping Force (IPKF) to the country to counter balance the Tamil demands for autonomy with Colombo's objective of maintaining its territorial integrity and national unity (Paranjpe and Thomas 1991, 181). His successor, Ranasinghe Premadassa, was less inclined to believe in Indian benevolence and deliberately stayed away from the country during the signing of the Indo - Sri Lanka peace accord in 1987 and later asked the IPKF to leave Sri Lanka during his presidency.

3.3.2 Conflict over Resources

The general suspicion towards India is also reflected over sharing of natural resources, which could have been mutually beneficial to the countries concerned. The common fear of its neighbours is that India will exploit the situation to its advantage and they might lose their limited bargaining power in future dealings with India. The Ganga - Barhmaputra - Meghna Basin that flows through the subcontinent is one of the richest river systems in the world, which has the potential to meet the demands of arable land, water and energy needs for of the millions of people in Bangladesh, Bhutan, India and Nepal.

There is a widespread belief in Nepal that the first two Indo - Nepal water projects involving the rivers of Kosi and Gandak in Nepal, were not in Nepal's favour. Since then, any discussion on sharing of water resources with India evokes the fear of a sell out to India, as did the Tanakpur Agreement signed by an elected government in Nepal. Even the 1996 Mahakali Treaty with India, which was ratified by the joint Houses of the Parliament and would provide 6,480 MW of electricity, has not yet been implemented because of the lack of a detailed project report due to differences between the two countries over various issues.

For Bangladesh, the question of common water resources management remains an 'important and sensitive' issue over which talks have been going on for the last seven years. The negotiation took a serious turn when India announced its intention to develop a river linking project, through which Bangladesh fears it might lose out as a lower riparian state. The general air of mistrust is also reflected on the question of gas export from Bangladesh. Gas export to India has, however, become a politically sensitive issue for Bangladesh, to which no government in the country would like to commit, not unlike the controversy over water resources in Nepal.

3.3.3 Failure to Exclude the External Powers and Inability to Solve Problems

As noted above, one of the main objectives of India is to exclude, and if not possible at least minimize, the presence of foreign powers in South Asia so that the other states will accept the subsidiary roles implicitly assigned to them by the aspiring hegemon. Not only has India not succeeded in keeping the international powers away from the region, but has also exposed its own limitations as a hegemonic power by not being able to resolve regional problems to which it has committed its resources and manpower, thus undermining its credibility. This precarious situation, left open by India's inability to exercise its power in the region and the ability of the other states to challenge its authority at different intervals, has helped to sustain the level of discord in the region.

Pakistan, more than any other power in the region, has taken advantage of the international situation to obtain support from external powers. During the Cold War, it joined both Southeast Asia Treaty Organization (SEATO), and Central Treaty Organization (CENTO) as a means of counter-balancing the perceived Indian hegemony through the infusion of large-scale American aid. It was also able to capitalize on the rift in Sino-Indian relations after the 1962 conflict and establish a 'tested friendship' with China, thus developing an alternate base of moral and economic support to counter Indian influence. In the mid 1970s, during

General Zia - ul Haq's regime, Pakistan was able to reap benefits from US assistance, worth billions, when its strategic importance was enhanced by the Soviet invasion of Afghanistan. In the global campaign to root out Al Qaeda, after the September 11 attack on the US, Pakistan was considered to be an important 'non - North Atlantic Treaty Organisation (NATO)' ally, whose role was crucial in eliminating the Taliban and the terrorist infrastructure from Afghanistan. Thus, it would be safe to say that since the partition of the subcontinent, Pakistan's ability to play the external powers to its advantage has sustained its deep rooted rivalry with India.

Similarly, taking on the example of Nepal, it is interesting to note that the Himalayan state intermittently throws the 'China Card' on the bargaining table vis - à - vis its negotiations with India on bilateral issues. This strategic option of knocking on China's door for assistance during difficult times with India has been a key bargaining tool for the leaders of the landlocked Himalayan country and presumably gives sustenance to its defiance to India.

4. INTRASTATE CONFLICTS

Intrastate conflict is an equally serious problem in South Asia. Conflicts of such nature have three fold implications for the region. First, it tends to sap the development resources of the countries in the region; secondly, it weakens the movement towards strengthening liberal democratic structures; and thirdly, it raises the possibility of inter - state conflicts with the spill over effects of 'cross - border terrorism'. In South Asia, the intrastate conflicts are largely manifest in acts of terrorism perpetrated by disenchanted groups of people against the state machinery. The forms and patterns of terrorism experienced in South Asia have been varied ranging from religious extremism to those resulting from ethnic, regional, systemic and politic - ideological rebellions and conflicts (Muni 2006, 11).

A recurring theme that emerges in understanding terrorism/ insurgency in South Asia is the role of State and the governance factor therein. In this context, terrorism/insurgency is not just about an event that takes place at a certain moment in the history of a nation, but a process in which the state, for various shortcomings of its own, inadvertently provides the breeding ground for a self destructive cycle that it is unable to manage after a while. Hence, terrorism can be largely attributed to governance or rather the mis - governance factor which is manifested in the failure of the state to redress the grievances of its citizens; intolerance by dominant groups in society of the demands of the minority and less privileged groups; and the lack of vision and insecurity of political leaders and their tendency to search for popular short - term, quick - fix solutions (including the use of force) that only exacerbate the situation. The role of state in sustaining the environment of discord in internal conflicts is highlighted in this bold comment by the then Sri Lanka's President Chandrika Bandaranaike Kumaratunga in her address to the SAARC Summit held in Kathmandu in January 2002, soon after 9/11. She said:

> "Someone once said, 'hope betrayed transforms itself into bombs'. I would add that, perceived injustice, if it is allowed to continue unresolved, would transform itself first into despair and then into violence...
> ..... it would be useful to remind ourselves that... the terrorists did not cause the partition of India and create the tragedy of Kashmir as a buffer zone. To come closer to home, neither did the LTTE nor the armed Tamil militants create the circumstances for the marginalisation of the minority communities of Sri Lanka. Violence – social, political or physical – perpetrated by the state or the agents of the state against other states or its own people is the womb of terrorism, humiliation is its cradle and continued vengeance by the state becomes the mother's milk and nourishment for terrorism (Muni 2006, 16)."

Indeed, few heads of state would have courage to go to this length in holding the state responsible for terrorism.

4.1 Diagnostic Events

The nation building process has not been an easy one in South Asia. Very often due to either intentional or unintentional behaviours of rulers in power, the state has failed to show sensitiveness to the need of the various regions, ethnic groups and regional minorities, which has led to armed rebellion against the centre. The explanation for insurrection varies from country to country depending on specific time and location, but usually the counter-terrorism policy of the South Asian countries has proved to be more counter-productive than warranted and has inflamed the conflict further.

In Pakistan, the 1950s witnessed the language riots when the government attempted to make Urdu the national language, which infuriated the Bengali-speaking people who constituted majority of the Pakistani citizens. The crises between the East and Western wings reached a breaking point when the Awami League of East Pakistan led by Sheikh Mujibur Rahman won the elections in 1970 and the West Pakistani rulers refused to handover power to a legitimately elected government and instead unleashed the military forces to counter the crisis. The outcome was that after twenty-four years of being treated as a colony, the Eastern wing seceded from Pakistan in 1971. A different kind of a tussle between the state and federating units was witnessed in Baluchistan in the 1970s which resulted in nearly 10,000 deaths, while the 1980s saw the Sindh province up in arms against the government in the Movement for the Restoration of Democracy (MRD) that led to the confrontation between the makeshift Sindhi guerrilla outfit and the army. In the early 1990s, the rebellion led by the Muttahida Quami Mahaz (MQM) in Karachi, which initially started in opposition to the urban-rural quota in government jobs and college admission in Sindh grew into a reign of terror in Karachi. The fact that the state in Pakistan clashed with virtually all of its sub-national groups, showed the failure of the rulers to evolve a federal structure with maximum provincial autonomy and a fair distribution of resources (Ahmed 2006, 12).

The conflict in Sri Lanka, which is largely ethnic based, can be attributed to the inability of political elite representing the country's distinct ethnic communities to agree on a power-sharing formula over the past five decades. It can be argued that in large parts, the difference between the Tamils and the Sinhalese lies in the self-perception of their respective communities in which each see their identity threatened as a minority. For the Sinhalese, they are susceptible to the notion that they were the chosen people with a mission to preserve Buddhism in Sri Lanka, which has historically faced the threat emanating from their traditional 'national enemy', the 40 million Tamils in South India.

From the Tamil perspective, they see a systematic policy being churned out by the Sinhalese dominated state to marginalize them from the political processes of the country. As Ketheswaran Loganathan succinctly puts it, "the primary causes of Tamil militancy were clearly institutionalized discrimination, Sinhala chauvinism, and state-sponsored anti-Tamil programs (Muni 2006, 197)." In 1948, the up-country Tamils were deprived of their citizenship, and were disenfranchised the following year. In 1956, the country's leadership abandoned the two language policy and made Sinhala the only official language of the country. But in the 1970s, two more watershed events led to further alienation of the Tamil communities. The first was the linking of Buddhism to the state in the 1972 Constitution and the second was the implementation of discriminatory educational policies, most inappropriately labelled by the government as 'standardization' that would in essence squeeze out Tamil students to make room for Sinhalese ones under the rationale for affirmative action for the educationally underprivileged (Muni 2006, 197-98). Taken together with the indiscriminate targeting of Tamil lives and property by the Sinhalese mobs in various instances, to which the state turned a blind eye, the seeds of a protracted conflict between the two communities were sown, with the LTTE spearheading the demand for secession.

India's case is unique in South Asia since insurgencies are modulated by different compulsions in different regions. In some areas it is based on ideological motives but the ideologies are mainly driven by irredentist aspirations. In some cases religion provides the motive force, while political aspirations provide the underlying sustenance to militancy. And in other parts of India, terrorism stems from ethno-centric and parochial motives, seeking to break out from the majority fold, which they consider dysfunctional to their economic development as a separate ethnic entity (Ahmed 2006, 8).

India's experience in the Northeast, which is comprised of the seven states of Assam, Arunachal Pradesh, Manipur, Meghalaya, Mizoram, Nagaland and Tripura, underscores the difficulty in tackling the insurrections that are multifaceted and multidimensional in character. With the indigenous Indian elite as the socially cohesive and powerful group in full control of the political structure and system, marginalisation of the North - Eastern region remains a stark feature of the Indian political culture (Rizal and Yokota 2006, 223). Except for Arunachal Pradesh and Meghalaya, the long standing movements, either for autonomy or independence, have graduated into violent militant movements over time. More importantly, there is violence at many levels in all of these seven states. There is conflict between the centre and the states, between the states themselves, between tribes within the states and tribes in other states, between tribal and non - tribal actors, and between indigenous groups and 'outsiders (Ahmed 2006, 17).' Mizoram is the only state where militancy has been contained.

Although each case of conflict has its own causes that are distinct from others, the failure of the state to redress the grievances is due to its inability or apathy to identify the distinctive nature of the conflict. This tension is further aggravated when dissident groups feel that all other constitutional and legal alternatives appear to be getting them nowhere. Very often, policy based on haphazard reactions by states as a response to such violence through military and legal means has only helped to inflame the situation further. State's heavy handed measures meant to swiftly quell the insurrections, such as disappearances and custodial deaths, fake encounters and extra judicial killings, have had reverse effects. Instead of weakening the resolve of the militants, these measures have only helped to strengthen them and provide sympathy to the underdog.

4.2 The Marginalization Factors

In South Asia, the inability or the reluctance of the dominant groups in society to provide equal political space to incipient political elements has led to insurrections on several occasions. The Maoists uprising in

Nepal exemplifies this particular case where the Maoists had already joined the parliamentary process in the country, but were eventually excluded from mainstream politics.

In January 1991, when Nepal was just entering an era of multi-party democracy after the then King handed over the power to the people, the Communist Party of Nepal (CPN) – Unity Centre (the overarching body of like-minded extreme left of the centre groups under which the Maoists operated) formed the United People's Front Nepal (UPFN) to "expose the inadequacy of the multiparty system" by simultaneously adopting a resolution to form the people's army along with the decision to participate in elections. In the 1991 elections, the UPFN was able to acquire nine seats. However, within a few years, there emerged a rift within the UPFN. But when one of the present Maoist leaders, Baburam Bhattarai,[4] attempted to register for the next elections, the Election Commission refused to accept his faction and recognized only the Vaidya faction, which was the other faction splintered from the original UPFN, thus marginalizing the former. To add insult to the injury, subsequent strong measures taken by the state against the UPFN party workers in the early 1990s, including their harassment, arrest, torture and killings through police operations strengthened the Maoist's resolve to leave behind mainstream politics and opt for extreme counter measures, thus initiating the more than a decade long people's war which caused a death toll of more than 10,000 Nepalese and severe set backs to the already fragile economy of the country.

4.3 Insecurities of Political Leaders and Lack of Political Vision

The perceived insecurity of political leaders in South Asia and their determination to hold on to power at all costs have inadvertently sown the seeds of terrorism and perpetuated conflict even further.

In Pakistan, in the absence of popular legitimacy, General Zia-ul

---

4 The erstwhile Maoist leader is now the finance minister in the Nepal Government, after the landslide victory the party enjoyed in the Constituent Assembly Election held in 2008.

Haq's regime attempted to convert the state and society into a theocracy to an extent not witnessed before. His policy of subsidizing religious seminaries (*madrassas*) in small towns and rural areas, with the generous money that the US and Saudi Arabia had funnelled into Pakistan to create Afghan *Jehad* against the Soviet occupation of Afghanistan, led to the rapid growth of militant religious organisations, which were often competing with one another through violent means.

Between 1979 and 1990, the country witnessed a marked increase in the number of sectarian parties, while Jehad - related organizations increased considerably even more. The extent of terror and violence unleashed upon society due to the rise in the number of such organizations can be gauged from the large number of people being killed in sectarian terrorism. Pakistan today has around 10,000 *deeni madaris* (religious seminaries) where one million students receive religious instruction. About 7,000 students annually graduate from the seminaries and fail to find employment in Pakistan's weak economy. Most of them join the *Jehad* in the absence of opportunity to secure gainful employment. In the past, many *Jehadi* groups had openly admitted their connections with Osama bin Laden, but after the events of 9/11 such links are mostly denied. Today, the legacy of General Zia's use of religion to prop up his regime has created a 'monster' that has returned to haunt the state which created it in the first place (Ahmed 2006, 16 - 21).

In Sri Lanka, one can find a history of broken promises made by the ruling group to live up to agreements made with the Tamil community. The process of negotiations by the government with the Tamil political leadership shows how easily political leaders in Colombo have found it expedient to sacrifice long - term benefits for short - term political security. The inability of the government to come up with substantial initiatives to address the Tamil issue essentially manifests itself in two specific characteristics. First, agreements with the Tamils could not be implemented due to the instability of the government leadership to obtain the backing of their own party, let alone the opposition. And second, the two major Sinhala - dominated political parties, Sri Lanka Freedom Party (SLFP) and United National Party (UNP), do not allow political settlements to be expressed since it is viewed as an opportunity to undermine the role of the other party when it is in power. This is ironic since these parties endeavour to reach a settlement when they are in power, but consider it necessary to thwart or oppose a settlement when they are in opposition. The party in power then opts for an easy way out of the dilemma by withdrawing its proposal, and justifies its action on the ground that they cannot obtain the support of the people (Ahmed 2006, 16).

4.4 The Response Strategy to Terrorism in South Asia

The response strategies pursued by the South Asian states towards the varied challenges brought about by terrorism/insurgency fall into four broad categories (Muni 2006, 18 - 21).

The first strategy is based on the use *of force*. This strategy which involves the use of superior counter - force to suppress terrorism and insurgency is invariably pursued by all the South Asian states. The use of force being either inadequate, or excessive, or inappropriate; compounded by lack of proper coordination and understanding between different instruments and agencies of force, i.e. between police, paramilitary and military forces, between security agencies and political as well as administrative decision - making processes; has ironically helped the insurgency gain legitimacy, social support, and greater resilience. The second strategy relates to the *law and order* approach where terrorism is dealt with as a crime and sought to be curbed through legal and police methods. Almost all the South Asian states have enacted special laws and raised specialized forces in pursuance of this strategy but the impact of these laws in curbing terrorism has been far from being satisfactory. The third strategy is the *political and constitutional* approach to address the root causes of insurgencies and terrorism. Under this approach, steps to initiate talks and peace processes in search of negotiated settlements have been taken, and in some cases, accommodation through constitutional changes have also been offered and achieved. This strategy has garnered more positive outcomes by enabling the state to win the hearts and minds of insurgency -

affected people; and also to isolate terrorists and insurgents and erode the social support for their cause. The fourth approach, and closely linked with the political and constitutional approach, is the strategy of responding to terrorism through *socio-economic development* and *cultural accommodation*. The third and fourth approaches tend to serve long term strategy and deal with the preventive aspects of terrorism and conflicts. However, due to the lack of strategic patience on the part of political regimes and leadership, and the lack of adequate financial resources required to address the underlying social and economic issues, compounded by widespread corruption in government machinery, have led to the futility of these approaches.

In South Asia, one can discern a pattern to how state machinery responds to each new threat posed by terrorism or a multiplicity of such threats. First, with sheer neglect of the situation that has been brewing all throughout and then with what can be amounted to utter shock and followed by administrative collapse. This is coupled with inevitable confusion on whether the threat should be treated as a law and order problem (the root cause approach) or a high security risk (the military option), and these are issues which political leaders hardly see eye-to-eye. Hence, very often, terrorism takes its roots in an environment of political indifference, ambivalence, cynicism, or even political patronage before the state realizes the enormity of the task it will need to face. Even at a later stage when the level of violence perpetrated by both the non-state actor and the state becomes increasingly costly and intolerable, the state continues to function without a clear cut approach to terrorism by wavering between a policy that aims either for a political or military solution, or a combination of both. Moreover, there seems to be no mechanism of institutional learning within and among the states in South Asia in dealing with the threat of terrorism as each new theatre finds the state virtually setting about reinventing the wheel.

4.5 Handling the Maoist Insurgents in Nepal

In the case of Nepal, the state's response to the ever increasing Maoist threat shows a number of distinct characteristics as outlined in the preceding paragraphs. In the initial phase, the failure of the political leaders to understand the nature of the conflict led to a haphazard reaction that resulted in the indiscriminate use of the police force in two major 'search and destroy' operations that had disastrous results. It is widely believed that since the operations made little distinction between the innocent bystanders and the insurgents, such arbitrary use of state's force only helped to alienate the population from the centre to the extent that many neutrals were inadvertently pushed into the Maoist fold.

During the next few years, two different committees were set up by the government to find a solution to the Maoist problems in Nepal. After a thorough analysis of the Maoist situation, both the Dhami Commission Report (1997) and the Deuba Commission Report (2000) recommended an overhaul in the socio-economic structure which was in line with some of the insurgents' demands. The Deuba Commission's analysis went even further, suggesting that the ineffectiveness of the government was making the insurgency larger than life, and that dialogue should be the basis for resolving the problem (Muni 2006, 251-252). Although the recommendations were pretty substantive and dealt with a host of key underlying issues that it believed went to the roots of the ineffectiveness of the government, Girija Prasad Koirala, the prime minister at the time simply chose to ignore the Deuba report and nothing more has been heard of it since (Muni 2006, 252).

The lack of political resolve in addressing the Maoist issue was demonstrated by the fact that government was unable to come up with specific bargaining points with the rebel group through effective dialogues and nor was it able to muster consensus about coming down heavy-handed militarily with the rebels. Even after the Maoist threat was looming large all over the country, the government was unable to mobilize the national army in a coherent manner. It couldn't provide the army with clear cut mandates, such that the army was initially reluctant to get involved in the insurgency and asked that there be consensus among the political parties vis-à-vis its mobilization with specific guidelines from the government before it could move in. Hence, the ambivalent attitude of the leadership towards the armed rebellion during its formative years enabled a small fringe outfit to grow into a fearsome military machine within a few years (Shah 2004, 206). This resulted into Nepal being rapidly engulfed into a protracted war with Maoist insurgency that claimed thousands of lives and property worth millions.

4.6 Handling the Northeast Insurgents in India

In India in the Northeast, the military approach has made little headway due to the government's inability to create a unified command structure with proper coordination with the civilian authorities in most of the states except Assam. Furthermore, the old British Army doctrine that 'if you have them by the balls their hearts and minds will follow', though perhaps a successful colonial device, is not a successful method of dealing with ethnic strife in democratic countries that are trying to resolve internal problems of sub - nationalism (Muni 2006, 97). Government's inability to evolve an effective counter insurgency policy and lack of co - ordination at various levels is widely evident in the Northeast India. State armed police battalions are badly trained and inadequately equipped with outdated equipment. Another problem is the lack of adequate manpower in the police force, as on the pretext of providing security or batmen (orderly) duties, almost 20 percent of armed police manpower in the north - east is engaged in the households of senior officers, their duties including working in the poultry, piggery, and dairy farms or other businesses of these officers, along with their wives and other family members. The morale of the security forces is further degenerated by the lack of effective political leadership which, often hand in glove with the extremists, has never made the goals and objectives of the police force clear. This has prompted police officers to remain passive onlookers most of the time (Muni 2006, 97 - 100).

The 'developmental model' in the Northeast which predicated that massive developmental investment will eliminate the sources of popular discontent has also proved ineffective since the little surpluses that are left for this purpose is appropriated by the militants through extortion and 'taxation', and it is further offset by the flight of private capital in an environment of political uncertainty and widespread extortion (Muni

2006, 101). Other non - military strategies, such as amnesties and offers of rewards, bribery and corruption, devolution of power, empowerment and creation of new States, electoral politics, negotiations across the table and secret negotiations in India and abroad, etc. – offer only temporary respite from violence, but have not led to the resolution of conflict. To that end, it can be argued that the resolution of the Mizo insurgency in the state of Mizoram, the only case in the Northeast where the conflict was settled, was not because of the developmental approach, but because the Bangladesh war of 1971 led to the closure of the Mizo National Army camps in East Pakistan (Muni 2006, 101 - 102).

4.7 Bangladesh

Bangladesh in recent years has suffered serious loss of face and earned for itself a bad name and reputation as a lawless and violent nation (Muni 2006, 180). Militancy in Bangladesh displays some of the characteristics of terrorist organizations, but the threat to the country is perceived more from societal violence that is sustained by the animosities among the political parties in the country, where political vendettas play a strong role. It is indeed disconcerting that since both sides in the political divide use the terrorist elements to intimidate the opponent, society becomes almost a hostage to the political game - play (Muni 2006, 164). With the polarization and subsequent criminalization of politics in Bangladesh, this has led to the criminalization of educational institutions and student wings of the political parties have emerged as their main bastions of power (Chari 2001, 40). Thus the academic sphere has also been severely affected resulting into a heavy brain drain.

As mentioned above, the primary concern for Bangladesh is more for societal violence and criminal imperatives that are generated out of the confrontational nature of the political sphere. In Bangladesh, the group that comes closest to what might be called a terrorist organization is the *Sarbahara Party*, the self styled left radicals (Muni 2006, 170) whose aims and objectives are similar to those of the Naxalites in India, but has the "Robin Hood" image of helping the poor and not resorting to wanton violence. Another group that is emerging now is the Swandhin

Bangabhumi Movement that is reportedly sponsored by India, with the intention of carving out a chunk of the south western district that is a predominantly Hindu dominant region, into an independent country. The insurgency in the Chittagong Hill Tracts (CHT) is in a state of limbo and there is no guarantee that the situation will not turn violent in the future.

The Bangladeshi government's response to terrorism from the criminal elements has met with limited success. Most security operations against the militants have failed to produce the intended results due to a faulty strategy, lack of intelligence and alleged police tip - off to criminals about the planned operation before it is launched. As a result, such operations have proved to be largely ineffective in apprehending major ringleaders or recovering any significant amount of arms and ammunition. The police, in particular, are known to have their own links with criminals and politicians, often living beyond their means, but incapable of waging Bangladesh's battle against terrorism (Muni 2006, 177).

4.8 Pakistan

In Pakistan, although the government has repeatedly pledged its intention to eliminate terrorist organizations and to eradicate extremism from its policy, the government's response to terrorism is still deemed far from adequate. It has not fully clamped down on local terrorist and extremist groups, many of which have links with Al Qaeda. The government's seemingly half hearted move to ban a number of radical Islamic groups in January 2002, including the Jaish - e - Mohammad and the Lashkar - e - Toiba, held responsible by New Delhi for the December 2001 attack on the Indian Parliament, has not yielded positive results as many of these organizations simply re - emerged under changed names (Muni 2006, 117).

Although the government has taken some measures to check the infiltration of militants across the Line of Control that divides India and Pakistan, it has not taken any strong measures against the extremist networks that sustain the Kashmir *jihad* and there is a clear ambiguity in the military's policies towards the external *jihad* in India - administered Kashmir and in Afghanistan. The recent Pakistani government offensive into the Swat valley to root out Al - Qaeda, although demonstrating renewed resolve on the part of the government to check the growth in militancy, is yet to produce substantial results. However, it is encouraging to see that the operation has enjoyed an unusual level of support in Pakistan, even from conservative forces previously reluctant to criticise the Taliban (Walsh 2009). Furthermore, the government of Pakistan has not been able to effectively monitor and regulate terrorist funding that might be diverted from the *jehadi madrassas* to the Taliban and thereby to Al Qaeda patrons. And like most other governments in South Asia, Islamabad has also not enacted effective anti - money laundering legislation that might be used to clamp down terrorist money - laundering networks which operate through unofficial channels; known locally as *hundi* or *hawala* (Muni 2006, 133 - 134).

4.9 Sri Lanka

In Sri Lanka, the government initially came up with a two - pronged strategy (Muni 2006, 202) to deal with the nascent Tamil youth militancy in the mid - 1970s, which at first was to initiate a process of finding a political settlement and then to facilitate it by softening up the Tamil militancy. However, the strategy did not succeed in either appeasing or suppressing Tamil aspirations or revolt (Muni 2006, 205). When the policy of political and physical intimidation of the Tamils by successive governments failed to stop the spate of violence, it responded by further intensifying its strategy of collective punishment to terrorise the civilians into submission. In 1978, the LTTE was banned, and in July 1979 the Prevention of Terrorism Act (PTA) was passed in the Parliament. Many have observed that this was the beginning of the dark days for the Tamil people as all legal and constitutional safeguards with regard to arrest; detention and protection against self - incrimination were abrogated (Muni 2006, 205).

The recent military success of the Sri Lankan government against the LTTE in which they claim to have crushed the insurgent rebels for good is a significant turn of event in this more than five decades long secessionist movement. However, the long term implications for a sustained peace process from this military victory will depend to a large extent on how well and positively the Sri Lankan government capitalizes on this operational advantage. Hence, much will depend upon the subsequent political moves of the Sri Lankan government to sow seeds of confidence among the Tamil population, and also to a large extent on whether Vellupillai 'Prabhakaran', the insurgents much revered leader was indeed the centre of gravity for the secessionist movement.

5. THE FAILURE OF SAARC

The South Asian Association for Regional Cooperation (SAARC) is an economic and political organization of eight countries in Southern Asia. In terms of population, its sphere of influence is the largest of any regional organization encompassing almost 1.5 billion people. It was established on December 8, 1985 by India, Pakistan, Bangladesh, Sri Lanka, Nepal, Maldives and Bhutan. In April 2007, at the Association's 14th summit, Afghanistan became its eighth member.

5.1 Genesis of SAARC

The formation of the SAARC in 1985 marked a watershed event in the regional dynamics of the South Asian subcontinent. This historic step reflected the first institutionalized effort to overcome petty indifferences and thus forge multilateral cooperation among the countries of the region.

Regionalism in South Asia has its own pattern (Chaudhury 2006, 51). In this context, it is interesting that SAARC was different in many ways as a regional organization from the outset. Firstly, the strategic backdrop behind the genesis of SAARC was different. Unlike other regional organisations in the world that largely grew out of a necessity to counter outside threat perceptions, SAARC was not the outcome of a strategic need to form a regional alliance to counter any common external threat nor was it initiated by any external 'big power', and nor was it the brainchild of the regional super power, India. The organization was largely the outcome of a regional strategy based on the need to counter the growing military strength and influence of a regional power within the region [India], and the initial proposal for the organization came from Bangladesh, one of the smaller neighbours. Secondly, SAARC began its journey with a bumpy start as the two key stakeholders of the region, India and Pakistan did not favour the concept of a regional alliance which they regarded as not in accordance with their national interests. Hence, they were not part of the initial steps in setting up of the organization.

Against this backdrop, India's suspicion towards this regional development was natural and hence, it was hardly surprising to anyone that India came up with a lukewarm response to the concept of the regional alliance. India, as the largest state in the region was 'less-than-enthusiastic' about the whole matter and was reluctant to be a partner in the regional organization. India initially responded with utter indifference followed by hesitation based on its apprehension to the potential notion that its neighbours could collectively scuttle its 'beneficial bilateralism'; and use the proposed organization as a tool to undermine its vital national interests (Chaudhury 2006, 62).

However, despite its attitude towards the alliance, India did not, or to put if more aptly, could not altogether reject the proposal of the regional organization. India's eventual acceptance of the proposal can be attributed to two factors. First, the idea of such an organization was too powerful to reject at that juncture, as India envisaged the potential to convert the agenda of the proposed organization to pursue its own regional policy (Chaudhury 2006, 63). The other factor was that the total rejection of the idea could also lead to India's isolation in the region, which would indeed be detrimental towards its overall standing in the region in the long run. Thus, India's eventually accession to SAARC was full of trepidation regarding the whole affair and was carried out in a tardy and grudging manner.

Indian apprehension was reflected in the preconditions made by New Delhi for its proposed accession to the organization. The conditions emphasized two major points. First, India demanded that the proposed organization would not discuss bilateral and contentious issues; and at its behest, bilateral issues were kept out of the domain of SAARC. It is interesting that Indian inclination towards the apolitical nature of the regional alliance was largely a resultant of it premonition that the organization would inadvertently turn into a forum for discussions of political debates where the smaller states would be able to exert pressure on India and thus check its hegemonic aspirations. The second condition proposed by India was that all decisions of the organization should be unanimous.

It was not only India who came up with a lukewarm response to the proposal for a regional organization in South Asia. Pakistan, the other key player in the region was also apprehensive about the whole concept; and for its own reasons. Firstly, the ever prevalent bad blood between India and Pakistan was a key raison d'être behind the hesitant attitude of Pakistan towards SAARC. It is interesting that both India and Pakistan, two arch rivals in the region saw the attempt to establish a regional organization to be the malicious handiwork of their respective enemy number one; and saw detrimental implications of the regional concept towards their own national interests. Hence, Pakistan, for her part was apprehensive that the proposed organization would only serve the purpose to further strengthen India's national interest in the region by giving India a more proactive forum to better voice and force her strategic interests upon other lesser players of the region. After two major military setbacks at the hands of the Indian army in 1965 and 1971, it was not surprising that Pakistan would no longer be interested in any perceived attempts to further degrade her status in the region. Secondly, Pakistan was more inclined towards increasing her proximity with the Middle East countries, which would serve her two key strategic interests i.e. to strengthen the country's Islamic links in the Persian Gulf region and to further her economic interests by taking advantage of the growing importance of OPEC in world politics, which had been burgeoning since 1973.

The exclusion of bilateral and contentious agendas from any discussions in the SAARC forum and the need for total consensus in all decisions have rendered decision-making process in SAARC ineffective and impractical. Many contentious issues in SAARC, both at the inter-state and intrastate level, remain largely unresolved due to the inability of SAARC to address such issues, however pertinent they may be for enhancing regional stability and cooperation. Furthermore, the categorical removal of decision making process based on majority votes due to insistence on total consensus among all member states has obviously been another setback towards the progress of the organization, as it is inevitable that decisions will be tied down due to the inherent difficulty in reaching a total consensus in such a diverse organisation.

5.2 State Sovereignty vs. Supra Nationality

The lack of confidence among member states was also manifested in the form of ingrained sensitivities towards their state sovereignty, especially the smaller ones. It can be argued that this attitude towards state sovereignty in the region was an outcome of the colonial legacy; as most of the South Asian countries were colonies not so long ago. Hence, they cherish their new-found sovereignty to such an extent that they are hyper sensitive toward one another that may sometime smack of 'reflexive nationalism (Chaudhury 2006, 243).' As a consequence, state sovereignty has assumed immense importance for the countries of the region, which is not negotiable, at least with respect to the other neighbouring countries of the region (Chaudhury 2006, 248). This tendency of the South Asian nations to be reluctant to shed their reticence of state sovereignty has made it difficult for them to move towards the politics of supra-nationality; as has been the case in other regional organizations such as the European Union. This has seriously hindered the progress of SAARC towards attaining regional integration.

Thus the asymmetric situation in favour of India has not yet allowed the SAARC and regional cooperation in South Asia to take off (Chaudhury 2006, 249).

6. CONCLUSION

In South Asia the inherent conflict dynamics that revolve around a milieu of suspicions and hatred, built over decades, will not disappear overnight. It has made it difficult to kick start a viable and sustainable peace building process in the region. The troubles in the region, its endemic tensions, mutual mistrusts and occasional hostilities can be largely considered as products of the contradiction of India's security perception and interests with that of the rest of the countries of the region. Due to the omni - present suspicion of India's motives, other regional powers in South Asia perceive threats to their security coming primarily from India, which for its part, considers its neighbours as an integral part of its own security system. Hence, the perception of India as a regional power that demands habitual obedience from its neighbours (Baral 2001, 200), has given it the image of the proverbial Big Brother with all its negative connotations (Muni 1980, 39). This has inadvertently exacerbated the complexity of the environment.

At the interstate level, the asymmetrical power balance in the region, which is manifest with Indian preponderance, is largely responsible for sustaining the environment of mistrust and suspicion in the region. Disparity in the size and resources of India compared with the rest of the states in the region, have invariably created a sense of insecurity among the lesser powers, thus making the prospect of developing confidence building measures a problematic one. Furthermore, the inner contradictions of India's regional policies based on its hegemonic aspirations, on one hand, and its representation of itself as the 'largest democracy' have further tainted the strategic landscape of the region and arguably have contributed to making South Asia one of the world's most volatile and violent regions. The hegemon - subsidiary relationship in the region between the aspirant hegemon, India and the secondary powers that come up with knee jerk reactions in defiance to the Indian aspirations; has fed a vicious cycle of mistrust and fuelled an environment of intractable conflict in the region.

In the intrastate domain, the predominant role of the state machinery in managing internal conflicts has fallen far short of resolving the root causes of the conflict. The failure can be mainly attributed to the inability of the state to identify the root causes of the problem which are inherently distinct from others. State measures to address such internal crises lack coherence and earnestness; and their incompetence are reflected in their knee jerk policies of quick fix solutions, mainly through military and legal means. Without any substantial endeavours to identify and redress the inherent nature of the grievances underlying the conflicts, which are distinct from each other, the governance factor has contributed paradoxically to sustaining the environment of discord in the region.

SAARC as a regional organization has completed more than two decades of its existence since its inception in 1985. The organization which grew in a particular strategic context, in which the smaller countries of South Asia came together to resist the potential hegemonic behaviour of India, has largely been unable to achieve much as compared to its regional counterparts in other parts of the world. The dismal failure of SAARC can also be attributed to the asymmetric power structure in the region, which has made it difficult to build a relationship based on mutual confidence and work towards regional integration by shedding the reticence of state sovereignty. Therefore, genuine initiatives to overcome the atmosphere of suspicion and build confidence among the countries of the region are needed. SAARC could reach the next level of regional cooperation and integration if the pre-fixation on state sovereignty could be replaced with the concept of supra-nationality similar to the European Union. SAARC should be a made a forum to discuss all contentious issues and decisions have to be taken based on majority vote instead of the quite-difficult-to-achieve total consensus. Unless such steps are taken by the countries and the people of the region, SAARC is likely to continue as a mere talking shop for the dignitaries of states and governments in South Asia.

In such a scenario, the plight of the millions in South Asia will continue unchanged.

REFERENCES

Ahmed, Imtiaz. 2006. *Understanding Terrorism in South Asia: Beyond Statist Discourses.* New Delhi: Foundations Books.

Banerjee, Dipankar, ed. 1998. *Comprehensive Security in South Asia.* New Delhi: IPCS.

Baral, Tara N. 2001. "Perceptions of Small States on Confidence - Building in South Asia." In *The Challenge of Confidence - Building Measures in South Asia*, edited by Moonis Ahmar, 188 - 203. New Delhi: Har - Anand Publications.

Chari, P. R., ed. 2001. *Security and Governance in South Asia.* New Delhi: Manohar.

Chaudhury, Anasua Basu Ray. 2006. *SAARC at Crossroads: The Fate of Regional Cooperation in South Asia.* New Delhi: Samskriti.

Dahal, Dev Raj, and Nishchal Nath Pandey, eds. 2005. *Comprehensive Security in South Asia.* New Delhi: Manohar.

Dahal, Shiva Hari, Haris Gazdar, S. I. Keethaponcalan, and Padmaja Murthy. 2003. *Internal Conflict and Regional Security in South Asia: Approaches, Perspectives and Policies.* Geneva: United Nations Institute for Disarmament Research (UNDIR).

Datta - Ray, Sunanda K. 1984. *Smash and Grab: Annexation of Sikkim.* New Delhi: Vikas.

Freedman, Lawrence, ed. 1998. *Strategic Coercion: Concepts and Cases.* Oxford: Oxford University Press.

Hunt, T. 2000. "President - Wallah: India Is the Jewel in U.S. Leader's Asia Trip." *The Guardian*, March 20, 2000. Http://www.guardian.co.uk/Archive/Article/0,4273,3976010,00.html.

Huntington, Samuel P. 1991. *The Third Wave: Democratization in the Late Twentieth Century.* Oklahoma: University of Oklahoma Press.

International Institute for Counter Terrorism. Accessed February 10, 2009. http://www.ict.org.il.

Keohane, Robert O. 1984. *After Hegemony: Cooperation and Discord in the World Political Economy.* Princeton: Princeton University Press.

Khatri, Sridhar K. 1998. "Nepal in the International System: The Limits of Power of a Small State." In *The Political Economy of a Small State,* edited by Ananda Aditya, 5 - 24. Kathmandu: NEFAS.

Muni, S. D. 1980. "South Asia." In *Conflict and Intervention in the Third World*, edited by Mohammed Ayoob. London: Croom Helm.

Muni, S. D., ed. 2006. *Responding to Terrorism in South Asia.* New Delhi: Manohar.

Myers, David J. 1991. "Threat Perception and Strategic Response of the Regional Hegemons: A Conceptual Overview." In *Regional Hegemons*, edited by David J. Myers, 1 - 26. Oxford: Westview Press.

Naik, Niaz A. 2003. "Security Organization for South Asia (SOSA): Mechanism for Conflict Resolution in South Asia." In *Terrorism in South Asia: Impact on Development and Democratic Process*, edited by Sridhar K. Khatri and Gert W. Kueck. New Delhi: Shipra Publications.

Panda, Rajaram. 1984. "Recent Developments in South Asia." *Asia Pacific Community* 24 (Spring): 49 - 73.

Paranjpe, Shrikant, and Raju G. C. Thomas. 1991. "Indian and South Asia: Resolving the Problems of Regional Dominance and Diversity." In *Regional Hegemons: Threat Perception and Strategic Response*, edited by David J. Myers, 161 - 189. Oxford: Westview Press Inc.

Ramana, P. V. 2006. "Naxalism: Trends and Government Response." *Dialogue* 8, no. 2 (October/December): 58 - 69.

Rizal, Dhurba, and Yozo Yokota. 2006. *Understanding Development, Conflict and Violence: The Cases of Bhutan, Nepal, North - East India and the Chittagong Hill Tracts of Bangladesh.* New Delhi: Adroit Publishers.

Shah, Saubhagya. 2004. "A Himalayan Red Herring? Maoist Revolution in the Shadow of the Legacy Raj." In *Himalayan People's War: Nepal's Maoist Rebellion*, edited by Michael Hutt, 192 - 224. London: Hurst & Company.

Walsh, Declan. 2009. "Pakistani Civilians Flee Swat Valley as Major Ground Offensive Draws Closer." *The Guardian*, May 10, 2009. http://www.guardian.co.uk/world/2009/may/10/pakistan - taliban - swat - valley.

Wikipedia. n.d."Naxalite." Accessed April 7, 2009. http://en.wikipedia.org/wiki/Naxalite.

Ziring, Lawrence, ed. 1978. *The Subcontinent in World Politics: India, Its Neighbors and the Great Powers.* New York: Praeger.

III

CONFLICT OF NUCLEAR CONFRONTATION IN SOUTH ASIA

1. INTRODUCTION

One of the major issues facing the post-Hiroshima modern international system has been controlling the spread of nuclear weapons. An immediate solution proposed by the only proprietor and employer of the nuclear weapons, the USA was to submit all nuclear weapons and related material to an international body. As expected, this suggestion was rejected by USSR owing to the distrust and antagonism that existed between the rivals in conflict. Ever since, the same has been the persistent behaviour of adversaries in the conventional as well as the nuclear conflicts. India and Pakistan are two such well known antagonists of South Asia who were born into a conflict. Kashmir has been a political and military dispute for over six decades now. In 1998, both the countries openly demonstrated their nuclear capability to the world and added another critical dimension to the already volatile security environment of the South Asian region. Since then, the world has been witnessing with extreme concern, swings of crisis and stability in this area. The world has found it difficult to reconcile with the nuclear status of these hostile neighbours and worries about the future of this explosive combination of antagonism and nuclear capability.

This paper seeks to analyse the worrisome phenomenon of nuclearisation in South Asia. In doing so, the perspectives of both the countries will be considered and the opinions of both the nuclear optimists as well as the pessimists will be applied to present a broad-spectrum view. The paper will first examine the prevalent security environment of South Asia. In that, it will first analyse the security and threat perceptions of both the countries and then study the individual nuclear doctrines which have evolved out of these perceptions. Second, the paper will analyse what impact has nuclearisation had on the security environment of South Asia. For this propose, it will deliberate how the South Asian states differ from the Nuclear Weapons States (NWS) of the Cold War. Subsequently, both the nuclear doctrines will be analysed from the opponent's point of view, to identify the contentious issues. Later, an overall assessment will be made on the impact of the nuclear weapons on the regional security environment. In the last part, the paper will undertake a historical analysis of four case studies of recent crises to determine the efficacy of nuclear weapons as deterrence in South Asia. Then, inferences from these case studies will be extrapolated to predict few probable future scenarios. Finally, nuclear deterrence theories will be applied on these inferences to predict the likelihood of the stability of nuclear deterrence in South Asia.

This paper will maintain that, there is an inherent contextual dissimilarity in the perceptions of both the countries which threatens the South Asian security. India feels threatened from China and Pakistan, while Pakistan's security concerns are Indo - centric. It will be argued that Indian quest for nuclear capability is underlined by a combination of perceived threats as well as ambitions for enhanced global stature while Pakistan's nuclear arsenal is its key deterrent against India. Pakistan has enunciated a straight forward nuclear doctrine of 'first - use' in case the integrity of Pakistan is threatened. While for India with a sizeable arsenal of nuclear weapons and vast strategic depth, 'No First Use' (NFU) doctrine is a practical choice. It will be maintained that there are numerous ways in which the developed nuclear states fear the actions and interactions of new nuclear states to be different. It will be inferred from the analysis of the historical cases that nuclear deterrence has been robust enough to shape the outcome despite the organisationally biased behaviours. It will also be argued that it was primarily the nuclear factor that deterred both states from going to war and the presence of nuclear weapons has been the most significant factor in bringing these crises to a close. It will be presented that nuclear predictors have divided the future nuclear possibilities of South Asia into three practical scenarios. They are categorised as purposive, inadvertent and accidental. It will be maintained that purposive and inadvertent uses seem improbable for the future while the making of a 'crude dirty bomb', by a non - state actor cannot be ruled out. Conclusively, it will be opined that, for the foreseeable future, the majority of indicators point towards a greater probability of a stabilised nuclear deterrent in the South Asia. However, the situation can be further consolidated by pursuing CBMs for securing the stability in the region.

It is important to note that this paper deals with the mindsets, attitudes, behaviours and dynamics specifically in South Asia only. By implication, the inferences and logics may not therefore be generically applicable to different rivals, regions or environments. This paper assumes that the reader has adequate background knowledge about the progression of nuclear programs of both the countries as well as of the basic nuclear deterrence theories. Owing to the paucity of space, details regarding capabilities and programs have not been included. The focus has remained on the issues of employment of the nuclear weapons.

However, the following generic status of capabilities is considered valid while discussing the subject. As per a SIPRI source (Badri - Maharaj 2000, 63), India's nuclear stockpile will include a sizeable number of enhanced fission weapons in the 100 - 150kts range, good numbers of small fission weapons in the 20kts range and sub - kiloton tactical weapons and maybe few large super - boosted fission weapons in the 200+kts range. This combination of a reasonably comprehensive variety of weaponry would probably not demand the development of a fusion or an expensive thermonuclear arsenal. However, the capability to produce such device has been demonstrated in one of the five tests in 1998. Additionally short and intermediate range nuclear capable ballistic missiles also form a part of nuclear delivery systems.

Whether India will choose to develop such a nuclear arsenal will depend entirely on its security perceptions and domestic politics. However, the fact remains that substantial capability and capacity exists in India to develop and deploy an effective and sizeable nuclear arsenal without further publicity.

For Pakistan, the same SIPRI (Badri - Maharaj 2000, 90) source assumes that, the available material could produce 60 - 65 fission weapons, considering an average weight of 15kgs used in a single weapon. Pakistan's weapon program is quite modest in scale and quantity. Pakistan lacks self - sufficiency in fuel, nuclear industry and simulation facilities of thermonuclear devices (Barnaby 1998). Pakistan also cannot use reactor grade plutonium for weapons. However with access to plutonium, and test results of 1998 boosted - fission device, Pakistan has developed the capability to make these weapons with an estimated yield of up to 150kts. Even though Pakistan's capacity to produce nuclear weapons is much lesser compared to that of India, yet its ability to produce meaningful numbers and types of weapons has provided it with the 'minimum credible deterrence'. Short and medium - range nuclear capable missiles also form an important part of the delivery systems of Pakistan.

2. SOUTH ASIAN SECURITY ENVIRONMENT

The security situation in South Asia underwent a paradigm shift when in 1998 India and Pakistan revealed their nuclear capability to the world to proclaim the status of de facto nuclear states. Ever since, two mutually contradictory developments have taken place: one conflicts like Kargil and 2002 stand - off and second, efforts to improve relations like Lahore and Agra summits. This contradictory combination of recurring conflicts and peace efforts proves that a wide communication gap exists between the two antagonists which outsiders often rush to fill in before a crisis spirals out of control. Crisis tend to justify the nuclear pessimists' perception of inadvertent nuclear exchange while the peace efforts and the absence of a full scale war despite few 'near misses' give confidence to nuclear optimists' conviction that nuclear deterrence is working for South Asia. Immediately after the nuclear tests, a quick succession of crisis erupting in the region gave rise to apprehensions about hasty intended or inadvertent exchange of nuclear weapons. Crisis stability was seen to be becoming a problem. However, both the states demonstrated excellent restraint realising that a nuclear escalation would be mutually destructive. As more time has passed, both states and the world at large, appear to be reconciled with the reality of nuclear status of each other. Since 2002 stand - off, there has been no serious confrontation; rather the emphasis has shifted towards engagement and restraint. This may be termed as the natural outcome of the deterrence created by the arrival of nuclear weapons in the region. Nuclear optimists may feel good about this analysis; however certain potential nuclear dangers have also been identified during these crises, which will be discussed later. There is an inherent contextual dissimilarity in the perceptions of both the countries (Khan 2002, 133). The South Asian security is threatened by the contradicting security perceptions of Pakistan and India. It is therefore important to understand the basic differences in the security and threat perceptions of both the countries.

2.1 Pakistan's Perspective

Pakistan's threat perception has always been and still is Indo - centric. No other country features in the security assessment of Pakistan as crucially as India. Pakistan has always been driven by the security concerns generated by India. Apart from many other post - independence issues, Kashmir has been the biggest problem. Both have fought three full scale wars and four 'almost - wars' over the issue. The separation of East Pakistan due to Indian interference in 1971 followed by the 1974 nuclear tests, made the Pakistani leadership conscious of its vulnerabilities. Even though, immediately after the tests, Pakistan tried to get security guarantees from its allies and major super powers, it was not surprised by their refusal. It sought a nuclear umbrella but was disappointed by USA as well as China (Khan 2002, 138). Pakistan's subsequent efforts to have South Asia declared a nuclear weapons free zone through UN, joint ratification of NPT, a bilateral agreement on non - proliferation and an agreement not to produce weapons, were all rejected by India on the pretext of its security concerns with China. After exhausting all other options, Pakistan embarked upon its own weapons program in late 70s to create a minimum credible deterrence to deter a likely Indian aggression. Kashmir has remained a disputed issue due to diverging stances. India believes Kashmir is a territorial issue and is non - negotiable as it is an integral part of India. Pakistan considers Kashmir an outstanding political issue and wants Kashmiris to be given right of self determination according to the UN resolutions. Shimla agreement also asks for bilateral resolution and Nehru too committed to giving Kashmiris their choice (Peimani 2000, 27). India's recent stance that it has 18 separatist movements going on in the country and giving Kashmiris their right of self determination would be setting a wrong precedence, has made the resolution of the dispute highly improbable. Pakistan responds that India claimant of being a large democracy should act democratically and respect the demands of the majority of the Kashmiri as well as ethnicities to decide their own future. Pakistan's political, moral, diplomatic and alleged military support to the freedom struggle has also been another cause of severed relations between the two neighbours.

Since the Kashmiri freedom movement has gained momentum, swings in the relations have been witnessed from brief calm periods to protracted hostile interaction, characterised by military exercises, arms race, cross border skirmishes, hectic hostile diplomatic flurry to undo each other on international issues, threats of grave destruction, nuclear and missile tests, castigating media campaigns and prolonged military stand - offs on the borders. In the aftermath of nuclearisation of South Asia, Kashmir has attracted global attention as being a nuclear flashpoint. In the backdrop of these issues, Pakistan's nuclear arsenal is its key deterrence against India (Khan 2005). For Pakistan, it plays the same role as it did for the West against USSR. It deters a potential adversary with heavy superiority in the conventional as well as nuclear forces. The scope and status of Pakistan's nuclear capabilities illustrate well that Pakistan does not look beyond India.

Another reason that is generally imposed upon Pakistan for acquiring nuclear capability is its quest for prestige through being the first in the Islamic world to get a nuclear weapon. The esteem that is acquainted with the bomb has come as a spin - off of the weapon acquisition but was not the driving force behind it. It is a consequence but not the cause, therefore the perception of an 'Islamic Bomb' is more of a political proposition rather than a practical consideration (Khan 2002, 131).

2.2 The Indian Perspective

India perceives itself threatened from multiple sources. However, Indian quest for nuclear capability is underlined by a combination of considerations of the perceived threats and ambitions for enhanced global stature. In order to explain Indian framework of nuclear acquisition, at least six considerations can be identified.

First, China has been the key consideration in the Indian security calculus since early 60s. Indian apprehensions about Chinese nuclear weapons in the aftermath of Indo - China war of 1962 provide rationality for justifying its own pursuit of nuclear weapons. Design and shape of Indian long range missile program illustrates the Indian concern to address Chinese threat.

Second, Pakistan, owing to turbulent historical animosity and violent record of relationship over Kashmir since independence, has always factored prominently in Indian threat perception framework (Shah 2002b). This concern has grown especially during and after late 1980s when India came across credible information about Pakistan's ambiguous nuclear capability. Acquisition of nuclear - capable missile capability by Pakistan after nuclearisation in 1998, enabling it to hit targets deep inside India, has added to the security concerns in the face of its own missile program. Indian 'Prithvi' missile program being Pakistan - specific, demonstrates the significance of Pakistani threat for Indians.

Third, biggest security concern for India is Pakistan's expanded relations with China. India perceives this bilateral relationship as 'strategic convergence' against India, where Pakistan is playing proxy of China to counter it in the region (Malik 2001/02, 73 - 74). Of most concern is the Sino - Pak defence and nuclear cooperation. The perceived collusion between Pakistan and China has accelerated its military cooperation with Russia, Israel, and US especially (Khan 2002, 106).

Fourth consideration is not a threat but an ambition. The perception of a great power status looms large behind all dimensions of Indian foreign, defence and economic policies. The Indian intelligentsia and decision makers supplicate that India carries inherent credentials of a big power and therefore must act and be treated accordingly. It is perceived that it's geo-strategic location, population,size, culture, emerging role in science and technology, growing role in international politics, developing military infrastructure and improving economy, are all pointers towards the realization of a Great Power status. The quest for recognition as a de jure nuclear weapon state and campaign for UNSC seat are consistent with this objective (Mattoo 1999, 328; Chari, Cheeman, and Iftekharuzzaman 1996, 32).

Fifth security consideration is generated out of ambition. Consistent with its notion of being a great global power, India has historically had a hegemonic attitude and relationship in its regional neighbourhood. Its occupation of Sikkim, dismemberment of Pakistan, intervention in Sri Lanka, border and water issues with Bangladesh and uninterrupted influence in Nepal, explicitly validate its bullying attitude. India perceives its immediate neighbourhood as its exclusive zone and near abroad. Its relationship with all its small neighbours testifies that it has not reconciled with their status as sovereign states. Moreover, the Indira Doctrine in early 1980s (Mitra 2001, 64-65) and the Gujral Doctrine (Mitra 2001, 64) in 1997 reflect inherent Indian aspirations to dominate the region and dictate regional political order according to Indian desires. Indian intervention in almost all of its neighbouring states verifies the ambition to shape regional relationships accordingly. It is argued by the Indian policy and decision makers that South Asia is 'arbitrary construct' by the outsiders with a view to confining Indian role only in South Asian region (Majid 2002). Paradoxically, this has created another security concern for India as all neighbours have irritants in their relations with India and the regional environment is strained with mistrust.

Finally, the tri-angular interaction between India, China and Pakistan complicates regional security configuration. China, not being a part of South Asia only, acts in response to its external concerns and considerations especially from USA, Russia and Central Asia. Pakistan, more recently has its own security priorities towards West while India remains more ambitious to exploit its status and influence in the Indian Ocean and globally. Therefore, diverging and at times conflicting priorities make the regional security environment more complicated and less stable.

Therefore, in South Asia, divergence in threat perceptions, reinforced by some inherent ambitions for more power and influence, beget the underlying security dilemma of South Asia (Majid 2002).

Since the security models of Pakistan and India differ from each other, their doctrines on the employment of nuclear weapons also differ. India's security model is based on its multiple threats perception and on the ambition to extend its perimeter of security and influence much beyond its territorial boundaries. It has sufficient conventional capabilities to defend itself from China as well as Pakistan and therefore, does not depend on its nuclear weapons alone.

Pakistan's security model is based on the perception that India will continue to deny a resolution of Kashmir dispute and may not hesitate to attempt to dismember Pakistan which will employ all means short of a war to settle the dispute. Underpinned by its conventional inferiority, Pakistan depends upon the Nuclear weapons to deter any aggression (Ganguly and Hagerty 2005, 196).

In the aftermath of 1998 explosions, both India and Pakistan pronounced what was called the 'bare - bone' doctrines. These should however be regarded as hints rather than guides to what would actually emerge in a conflict. Nonetheless, any discussion about nuclear affairs in South Asia must refer to these doctrines. It is therefore pertinent to study and analyse the nuclear doctrines of both countries.

2.2.1 Pakistan's Doctrine

Pakistan has enunciated a straight forward nuclear doctrine of 'first - use' in case the integrity of Pakistan is likely to be threatened (Matinuddin 2002). Pakistan has not announced an elaborate doctrine except that its strategy remains premised on its basic security concerns, to establish a credible deterrence, preserve its strategic forces and its sovereign existence. 'It implicitly threatens nuclear reprisals for nuclear or conventional aggression (Ganguly and Hagerty 2005, 197).' In order to sustain a viable deterrent vis - à - vis India's much larger conventional and strategic forces, the calculus of Pakistan's nuclear threshold has been intentionally shrouded in vagueness. It implies nuclear weapons to be a deterrent and not the weapons of war but weapons of mass destruction. These will be used as a choice of last resort, when all other conventional means have failed to deter aggression (Jervis 2002, 40). It is a natural choice for a country like Pakistan, with relatively weaker conventional forces and no strategic depth. Nuclear weapons form the last option in order to avoid a total collapse or annihilation by a conventionally stronger nuclear adversary. First - use doctrine does not automatically imply that Pakistan will always be the first to use the nuclear option but it does imply that Pakistan retains the option of first use and is determined to use nuclear option if its integrity/survival is assessed to be threatened. First - use option is a direct function of the nuclear threshold and the capability of conventional forces. The stronger the conventional forces, the higher is the nuclear threshold. Therefore, in this option, there is an inherent interplay of conventional and nuclear weapons. Pakistan has also institutionalised its command and control by establishing the National Command Authority (NCA) in February, 2000. It is an elaborate set up to ensure safe handling and prevent unauthorised employment of the assets. The country's highest decision making body for strategic assets is the National Security Council (NSC). It comprises of the President, Prime Minister, Governors, Chief Ministers, Defence Minister, Foreign Minister, Interior Minister, Services Chiefs, Chairman NCA and the Chairman Joint Chiefs of Staff Committee. Any other member can be included as deemed necessary to consult about other matters such as technical or financial issues. It is a comprehensively balanced and a well represented body, in which final decision making is with consensus, so that a single element may not influence the process. The NCA is a military - civil supervisory body which is responsible for the overall development, custody, handling and employment of all the strategic assets. It is a national agency for integrating and supervising activities of different agencies working for development, R&D, and storage of the assets. The employment is specifically the domain of Strategic Plans Division (SPD), which is primarily a joint - services military body and co - ordinates the processes of Intelligence, plans, deployments, and operations of the nuclear forces. It controls all the nuclear warheads and their delivery systems. Redundancies regarding the survivability of the arsenal and command chain for decision making in cases of attrition are being incorporated but details are not available publicly. In order to preclude the possibility of unauthorised use and ensure a graduated escalation while retaining the escalation control, the warheads, missiles and the delivery systems are all stored and handled separately from each other. This however implies the requirement of a sorted out and well integrated C2 setup to ensure timely deployments should a requirement arise. At the same time requirements of authentication codes/identities in each of the separate chains provides an inherent security against unauthorised access.

2.2.2 India's Doctrine

India refined its initial Draft Doctrine and finally in 2002, declared its Final Nuclear Doctrine. It is a set of political principles and administrative arrangements to handle its nuclear assets. Again, it may be referred to as 'hints' rather than 'elaborate guidelines' regarding management of nuclear assets (Khanna 2000, 109). The main elements of the Doctrine may be summarised as follows:

- 'No First Use' (NFU) policy;
- Maintaining a minimum credible deterrent;
- Retaliatory attacks to be authorised by civilian political leadership through the NCA ;
- Non-use of nuclear weapons against non-nuclear states;
- Retention of option to retaliate with nuclear weapons if India or Indian forces anywhere are attacked with biological or chemical weapons;
- Continuance of control on export of nuclear and missile-related materials and technologies, participation in FMCT negotiations, observance of moratorium on nuclear tests and working towards universal nuclear disarmament (Pant 2005, 279).

The command and control is provided by a two-layered National Command Authority (NCA). It has a political as well as a military council. The political council includes members of CCS and national security advisor, while the Executive council headed by national security advisor, includes Chairman Chiefs of Staff Committee (COSC), Chiefs of three Services, heads of intelligence agencies and members of scientific community. The executive council advises the political council headed by the Prime Minister, on decision making. The Prime Minister is the sole authority for issuing orders to release nuclear weapons. The operational arm of the NCA is the Strategic Forces Command (SFC), which is a tri-services command with an independent C-in-C who reports to Chairman COSC. The SFC holds command over all nuclear related tri-services assets, warheads and delivery systems. For retaliatory strikes, alternate chains of command and infra structure is also being established with no specific details available (Pant 2005, 285).

NFU doctrine implies that nuclear weapons will be used only for retaliation against a nuclear attack on India or Indian forces anywhere. However, the option of nuclear response to biological and chemical weapons has been retained to deter such attacks. The NFU option is not only a policy declaration, but also entails force structures, deployment patterns, surveillance assets and readiness states commensurate to the NFU posture (Matinuddin 2002). The crux of the NFU Doctrine lies in the assurance of massive retaliation to an extent that the first strike choice appears too costly to the adversary, thereby deterring the use of nukes in the first place. For India with a sizeable arsenal of nuclear weapons and vast strategic depth, NFU doctrine is a practical choice. It allows India to keep its warheads de-mated from the delivery systems and hence maintain a lower readiness status of 'launch on strike'. India is developing a triad of nuclear delivery options, has the size and the strategic depth to disperse its assets and thus survive the first strike with a meaningful arsenal still surviving to deliver an effective second retaliatory strike (Pant 2005, 283). NFU by China, the presence of huge Himalayan Mountains between the two and China's logistical and operational difficulties to sustain a full scale war in Tibet affords India the opportunity to choose NFU while still improving its conventional capabilities. There is an increased interplay of conventional weapons with the nuclear ones in the NFU option. It is assumed that the conventional strengths would be employed to keep the conflict below the nuclear threshold with the threat of nuclear retaliation also supporting to deter the adversary from choosing the nuclear option (Matinuddin 2002).

As India develops minimum credible deterrence vis - à - vis China, it automatically caters for a smaller threat from Pakistan. Even though India has the capability to make and has tested low yield tactical nuclear weapons, doctrinally it renounces their use while China and Pakistan have retained the option of these weapons. The latest doctrine has done away with 'keeping an open - ended nuclear program', but opts to develop a triad of mobile land, sea and air based delivery assets (Pant 2005, 284). India not only supports US policy on the Ballistic Missile Defence (BMD) systems' deployments globally but is also pursuing a BMD program of its own. Endeavours include Israeli Green Pine radars, choice of Patriot/ Arrow systems, deployment of S - 3000V system and development of indigenous system by integrating Akash with Green Pine/Indra - II radars (Bhatti 2003).

3. WHAT IMPACT HAS NUCLEARISATION HAD ON SOUTH ASIAN SECURITY ENVIRONMENT?

3.1 How are the New States Different from USA and USSR?

While it is important and useful that the theory and lessons developed during the cold - war may be consulted so that new nuclear states do not repeat the same mistakes, it is equally important to appreciate the differences that exist in the context of the new nuclear states lest we do not make over - generalised assessments or draw wrong parallels and lessons. The new nuclear states (if any) in general and India - Pakistan in particular have a typical set of circumstances that are important to be considered for analysing the past, present and while predicting the future. There are numerous ways in which the developed nuclear states fear the actions and interactions of new nuclear states to be different.

First, the new states may come in hostile pairs and share contiguous borders. Worse still, they may have legacy of hostilities and given a chance, may like to settle old scores. Past does provide the example of China and USSR who shared a long border and were sufficiently hostile but treated each other with caution (Sagan and Waltz 2003, 12).

Second, many fear that some new states may be radical domestically and may use their nukes recklessly abroad also. Optimists argue that a state radical at home may not necessarily be radical abroad. Few like China and USSR were radical domestically and remained radical in their foreign policy also but not for long. In international system, radicalism can survive only if one is overwhelmingly strong. Nuclear weapons take away this luxury and bring the weaker states also at strategic parity with the stronger. Even the most trigger-happy war-monger will be faced with the question about the probability of his offensive capability to destroy all assets of the adversary in the first strike.

Third, some states may not have very well rooted governments and societies. Non-democratic governments and authoritarian regimes with societies that might not be very well developed polities fall in this group. Libya is a classical example. Despite being openly hostile in rhetoric and intentions, with Egypt, and having exchanged strikes, both did not let the conflict get out of hand. Qaddafi and Idi Amin of Uganda were the most notorious 'irrational' leaders, but they both showed restraint not because of thinking logically but when the cost of consequences was made to appear too high to them. Nuclear weapons provide precisely the same inherent coercive diplomacy and make the most irrational leaders 'sensitive to costs of misadventures'. Yet many Western strategists become fearful about South Asia when they let ethno-centric speculation replace evidence and view the third world nations as "lesser people without the law (Sagan and Waltz 2003, 14)."

Fourth, fear is if the nuclear weapons spread beyond a pair of hostile nations, implying that more than two nuclear nations become party to a conflict. A speculative example for South Asia could be Iran becoming a nuclear power and becoming hostile to Pakistan with nukes proliferating into the Middle East also. It will not be as simple as the present situation where it is clear who is deterring whom. Multi-party and multiple alignments may not only make the situation complicated but increasingly volatile also. Any one initiating a nuclear brinkmanship may trigger a chain reaction of nuclear responses. However, it may be recalled that USSR also faced a complex problem while calculating any response lest any move made in Europe might cause UK and France to react, thus causing US forces to react as well, while China being hostile too. Consequently, it may be inferred that complicated responses strengthen deterrence and discourage a nuclear option at the first place.

Fifth, in some new nuclear states, like Pakistan, civilian control of military may be weak, and nuclear arsenal may be in their custody. The military may be more inclined to use these offensively (organisational theory). However, evidence suggests that civilian control in USSR was not effective, given the occasional presence of military officers in Politburo. In China, the military and civilians are fused together as government branches (Sagan and Waltz 2003, 16). USA's history is full of examples where civilian control of military was practically ineffective. President Eisenhower, despite all his prestige could not change military's plans to fire hundred or thousands of missile if USSR attacked and till his last days he kept worrying about post-war ungovernable world. President Kennedy's Secretary of Defence McNamara and his team were convinced of two hundred missiles to counter USSR in counter valve strikes, but they asked congress to fund 1000 missiles because Air Force wanted a counter force strategy with targets in thousands. As president needed the support of Joint Chiefs to get a test ban treaty through senate, he approved what Air Force wanted. Eisenhower under his 'new look defence policy', gave the Air Force 50% in the budget against the previous 33% to each service. The Army forced the next President Nixon to revert back to the old distribution despite the civilian opposition. Like it is between states, it is also between civilian and military leaders that accommodations are made for each other to get the support. Civilian control is also maintained by a huge political effort and civilian and military tiers of state mostly accept each other's requirements. Even in democracies like USA, military makes its say in issues of national security (Sagan and Waltz 2003, 133). Like USA, it may be wrong to always associate democracy with peace and authoritarian rule with war. Civilian control does not guarantee prevention of war. Soldiers do not want to fight even the conventional war in uncertainty. Offensive employment of nuclear weapons increases uncertainty by factorials. Optimists argue that uncertainties about the destruction, course that a nuclear war may take and about enemy's reactions are strong enough to make a soldier think more rationally than a civilian who may not fully understand the fog of war. External factors also shape the behaviours of governments, whether civilian or military. No political, military and academic rhetoric is of significance in the face of nuclear reality. Disabling the organisational biases, it makes all to think sanely and transcends all rhetoric (Sagan and Waltz 2003).

Sixth, difference that is envisaged is the size of the arsenal. Unlike cold war, the numbers are expected to be small but yet each nation is expected to have sufficient weapons to survive a decapitating first strike and still have some for second strike.

Seventh difference that is expected is the fear of South Asian arsenal being not as safe as those of cold war antagonists. This perception is derived out of the absence of sophisticated provisions like Permissive Action Links (PALs) and Personal Reliability Program (Majid 2002).

3.1.1 Analysis on Both Doctrines

Having examined the security perspectives and specific differences from older nuclear states in context, it is now pertinent to examine the doctrines of both the countries from the opponent's point of view. First let us consider the Indian NFU Doctrine as seen from Pakistan's perspective.

Pakistan considers NFU Doctrine as a convenient choice rather than a compulsion for India given its circumstances. It is a country with a huge strategic depth, conventional superiority over Pakistan and parity - getting - superiority over China, big survivable arsenal with capacity to expand to much greater size, triad of second strike capabilities and Ballistic Missile Defence (BMD) systems in the near future and a growing long range ballistic and cruise missiles program. Pakistan sees the NFU declaration as a means to gain high moral grounds and projection as a mature/responsible nuclear state in the international community, while actually keeping same options open as the first-use doctrine (Matinuddin 2002). Doctrinally, NFU seeks to create deterrence by the assurance of a retaliation which will be so costly that the aggressor will be deterred from using nuclear weapons in the first place. Practically, in NFU, nuclear weapons will be used when the deterrence has actually failed to deter the aggressor despite the assurance of a costly retaliation. Thereby nuclear weapons are not used as political instruments of deterrence as declared, but as weapons of punitive war after the first strike. In NFU option, there is a sort of inherent acceptance that deterrence will fail despite the assurance of a devastating retaliation and only then nuclear weapons will be employed as punitive weapons of war. Deterrence is seen to be relegated to second degree unless the situation becomes too risky and a decision is taken to strike first or threat a first strike for deterrence (Matinuddin 2002). Second, the Indian doctrine of NFU has an important tenet of 'credible minimum deterrence'. 'Minimum', here is a fluid and dynamic term, which refers to the number of weapons or size of force structure required to deter an enemy. This number is dependent on a number of variables of strategic security environment and is therefore hard to quantify as any number can be justified on the basis of changing threat perception. Therefore practically, 'minimum' is a relative term providing an open check to maintain any size of nuclear force structure, as minimum for China would be 'maximum' for Pakistan (Pant 2005, 281). Another worrisome issue is the Indian political support of US BMD deployments and pursuance of its own BMD systems while maintaining the contradictory claim of maintaining a 'minimum credible deterrence'. On the one hand, India declares that it is compelled to match a bigger Chinese threat; otherwise it would not choose to maintain such an arsenal. On the other hand, it is trying to introduce BMD systems in the region which will force both China and Pakistan to increase their number of weapons to keep their deterrence viable. This again will be used as a 'compulsion', to escalate its levels of arsenal, thereby raising the threshold of 'minimum' nuclear weapons in the region and triggering a nuclear arms race (Bhatti 2003).

From Pakistan's perspective, a NFU doctrine retains the option of seeking a political objective by exploiting its conventional superiority. Against the projected goodness of the concept, practically NFU does not restrict/bind the country to stick to NFU. The Indian NFU Doctrine is more of an eye - wash as few provisions of the doctrine can easily be used to make a first strike even against a non - nuclear state. The provision of using nukes against a biological or chemical attack even by a non - nuclear state is one example. Bharat Kannard, calls NFU a hoax, as "it is one of those restrictions which countries are willing to abide by except in war (Majid 2002)." Experience shows that nations do not regard all agreements as sacrosanct for all times to come, especially in war. For example, President Bush has changed the rules for the ABM Treaty as according to him USA's security is threatened by rogue states acquiring long range missiles. Russia has also modified its nuclear policy because of developments on its borders. It is also not clear whether India would react to TNWs with its declared massive retaliation or with TNWs of its own whose usage it doctrinally renounces (Pant 2005, 284) but yet has the capability to make them as demonstrated in one of the tests in 1998. A declared NFU does not have credibility if it does not bind the state by domestic or international legislations and if it has provisions set - in to allow exploitation for first strike. There are no UNSC resolutions which would punish a violator of a no first use policy nation. To be effective and taken seriously a no first use declaration should be underpinned by domestic legislations and international guarantees, without which it loses its credibility (Matinuddin 2002). Furthermore, NFU should not only be a policy declaration or a doctrinal rhetoric; it should be practically backed by corresponding force structures, weapon designs and projects. If no first use declaration is accompanied with augmented production of fissile material, ever increasing stock piles of nuclear weapons, enlarging the ranges of missiles, adding the lethality of atomic devices and working towards a nuclear missile defence programme, then the intentions of not being the first to use nuclear weapons despite the declaration of NFU become suspicious. Therefore, from Pakistan's perspective, India does retain the first strike option and will consider using it especially in the face of an imminent nuclear strike (Pant 2005, 283).

In broader security perspective also, NFU does not contribute to the over all security of the region, as it does not prevent the upgrade and increment of existing nuclear arsenals and the conventional forces. It is not a step towards disarmament and arms control. Herman Khan maintains that for a conventionally weaker state, "It is a preemptive to surrender". NFU increases the chances of conventional attacks, subversion and Low intensity conflicts. By renouncing the use of all the forces at its disposal a militarily weaker nation like Pakistan cannot defend itself. Carol Khan of the Hudson Institute in her article Thinking About Nuclear Morality brings out the facts that a NFU policy, no matter how well designed, will not by itself change the military balance, will not relieve the need for a first rate nuclear capability and will not reliably preclude the use of nuclear weapons. It will not eliminate the risk of unlimited escalation. It will not significantly reduce defence budgets. "NFU is not a panacea for American and NATO defence problems" says Carol with some justification. Neither is it a panacea in the Indo Pakistan context (Matinuddin 2002).

Now let us examine the Pakistan's first - use doctrine. The ICJ gave a ruling in July 1996 that "the use of or threatened use of nuclear weapons is illegal in all but one possible circumstance: a threat to the very existence of the state". If nations much stronger than Pakistan retain the right to use nuclear weapons first against another nuclear power when confronted with a hostile neighbour, there is no reason for Pakistan, which is militarily weaker than India, not to adopt a similar policy.

Again, given the strategic circumstances of hostile legacy with India, lack of strategic depth, conventional inferiority, absence of a triad of delivery options, small arsenal, nominal second - strike capability and limited capacity of nuclear program, first - use option of using nuclear weapons to deter even a conventional aggression seems to be the only viable option available to Pakistan (Matinuddin 2002). Doctrinally, the nuclear weapons are to be used as a deterrent and not as weapons of war, therefore Pakistan cannot and does not accept a bilateral NFU offer by India, as it would erode the very essence of its nuclear deterrent posture. The ambiguity on different aspects of the nuclear policy is intentionally left in place to complement the efficacy of deterrence (Cheema 2002). Given these circumstances, there may not be any conceptual dilemma on the Indian side regarding the choice of options; however there are a lot of apprehensions regarding the context and conduct of Pakistan as a nuclear state.

It is often alleged that Pakistanis are an irresponsible nation and have proliferated in the past therefore cannot be trusted with nuclear weapons. First, these events happened during the 80s when nuclear activities were not as closely regulated as they are now. Admittedly Dr Khan was given a remarkable degree of autonomy because of the importance of his work for national security. Yet once government of Pakistan discovered his illegitimate activities, it took appropriate action against him. The government even passed legislation to effectively check nuclear commerce. There is hardly any other nation in the world that has such legislation (Cheema 2007). Additionally, no other nation has punished any important figures except imposing bans and restrictions on few firms, despite the fact that the list of people involved extended from India to Europe and USA. Dr Qadeer did not buy, make and deliver everything all by himself. There was a long chain involved but nothing has been made public about its final disposal. All other so-called 'responsible states' have yet to demonstrate their resolve to control proliferation. It may be relevant to mention that USA is prepared to especially change the rules for providing nuclear fuel to non-NPT signatory India, whose program it once opposed, because now it suits USA's economic and political interests. Being a super-power does not put anybody above the law and even in an anarchic world rules of the game must apply equally to all. Rodney W Jones of The Henry Stimson Centre writes, "While sensational disclosures of this kind have not arisen in the Indian context, concerns exist about the generic integrity of Indian nuclear security measure against insider threats (Krepon, Jones, and Haider 2004, 51)."

The second source of apprehensions revolves around the argument that the radicals would win the elections and come into power. Nothing could be more ludicrous. To stress those radicals would win the elections and come to power amounts to reflecting complete ignorance about the country and society. The results of February 2008 elections have testified that the Pakistani nation has chosen the most liberal of parties. To top it all ANP, which is the most secular party and has never made it to the government has been elected to power in the frontier province, one that is widely publicised as the most fanatic area in the back drop of war on terror. Another aspect of this issue is that terrorists might takeover the nuclear weapons of Pakistan. Again, nothing could be more absurd than this. It is one of the inherent advantages of Pakistani set up, where nukes are handled by military that security is extremely tight (Cheema 2007). A concept that is selling very well in US Wargames that 'a fanatic Corp commander takes over the nukes', again reveals total ignorance about the country's set up. Nuclear weapons fall no where close to the domain of Corp Commanders even after deployments. The elaborate set of checks and multi-person requirements in the authorisation chain of SPD, makes it impossible to imagine that a nuclear weapon or even material may be stolen. Not even a single incident of such security breach can be reported to date. Furthermore, USA needs to explore its security, in view of numerous examples of recent breaches. Most recently, it was in August 2007, that an American B52 bomber carrying cruise missiles took on a usual flight without the knowledge of responsible US officials (Cheema 2007).

Another apprehension, which is well taken, is the absence of a credible intelligence/early warning system. This fact is recognised in Pakistan that first-use doctrine entails a reliable intelligence set-up to preclude the risk of an unintentional or misperceived use of nuclear weapons especially considering the minimum flight times available in case of India and Pakistan. However, Pakistan will have to rely on the present means available as induction of modern space based assets does not appear possible, for the foreseeable future. Nonetheless, recognition of this short coming makes the decision makers more cautious and adds to the prevention of nuclear war (Pant 2005, 285). The targeting aspect is covered by the fact that both India and Pakistan, at present are relying on counter-value targets rather than counter-force. However, in due course of time, intelligence as well as accuracy is likely to improve.

Apprehensions about the military control and its tendencies to wage war have already been discussed in the previous section. However, the Kargil misadventure and 2002 stand-off have taught their lessons to both the sides. The fact that war did not break out in both the cases is a good enough reason for optimism in maturity of both sides. This is further supplemented by the fact that for the last six years of one decade of nuclearisation, no escalation has taken place despite the turmoil of GWOT in the region.

3.2 How Has Nuclearisation Impacted SA Security Environment?

Having examined security perspectives and both the doctrines, let us examine how nuclear weapons have impacted the South Asian security environment. The nuclearisation of South Asia has added another dangerous dimension to the antagonistic relationships that already existed amongst Pakistan and India. Even as both the countries have embarked on developing and refining their weapons and delivery systems, specially the missiles, certain loopholes and deficiencies still exist that may create undesirable situations and need to be identified. Considering the brief period that has passed after nuclearisation as well as the period of ambiguous deterrent that preceded it, at least seven nuclear danger areas merit immediate redress (Shah 2002b).

First, the intended or deliberate use of nuclear weapons can assume two forms: firstly, born out of the conventional superiority that India enjoys over Pakistan, a temptation to wage limited war against Pakistan with a hope of keeping it below the nuclear threshold, notwithstanding the Pakistan's stance of using nuclear weapons even against the conventional aggression. The situation may likely be worsened beyond expectations due to the 'Cold Start Strategy' being put in place to deny Pakistan the reaction time available for preparing a response. The security environment is likely to be hyped up as in response, Pakistan is likely to increase its readiness levels of at least the conventional forces. Three occasions testify this, the 'Brass Tacks' exercise of 1986-87, the 1990 Kashmir crisis, and early 2002 stand off between India and Pakistan. The urge to escalate tensions out of an alleged or unverified instance of terrorism, in pursuit of domestic or international goals may have a catastrophic effect if either side oversteps its limits in the heat of the moment (Shah 2002b). The second danger of intended use of nuclear weapons may arise out of considering a preventive/decapitating/pre-emptive strike on the nuclear assets of the adversary (Akhtar 2002a; 2002b). As both sides are considered to have developed sufficiently redundant/survivable arsenal and infrastructure, this was more relevant in the days of ambiguous deterrent, however, it may be still be an option exercised to deny the other side a critical capability such as a second strike asset. Again on at least three occasions India reportedly had planned or seriously considered to launch decapitating strike against Pakistan's nuclear capabilities: first, in early 1980s the then Prime Minister Indira Gandhi did not permit it; second, in 1986-87 Brass Tacks exercise, when Pakistan timely apprised India of consequences; and third, in 1998, on the morning of 28 May when Pakistan warned through Indian High Commissioner in Islamabad to abstain from misadventure (Sagan 2001).

Second, is the possibility of use of nuclear weapons out of miscalculation and misperception from either side. Even though both the sides have put in place some rudimentary C2 structures, the warheads are not mated with the missiles and the weapons are not mated to the delivery systems, yet there is a critical absence of credible intelligence and early warning systems. It is more applicable to Pakistan which needs to be extra vigilant and doubly sure before opting to go nuclear in any situation. Any unusual activity in the movement of the warheads, missiles or delivery systems may create undue escalation and response from the other side. Furthermore, both countries being contiguous to each other drastically reduce the flight times to few minutes. This is too short a warning time for anybody to analyse and make a rational decision. Thus there is an inherent vulnerability of miscalculation in the South Asian context. As the separation of components provides ample chances to control escalation through analysis of response, throughout the deployment chain, while the readiness status is being changed, both sides need to work out a mechanism (like hotlines between DGMOs that already exist), for communicating with each other despite hostilities. Presently, in the absence of credible intelligence and communication channels, any misperception has the potential to trigger a response that may accentuate the crisis on both sides.

Third, nuclear danger zone is the possibility of unauthorised use of nuclear assets. Peter D. Fever contends that nuclear weapons states cannot help facing the always/never dilemma: always means that nuclear weapons should be so developed and deployed that when they are applied, they yield intended result; simultaneously they are never used without competent authorization (Fever 1992/93, 163).Thus, always be used when required and never be used unauthorised, are two key issues, which largely compliment each other. Like nuclear pessimist Scott D Sagan contends that (Krepon, Jones, and Haider 2004, 51), in the absence of sophisticated provisions like those of Permissive Action Links (PALs), the chances of unauthorised access remain alive. Both countries have different security dynamics as Pakistan's weapons are predominantly in military custody whereas Indian assets are mostly in civilian custody but both have chosen to keep the arsenal as de-mated de-weaponised deterrent. The weapons are kept separate from their delivery system with the nuclear cores removed from the detonators. Besides, Pakistan, like the other nuclear weapon states, follows a two-man rule to authenticate the codes that call for the release of the weapons. The transportation of nuclear material is indeed considered to be relatively more difficult to protect. Not only Pakistan has already ratified the Convention on the Physical Protection of Nuclear Material (CPPNM) but has also secured specialized vehicles to further strengthen transportation security. Besides the PRP (Personnel Reliability Program) is fairly advanced but lacks psychological assessments as done in USA (Cheema 2007).

Fourth, nuclear danger emanates from the development and potential operationalisation of Tactical Nuclear Weapons (TNWs). These are designed to fill the gap between conventional and strategic nuclear weapons, which implies that conventional war is not likely to instantly escalate to use of strategic nuclear weapons. Even though, doctrinally both countries do not specifically advocate use of TNWs, the tests yield results of both countries confirm that this option has been kept open by both. Reportedly, during early 2002 stand off between India and Pakistan, both states moved their TNWs to launching sites. It can be argued that TNWs provide a better option of gradually controlling escalation while transiting from conventional to strategic nuclear weapons; it may well be argued also that possession of TNWs may tempt the early employment of nuclear weapons due to the very same reason (Krishnan and Gokhale 2002; Ali 2002).

Fifth, security implication of nuclearisation is the unprecedented danger of a nuclear arms race in South Asia. Even though as nuclear optimists like Kenneth N. Waltz opine that 'nuclear states need to race only to the second - strike level', arms race is a possibility if the states get into a MAD syndrome to match numbers (Sagan and Waltz 2003, 110). As Strobe Talbott, former US deputy secretary of state opines, 'like us if they lock themselves into a mentality of MAD - they may be tempted into a considerable escalation of arms - race'. In case of South Asia, there is a positive chance of an arms - race if India continues to pursue its Missile Defence Program. The strategic upshots on China and Pakistan will be that both will be drawn into an unending race to enhance numbers in order to keep their deterrence viable and India will justify doing the same as a response to Chinese arsenal (Sultan 2002, 131 - 37). Mutual invulnerability may embolden India to launch aggression against Pakistan, under the illusion of Limited War (Shah 2002a).

Sixth nuclear danger has recently emerged in the backdrop of post 9/11 GWOT and seriously concerns most of the Western security analysts. It is the possible theft by terrorists or access to nuclear weapons by extremist elements in the military/ruling elite (Hersh 2001; Santhanam and Rajagopalan 2001). In Pakistan, political and military rules alternate which can create a problem in transition of nuclear command authority. In India, the country's nukes are controlled by government scientists, and deployment orders come from the Prime Minister's office, while the armed forces are virtually kept isolated from the decision - process till the very end. Both the set - ups have their own limitations however, these apprehensions are inconclusive, as both states, so far, have not shown any slackness in custody/handling of their respective nuclear arsenals. As Rumsfield, the US Secretary of Defense, affirmed, "I think the countries that have nuclear weapons have a healthy respect for their power and the lethality of those weapons and the dangers that they pose to the world and take appropriate steps to assure that they are managed and handled in a way that reflects the dangers that weapons pose (DWS 2001)." Even then concerns about possible access of unauthorized and undesirable elements cannot be ruled out definitely.

Seventh, security implication is a by - product of nuclearisation of South Asia. As both countries achieve 'minimum credible deterrence' against each other, all will not become well. As the realisation of the catastrophic consequences of nuclear options becomes clear, both states may opt to choose other non - conventional, non - kinetic means to destabilise each other. The options may include proxy through a third state akin to alleged involvement of [14 - 18] Indian consulates in Afghanistan to destabilise and tie down Pakistan towards West. This will ultimately result in a more trust - deprived and fragile security environment which will be ideally suited to realise any of the potential danger areas discussed above (Majid 2002).

4. FUTURE OF NUCLEAR SOUTH ASIA

Having analysed the doctrines and understood the security context of South Asia, let us know explore whether nuclear weapons have proved to be a stable deterrent or not?

4.1 Has Deterrence Worked?

In order to rightly predict the future, it is imperative that we analyse the past. Instead of examining the last 60 years of hostilities, to stay within the scope of this paper, the analysis will cover the period from

1980s - 1998, the decades of ambiguous deterrent and from 1998 till the present day.

Since the beginning, the strategy of deterrence in South Asia has been based on uncertainty, since the adversaries did not know how long it would take to make the bomb and what would be the capability of the bomb. However, the presence of nuclear weapons capability was known to exist. Some called it 'non - traditional deterrence', due to absence of nuclear tests, nuclear doctrine and declared strategy. Others called it 'non - weaponised deterrent', due to absence of a weapon. While some did not agree to this term arguing that was where West wanted India and Pakistan to stay and not go beyond non - weaponised stage. Others did not agree to the strategy per se. Since 1971, two crisis were most important before 1998, the 'Brasstacks Crisis 'of 1986 - 87 and the 'Kashmir Crisis' of 1990 (Mohan and Lavoy 1995, 32).

The Brasstacks crisis started in1986, with a huge Indian exercise in Rajasthan area. It triggered Pakistan to deploy its own forces and situation escalated. It is important to note that India was still unaware of Pakistan's nuclear capability. The Pakistani nuclear factor figured in the crisis, when Kuldip Nayar, an Indian journalist was invited to interview Dr A Q Khan. In his interview, Dr A Q Khan stated." Nobody can undo Pakistan or take us for granted. We are here to stay and let it be clear that we shall use the bomb if our exercise is threatened". The statement not only communicated Pakistan's capability but also its intentions (Khan 2002, 159). As against some arguments, Brasstacks did not end before this was publicised. Second, Pakistani government wanted to avoid sanctions so it communicated its status by an informal interview. Even though, nuclear pessimists worried about the provocation of a pre - emptive war in Brasstacks, it is important to note that further escalation did not happen and the crisis ended without a war. Nuclear deterrent had worked for the first time.

In 1990, when Kashmiri's revolted against the Indian government, Pakistan was blamed for it and tensions escalated because of Indian heavy deployments in Kashmir and Rajasthan. Pakistan responded with open deployments of armoured units. Washington was made to believe by its intelligence that Pak Army Chief Gen Aslam Beg has ordered the bomb to be assembled. Secretary Robert Gates rushed to diffuse the crisis. However, both sides now agree that the escalation did not go to the extent of nuclear threat but the West was convinced that South Asia could see a nuclear war. On the contrary, this crisis is probably the best example of non - traditional deterrence working where both sides cognisant of each other's nuclear capability, but were still opaque nuclear states. Despite the fragile political structures in both the countries, none of the leaders exhibited irrational behaviour by trying a pre - emptive surprise attack on other's nuclear facilities. Again open rhetoric of nuclear response followed in the press. But neither side contemplated war in nuclear - capable region. Rather it was after this crisis that both sides signed two confidence building agreements in April 1991. Agreements to avoid aerial violations, advance notice of exercises and troop movements and pledge not to attack each other's nuclear facilities. Nuclear deterrent had worked again (Khan 2002, 160). To summarise both these crises, Devin Hagerty concludes his detailed study as," There is no more ironclad law in international relations theory than this. Nuclear states do not fight wars with each other (Sagan and Waltz 2003, 95)."

One year after India and Pakistan, gained nuclear status, in 1999, Kargil crisis took place. Pessimists like Scott D Sagan call it war because more than one thousand deaths occurred which qualifies it to be called a war in the political science terms (Sagan and Waltz 2003, 115). The optimists like Kenneth Waltz, call it a major skirmish. The crisis started as allegedly Pakistani backed forces crossed into the Indian side of LoC close to Kargil. Starting from May 1999, it ended in July when these forces withdrew, after heavy attacks from land and Air forces. Pakistani military, while covertly alerting the nuclear forces, blamed the civilian government for backing out while claiming that the aim to revitalise Kashmir issue in the international community was achieved. New Delhi, however called it stab in the back after CBMs like Lahore Declarations. Indians claimed that P M Vajpayee had informed Washington that it may cross the border and US spy satellites confirmed movements of armoured units in Rajasthan sector. From the Indian point of view, it was the threat of war with probability of nuclear response that forced the withdrawal (Sagan and Waltz 2003, 96). These different lessons, however, disturb the pessimists. It is argued that both sides were convinced that if their government showed resolve and threat to escalate the issue, it would force the other side to flex. It is contended that this tendency of testing each other's endurance has the potential to recur and to escalate any future crisis to nuclear levels. The second analysis is of the organisational theorists. They contend that Pakistani military exhibited its typical war-mongering attitude which confirms that organisational biases do play their role even between the nuclear states and may do so again in South Asian context. The optimists view that whatever the causes, the net result is that the crisis did not escalate to full scale war, and was far from nuclear exchange despite the rhetoric. This crisis also raised the concerns that the nukes provided Pakistan false optimisms about impunity of its actions convincing it to take critical chances expecting to keep the conflicts limited to low intensities (Sheppard 2002, 200). Even though both sides have reasons to believe in their own inferences, it may be correct to conclude that the reality is war and nuclear war did not happen. If it was sanity from the Pakistani government not to prolong it too much, nuclear presence still made that happen and proved that nuclear threat can and will mould the most rigid of organisationally biased behaviour. If it was the Indian threat that worked, deterrent worked again. Optimists have a reason to be optimistic on the basis of what actually happened whereas pessimists have to rely on speculations of what may have happened or may happen in future.

The last crisis occurred with attack on Indian Parliament by six terrorists in December 2001. It was followed by rapid deployment of forces from both the sides. The stand-off continued till late October 2002. For Pakistan it was a military as well as a politico-diplomatic crisis. It was already involved in war against terror on the western front and now had to face another front on the East. Furthermore, Indian government's intent was to project Pakistan as a state harbouring and supporting terrorists. In this back drop, despite a year long stand-off between two nuclear states, which have had a series of crises as discussed earlier, war did not break out. Pakistan had already started to crackdown on the militants, in the backdrop of GWOT, but refused to hand over the twenty individuals wanted by India.

The question is why did India choose to pursue a strategy of forceful persuasion instead of surgical strikes despite having the capabilities and conventional superiority? One explanation is that Kargil crisis had sufficiently emboldened Pakistanis that their nuclear posture had forced India to strictly contain the crisis on its side of LoC and to the area of conflict. India's unwillingness to expand the conflict elsewhere also convinced them that Pakistan's nuclear parity has successfully neutralised Indian conventional advantage. Second, the resolve to use nuclear weapons openly expressed by President Musharaf in his second speech and by Pakistani Ambassador to UN Munir Akram, made the intentions clear (Krepon, Jones, and Haider 2004, 109). It was felt in the Indian security circles that any large - scale conventional conflict would neither be controllable nor calculable. As an Indian diplomat stated," The idea that Pakistan will cooperate in a conflict and comply with India's wishes to fight a limited war is ridiculous. It will be naturally in their interest to keep any conflagration as unlimited as possible". The fear of Pakistan's resort to nuclear response was paramount in the minds of Indian decision makers which inhibited them from resorting to an all out war (Ganguly and Hagerty 2005, 180).

Another explanation is that Musharraf had started to comply by cracking down on the insurgents therefore the coercive diplomacy backed by a threat of war, worked and hence full - scale war was avoided. An optimist view of the crisis is that deterrence from Pakistani side and coercion from Indian side worked and war did not take place. The pessimist view is that dangerous tendencies of deploying weapons was repeated like Kargil and other Pakistani leaders in future may not comply so it would not be correct to take Musharraf's actions as a reference for future (Sagan and Waltz 2003, 100).

It is important to consider both analysis for own inference. It is worth noting that if Indian coercion worked, it did so because it was backed by a threat of nuclear force. If Musharraf complied, it proves two points: first, that nuclear threat or deterrence forced Musharraf to comply. Second, according to organisational biases theorists, Musharraf should not have complied and acted in the same war- mongering way as in Kargil, his compliance again proves that nuclear threat overcomes the organisationally biased behaviour and forces irrational actors to act rationally. The other argument that Pakistani deterrence worked and India did not cross the border is self-explanatory. Therefore the analysis of this case also endorses the inference from the previous cases that nuclear deterrence is robust enough to shape the outcome despite the organisationally biased behaviours. While US diplomacy has also played its role, it was primarily the nuclear deterrent that deterred both states from going to war in such a provocative and volatile environment, with unprecedented scale of conventional forces deployed at war readiness. The presence of nuclear weapons was the most significant factor in bringing the crisis to a close (Ganguly and Hagerty 2005, 182).

4.2 Future Scenarios

Many nuclear researchers have tried to pre-meditate and simulate how the future of nuclear South Asia would look like? During the 2001-2 crisis, the Natural Resources Defence Council (NRDC) simulated two nuclear war scenarios, based on assumptions that both nations had 50-75 fission weapons with yields estimated between 5-25 kilotons. It was a non-objective study based on the counter-value targets. Scenario-1, simulated 5 cities hit on each side with ten nuclear weapons of 15 kilotons each. An estimated 1,690,702 deaths (2,2021,106 injuries) in India and 1,171,879 deaths (1,361, 872 injuries) in Pakistan, were calculated. Scenario-2, simulated 24 weapons of 25 kilotons each over same five cities on either side. The results were horrific levels of death and destruction, 60.1 million people exposed to lethal radiations with 8.1 instant deaths. It would cause fallout within hundreds of kilometres. The study concluded that the devastation resulting from nuclear fall out would far exceed that caused by the blast and fire of the explosion. As it was a counter value simulation, 99% of Indian and 93% of Pakistani forces deployed outside the major cities would survive to continue the war. This study only highlighted the quantum of devastation likely to be caused by a nuclear attack. However, it did not consider other contributory factors of deterrence framework like doctrines of NFU and retaliation but focussed on mutual destruction only (Khan 2005).

Other nuclear predictors have divided the future nuclear possibilities of South Asia into three practical scenarios. The may be categorised as purposive, inadvertent and accidental. These are more or less based on the cases and inferences that have occured earlier. The first scenario evolves when India grows impatient with Kashmir insurgency. It orders attacks across LoC to crush the terrorist camps. Pakistan Army adopts an 'offensive - defence strategy' and takes the war across the border in Punjab plains. India gains in Kashmir as well as counter attacks across Punjab border, threatening Lahore. Pakistan seeing its options limited resorts to nuclear weapons (Ganguly and Hagerty 2005, 198). There are a number of questions that were asked as this scenario was debated by Indian leadership in Kargil crisis. Why would any country send a massive attack across the borders in face of possible nuclear response? Why would Pakistan respond else where when it might make its big cities vulnerable? Why would a nuclear option be considered in this close proximity of forces and cities? As this scenario made some irrational assumptions it is considered improbable for future.

The second scenario presents that a South Asian nuclear war erupts inadvertently when India and Pakistan end up in a future conflict. A miscalculation on one or both sides leads to conventional war and Pakistani intelligence suggests that India is considering pre - emptive strikes against its nuclear arsenal. Pakistani decision makers choose to use rather than lose the weapons and launch a counter force pre - emptive strike of their own. This scenario also appears illogical as none of the wars in South Asia have started inadvertently (Ganguly and Hagerty 2005, 199). How can these two states let themselves get into a nuclear war inadvertently? The second question is regarding the practicality of pre - emptive strikes. It needs to be considered that what are the chances of success? How many warheads does the other side possess? How many are weaponised? Are the exact locations known? What are the chances of survival? No military planner may be able to answer all these and many more practical questions that arise. No planner will also be able to guarantee a total devastation of adversary's arsenal, which for nuclear weapons is the minimum level of certainty required in the face of a possible nuclear retaliation. It would be ethnocentric to believe that South Asian decision makers do not understand these implications. Hence this scenario is also considered highly improbable.

The third scenario is most disturbing as it implies that the main danger in South Asia is of accidental war and unauthorised use of weapons by terrorists. Even though there is no evidence of accidental or unauthorised use of weapons, absence of sophisticated security features like PALs etc makes the analysts very uneasy (Ganguly and Hagerty 2005, 200). There is no reason to believe that Indian and Pakistani scientists and engineers cannot very well make safety features of their own, to be equally effective. However the likelihood of accidents remains worrisome. As discussed earlier, when the weapons are prepared for deployments during crisis, any inadvertent shock like fire, unintentional drop or stray electrical charge could directly or indirectly detonate the high explosive surrounding the weapons' fissile core. Even though not much is publicly known about the technical safety features of weapons in India or Pakistan, absence of any serious accidents provides hope for optimists. However, once an explosion takes place, it would be difficult to control the reactions of the other side, especially if the incident happens in close proximity of the adversary forces or population. While there is a lot of speculation prevailing regarding terrorists accessing Pakistani weapons no breach of security has been cited till date. Much has already been discussed earlier in this regard. Both sides are likely to strengthen and improve their security arrangements and command and control set-ups, as time progresses. It is opined that due to the unassembled arsenals and technical complexities involved, even if unauthorised access is contemplated, a specialist team with varying skills is required to put a weapon together (Mark et al. n.d.). Nonetheless, the making of a 'crude dirty bomb', by a non-state actor cannot be ruled out. Therefore, rationally the emphasis should be on checking the proliferation of chemical, radiological and biological agents, which may be acquired from the international black market for making a dirty bomb.

While discussing the probable future scenarios in the South Asian context, Theatre Missile Defence (TMD) is a system that is envisaged to become a part of the future strategic environment. Even though it would enhance the Indian strategic options, it will not make the Pakistan's strike capability completely redundant (Mark et al. n.d.). If either country is convinced about using the nuclear option, TMD would not prevent a major India - Pakistan nuclear exchange (Vanaik 2001). Lack of mutual distances reduces the efficacy of the early warning systems by making impossible the technical verifications of false alarms before a possible launch hits its target across the border. Moreover, satellites, EW capabilities, high precision interceptors and fail - safe command and control systems need to be developed to have an effective nation - wide area defence.

Introduction of a TMD or a BMD system would mean a sharp rise in the arsenal in the region to increase the probability of penetration of maximum no of weapons through the defensive system. It would also entail introduction of alternatives like cruise missiles in the scenario, a trend that has already been initiated. However, owing to the sheer magnitude of the task of defending all or even most of India's strategic assets, TMD/ABM system cannot provide an ideal solution and will have a limited effect.

Additionally, introduction of an ABM system would force the readiness posture of the nuclear missile forces to be upgraded to "Hair - Trigger - Alert" which might add to the probability of accidental firing as a missile in high state of readiness is more prone to accidental launch. Owing to its conventional inferiority and lack of BMD, the change of readiness status will be more relevant to Pakistan (Jaspal 2001, 28 - 43). So introduction of BMD will not only contribute to an arms race with different alternatives but also destabilise the environment by increasing the chances of accidental employment.

4.3 Will Deterrence Continue?

One of the most difficult things to do is to predict the future accurately. However past does give us clues to what future might bring. An analysis of the past does give us the trends of different parameters of the dynamic strategic environment. We have already inferred few facts and trends from the past in the previous section, so these can be useful pointers to link to the future probabilities.

To start with, in South Asia, from 80s till 1998 during the period of ambiguous deterrent, there has been no preventive attack from either side, despite proposals these were rejected. Second, irrational actors and organisationally biased leaders have also acted and reacted as rational individuals in Kargil and 2002 stand-off. Third, for the last six years, after 2002, despite regional chaos due to GWOT, there has been no nuclear or even conventional conflagration. This may be interpreted as that the two nuclear neighbours have come to accept the nuclear status of each other and have realised that nobody can and should be pushed into a corner whatever the asymmetry in the conventional status. The leadership in the area has matured with the time and realises the responsibility of being a nuclear state. Fourth, with every passing day of stability, each country is able to improve its handling, intelligence, C^2 and safety arrangements. This will further reduce any chances of accidental or unauthorised use of the nuclear weapons. Apart from refining their missiles programs as both nations achieve a reliable and multi-options second strike capability, the stability of nuclear deterrence will be fully established. Fifth, political environment in the region has changed. Pakistan has a democratic government in place and the apprehensions about any irrational organisationally biased actors are likely to be eliminated. Moreover, the communication and CBMs are likely to establish themselves given the time and the absence of a conflict, in the near future. All these indicators suggest that the likelihood of nuclear deterrence breaking down by design, inadvertence and accident remains slim at least for the foreseeable future. It is however useful to assess the situation against the stability criteria of the nuclear deterrence.

Within the rational deterrence framework, three operational requirements exist for nuclear deterrence to be stable. First, there must not be a preventive war during the period when one state is nuclear and the other is transiting but has yet not achieved the nuclear capability. Second, both sides must develop a survivable and sufficient strength of second - strike forces capable of delivering unacceptable damages. Third, the arsenal must not be prone to accidental or unauthorised use (Khanna 2000, 148). It almost appears self explanatory that the present situation shows positive trends against each of the three requirements for a stable deterrence.

However, everything is not positive. There are some negative developments also that need to be considered. The Indian pursuit of introducing a TMD in the region is likely to significantly destabilise the region. Although from national perspective India has the justification of securing its people against an attack, the overall stability of the region will be jeopardised. It will imply an arms race to increase the numbers and alternatives to ballistic missiles for delivery. At the same time, it implies destabilising the deterrence also. Vulnerability to a nuclear attack contributes to the stability of the deterrence by compelling not to initiate a conflict. If India feels sufficiently invulnerable to attack, it may be encouraged to try some misadventures in the area, thus destabilising the status - quo. Second, negative trend which the broader world community must realise is the growing gap in the conventional capabilities of both the countries. As discussed earlier, the more is the conventional parity between the two states the less is the chance of a rapid escalation to nuclear threshold and beyond. A better conventional capability provides the room for low intensity conflicts, border tensions and skirmishes and provides the chance for rational thinking and decision making, thereby practically raising the nuclear threshold. Therefore, the political considerations to deny Pakistan access to any meaningful Western capability will actually contribute towards keeping a lower nuclear threshold in South Asia, a situation that neither regional nor international players would prefer to see prevalent. A third negative aspect of deterrence is that states may choose to avoid open conflict but employ other unconventional ways like proxy wars through third parties to weaken/destabilise the adversary. It needs to be realised that ultimately it will destabilise the overall security environment.

An overall assessment of the pros and cons discussed above permit us to logically conclude that the majority of indicators point towards a greater probability of a stabilised nuclear deterrent in South Asia, for the foreseeable future. However, the situation can be further consolidated by pursuing CBMs for securing the stability in the region. A basic framework already exists which must be built upon. Treaties for advance notices of violations, tests and not attacking nuclear facilities also exist. Communication channels at all levels must be re-established to preclude any confusions over accidents and inadvertent mishaps. As an initial priority, the trust and reliability needs to be re-established in the area. Both states need to realise that the regional priority must get preference over wider interests. Latter must not be pursued at the cost of former. For instance, supporting US BMD for international political and diplomatic clout must be avoided. The core security issues like Kashmir along with other outstanding issues must be resolved by mutual agreement. Both countries must realise that nuclear option is only a one-shot system and none can win a nuclear war. It must be preserved only for the sake of preserving the peace dividend that its disuse delivers.

5. CONCLUSION

In 1998, the security environment in South Asia underwent a paradigm shift. Pakistan and India demonstrated their nuclear capability to each other as well as the wider world. The pursuit of nuclear weapons by both hostile neighbours evolved out of the different security perceptions that each country has. India feels threatened from China and Pakistan, while Pakistan's security concerns are Indo-centric. This difference of context not only led to the nuclearisation of South Asia but has also set into motion, a perpetual quest to match other's capabilities. Owing to its strategic depth, expanded nuclear arsenal, second-strike capabilities and multiple delivery options, India has chosen a 'No First Use' doctrine. Pakistan, due to its limited nuclear arsenal, lack of strategic depth and nominal second - strike capability, has opted for first - use doctrine. Indian quest for nuclear capability was underlined by a combination of perceived threats as well as ambitions for enhanced global stature while Pakistan's nuclear arsenal is its key deterrent against India. Even though nuclear weapons have established unconventional parity in the region, India's wider aspirations will continue to threaten this regional status - quo.

Geographical proximity, hostile historical legacy, lack of technological sophistication and limited arsenal make these states contextually different from the earlier nuclear weapons states. The modern nuclear states also view India and Pakistan with suspicion regarding their ability to handle the nuclear weapons with responsibility and security. Nuclear pessimists fear that the irrational and organisationally - biased behaviour in South Asia, especially from Pakistani military may initiate a nuclear conflict. However, a detailed analysis of the crises in the 80s and 90s, when these states were ambiguous nuclear powers, proves that even the option of preventive war was considered but dropped. Even after overt nuclear status, the two nations have experienced extreme crises. Despite examples of irrationality, nuclear factor forced both sides to exhibit restraint and no crisis ended into a major war. Despite engaging in limited conventional conflict in 1999 and year long all - out stand - off in 2002, both nations showed restraint and responsibility of not crossing the borders or attempting a first strike. Provocations and threats were not followed by actions. The overarching factor in determining the behaviour of both the states has been the presence of nuclear weapons. Despite examples for pessimists to infer from, the reality remains that there has been no nuclear exchange. All this happened in the first four years of gaining the nuclear status. The last six years have seen a much more mature and responsible behaviour from either side. Open provocations and misadventures have ceased. Both sides are cognisant of the threat that nuclear weapons pose to the region. Nuclear weapons have worked as the ambiguous deterrent as well as overt nuclear deterrent. As both countries pursue a second strike capability, nuclear deterrence is expected to stabilise further in South Asia.

India's pursuit of Theatre Missile Defence system, however, is likely to destabilise the region. Apart from arms race, it may encourage rogue elements to undertake irrational initiatives. Increasing conventional disparity to the disadvantage of Pakistan is also considered as another destabilising factor for the region.

Nuclear pundits predict possibilities of purposive, inadvertent and accidental scenarios in South Asia. Purposive and inadvertent uses of nuclear weapons seem improbable for the future while the use of a 'crude dirty bomb', by a non - state actor cannot be ruled out. When judged against the criterion of stable deterrence, most of the prevalent trends and indicators point towards a greater probability of a stabilised nuclear deterrent in the South Asia. However, the situation needs to be further consolidated by pursuing CBMs for securing the stability in the region. The indications are that both antagonists have reconciled with the nuclear status of each other. The initial hyper - sensitivities of opponents' weapons and over - enthusiasm of own weapon has subsided and rationality and responsibility has replaced it. Going through a series of a low intensity conflict and a major stand - off immediately after gaining nuclear weapons, has proved to be a blessing in disguise. It has groomed both the states, notwithstanding that both have learnt different lessons from these crises. There seems to be one common lesson which remains that nobody can win a nuclear war, it is only the disuse of nuclear weapons that brings peace. Neither complete destruction nor survival of either side can be guaranteed, however the losses incurred in any case will be too costly to be borne. Even a limited conflict between India and Pakistan would set in motion the developments over which they would virtually have no control. Therefore, in such a situation even a minor misperception concerning the concept of a limited war could certainly intensify the "fog of war" thereby reluctantly leading the states to a full - scale war.

As Robert Jervis has rightly pointed out that, "then, the rest would be in the dustbin of history." It is certainly in the interests of both India and Pakistan to fine - tune their bilateral perceptions, remove misperceptions, and realistically formulate their nuclear and conventional strategies with a view to stabilise the concept of mutual deterrence without ever resorting to threats of mutual annihilation. The core issue of Kashmir which keeps recurring along with all other outstanding issues needs to be resolved for a sustainable peace in the region. CBMs and mutual communications need to remain engaged to preclude any chances of confusions, mistakes and accidents. Nuclear disaster is something that contiguous neighbours in particular and the world in general, can ill afford.

Therefore, there is no "rational" rationale to formulate flawed strategies and to harbour wrong concepts regarding an all-out war or a limited conflict (Aron 2002, 77), because even a limited conventional conflict – either by India or Pakistan would surely lead to a non-winnable situation.

Even though South Asian situation is different, its short nuclear history of a decade only, has given us enough precedents to learn from for our future. At least one theme must be extrapolated from the past into the future i.e. the absence of a nuclear exchange. Fortunately, India and Pakistan have learnt from their nuclear predecessors, nuclear maturity for them has come at an early stage. Nuclear deterrent has worked for almost three decades now; there is no rationalization for it not to do the same in future.

REFERENCES

Akhtar, Humayun. 2002a. "Britain Urges India, Pakistan to Show Restraint." *The News*, May 21, 2002.

———. 2002b. "India Has No Good Options: WP." The Nation, June 21, 2002.

Ali, M. 2002. "Tactical N-Warheads Moved along Borders." *The News International*, May 28, 2002.

Aron, Raymond. 2002. *The Dawn Of Universal History: Selected Essays From A Witness of the Twentieth Century.* New York: Basic Books.

Badri-Maharaj, Sanjay. 2000. *The Armageddon Factor: Nuclear Weapons in the India-Pakistan Context.* New Deilhi: Lancer Publishers.

Barnaby, F. 1998. "Discrepencies Claimed in Islamabad's Nuclear Tests." *Jane's Defence Weekly (JDW)*, June 10, 1998.

Bhatti, Maqbool. 2003. "Ballistic Missile Defence: China and South Asia." Islamabad Policy Research Institute (IPRI) Paper 6 (October). ISBN: 969-8721-05-3.

Chari, P. R., P. I. Cheema, and Iftekharuzzaman., eds. 1996. *Nuclear Non-Proliferation in India and Pakistan: South Asian Perspectives.* New Delhi: Manhor Publishers.

Cheema, Pervaiz Iqbal. 2002. "Nuclear Ambiguity Versus Transparency." Islamabad Policy Research Institute (IPRI) Paper 4 (December). ISBN: 969-8721-03-7.

———. 2007. "Unrealistic apprehensions." *Pakistan Observer*, December 26, 2007.

Dawn Wire Service (DWS). 2001. "Pakistan N-Arms in Safe Hands: Rumsfeld." *Dawn*, November 6, 2001.

Fever, Peter D. 1992/93. "Command and Control in Emerging Nuclear States." *International Security*, no. 17 (Winter).

Ganguly, S., and Devin T. Hagerty. 2005. *Fearful Symmetry: India-Pakistan Crises in the Shadow of Nuclear Weapons.* Seattle: University of Washington Press.

Hersh, Seymour M. 2001. "Watching the Warheads." *The New Yorker*, November 5, 2001.

Jaspal, Zafar Nawaz. 2001. "India's Endorsement of the U.S. BMD:

Challenges for Regional Stability." *Islamabad Policy Research Institute Journal* 1, no. 1 (Summer): 28 - 43.

Jervis, Robert. 2002. "Mutual Assured Destruction." *Foreign Policy* no. 133 (November/December).

Khan, Saira. 2002. *Nuclear Proliferation Dynamics in Protracted Conflict Regions.* Hants: Ashgate.

Khan, Zulfqar. 2005. "India - Pakistan Nuclear Rivalry: Perceptions, Misperceptions, and Mutual Deterrence." Islamabad Policy Research Institute (IPRI) Paper 9 (January).

Khanna, V. N. 2000. *India's Nuclear Doctrine.* New Delhi: Samskriti.

Krepon, Micheal, Rodney W. Jones, and Zaid Haider., eds. 2004. *Escalation Control and the Nuclear Option in South Asia.* Washigton D.C.: The Henry L. Stimson Center.

Krishnan, M., and Nitin A. Gokhale. 2002. "Small Is Scary." *Outlook*, June 10, 2002.

Majid, A. 2002. "Nuclear Risk Reduction in South Asia." Islamabad Policy Research Institute (IPRI) Paper 4 (December). ISBN: 969 - 8721 - 03 - 7.

Malik, A. I. 2001/02. "US - Indian Convergence of Interests: Challenges for Pakistan." *National Development and National Security* 10, no. 38 (Winter): 73 - 74.

Mark, Carson J., Theodore Taylor, Eugene Eyster, William Maraman, and Jacob Wechsler. n.d. "Can Terrorists Build Nuclear Weapons?" Washington D.C.: Nuclear Control Institute. http://www.nci.org/k - m/makeab.htm.

Matinuddin, K. 2002. "Logic of No First Use of Nuclear Weapons." Islamabad Policy Research Institute (IPRI) Paper 4 (December). ISBN: 969 - 8721 - 03 - 7.

Mattoo, A., ed. 1999. *India's Nuclear Deterrent: Pokhran and Beyond.* New Delhi: Har Anand Publications.

Mitra, Subrata K. 2001. "From Divergence to Convergence, and Back Again: Some Structural Constraints on Stability in India - Pakistan Relations." *IPRI Journal* 1, no. 1 (Summer): 53 - 75.

Mohan, C. Raja, and Peter Lavoy. 1995. "Avoiding Nuclear War." In *Crisis Prevention, Confidence Building, and Reconciliation in South Asia*, edited by Micheal Krepon and Amit Sevak. New York: Martin's Press.

Pant, Harsh V. 2005. "India's Nuclear Doctrine and Command Structure: Implications for India and the World." *Comparative Strategy* 24 (3): 277 - 293.

Peimani, Hooman. 2000. *Nuclear Proliferation in the Subcontinent: The Self-Exhausting Superpowers and Emerging Alliances.* Westport: Preager.

Sagan, Scott D. 2001. "The Perils of Proliferation in South Asia." A paper presented in a workshop on *Nuclear Risks Reduction in South Asia.* Islamabad Policy Research Institute (IPRI), March 21 - 22, 2001.

Sagan, Scott D., and Kenneth N. Waltz. 2003. *The Spread of Nuclear Weapons: A Debate Renewed.* New York: W. W. Norton & Company.

Santhanam, K., and Rajesh Rajagopalan. 2001. "Security of Pakistan's Nuclear Arsenal." *The Hindu*, November 10, 2001.

Shah, Mazhar Hussain. 2002a. "Challenges to Nuclear Deterrence in South Asia." *Pakistan Observer*, June 14, 2002.

———. 2002b. "Securing Nuclear Stability in South Asia." Islamabad Policy Research Institute (IPRI) Paper 4 (December). ISBN: 969 - 8721 - 03 - 7.

Sheppard, Ben. 2002. "Ballistic Missiles: Complicating the Nuclear Quagmire." In *Nuclear India in the Twenty - First Century*, edited by D. R. SarDesai and Raju G. C. Thomas, 189 - 209. New York: Palgrave MacMillan.

Sultan, M. 2002. "Emerging NMD Technologies & India: Impact and Options for Pakistan." *Strategic Studies* 22 (2): 125 - 50.

Vanaik, A. 2001. "Ballistic Missile Defence: Consequences for South Asia." Fact Sheet produced by the Indian Coalition for Nuclear Disarmament and Peace (CNDP).

IV

SOUTH ASIA'S PRECARIOUS RIVALRY:
India, Pakistan and Nuclear Weapons

1. INTRODUCTION

Home to over one - fifth of the world's population including the largest portion of the world's poor, the Indian sub - continent has long been in a vicious circle of conflict. However since 1971, there has not been state - on - state war between the two (Sagan and Waltz 2003, 115). In this sense, Indo - Pakistani relations have improved. This period represents a time when Indian and Pakistani nuclearization process was in the offing. The two states displayed restrained conflict behaviour in crisis both before and after May 1998 nuclear tests. Superficially, the activity appears to show a significant thawing in relations; however deeper analysis of the situation is not so optimistic. 19 years since nuclearization, the triggers of conflict between them still remain. Importantly, the introduction of nuclear weapons has further complicated those triggers. Severn decades since their independence from the British in 1947, enduring hostile relations have institutionalized mutual animosity at every level. War rhetoric continually threatens security and stability of the region. Ganguly and Kapur acknowledging the criticality of Indo - Pakistani conflict relations assert: "Such a violent relationship, when combined with nuclear weapons, could prove to be a combustible mix (Ganguly and Kapur 2010, 2)."

Despite this, the sustained economic growth of India and Pakistan's pivotal role in the US - led 'War on Terror' in Afghanistan in recent decades have made the South Asian security framework a subset of the global security complex. Nonetheless, Indian and Pakistani nuclear behaviour does not fit with the traditional models of nuclear weapons in international relations that are based on the Cold War nuclear rivalry; thus the two states are continuously threatening to disprove the very essence of nuclear deterrence. Furthermore, the security dilemma in South Asia is continuing to deepen. India's sustained economic growth and its strategic considerations are augmenting its military modernization; thereby further increasing Indo - Pakistani conventional asymmetry in favour of India. Accordingly, Pakistan increasingly considers its reliance to be more on its nuclear deterrence for maintaining the regional balance of power.

The 19 years of nuclear experience offers a puzzling picture about future South Asian security and stability. Optimists argue that both India and Pakistan "will be deterred from starting any military conflict in which there is a serious possibility of escalation to the use of nuclear weapons (Sagan 2001, 1)." Therefore, they claim that nuclear weapons have ended the probability of another Indo - Pakistani war, despite their antagonistic past. On the other hand pessimists caution that nuclear weapons will destabilize South Asia. Sagan argues, "India and Pakistan face a dangerous nuclear future. ...Imperfect humans inside imperfect organizations...will someday fail to produce secure nuclear deterrence (Sagan and Waltz 2003, 106 - 07)." Furthermore, the absence of direct state - on - state war in the past also does not completely negate the possibility of war between India and Pakistan in the future. The Kashmir issue and dangerous deployments on the either side of the Line of Control (LoC) are some of the ongoing alarming potential triggers between the two states. Beyond these direct triggers, both states exist within a mosaic of regional interstate and intrastate conflict. Aside from the fearful Indo - Pakistani rivalry, intrastate conflicts continuously threaten to bring them to confrontation.

South Asia as a region is a recent phenomenon and its definition varies. For the purposes of this paper, South Asia will be considered to be comprised of the eight member states of the South Asian Association for Regional Cooperation (SAARC): Afghanistan, Bangladesh, Bhutan, India, Pakistan, Nepal, Maldives, and Sri Lanka (SAARC n.d.).

Following a brief introduction of the historical rivalry between India and Pakistan, this paper will evaluate the security situation spanning from 1980s through to 2017. In doing so, the evolving strategic context will be put into perspective and nuclear weapons will be central within the wider thesis of nuclear deterrence and the associated dilemmas. The section will then conclude establishing Indo - Pakistani motivations to 'go nuclear', simultaneously evaluating their nuclear doctrine/policy.

2. THE NUCLEARIZATION OF SOUTH ASIA

As will be explored in a later part of this section, the nuclear aspirations of India and Pakistan were not a 1990s evolution and instead date back to the 1950s and 1960s respectively. It is widely believed that by the late 1980s both had acquired a de facto nuclear capability though it was not until 1998 that confirmation was made available (Ganguly and Kapur 2010, 37). Therefore, Indo - Pakistani nuclear relationships can be accounted in two distinct periods: pre - 1998 and post - 1998 periods. The former period is characterized by a relatively peaceful relationship, while the latter again constituted two distinct sub - periods: the immediate post - 1998 period characterized by two near - war situations and a period of improved relations that continued for most of the last two decades.

The absence of a hot war from 1971 to 1998 could be argued to have taken place within the logic of nuclear deterrence in the South Asian context. It is also true that the asymmetric power relations, evident after the 1971 war prevented Pakistan from resorting to direct war with India. Therefore it provided Pakistan an alternative motivation to engage in asymmetric warfare with India; instances being Pakistani proxies in Punjab and Kashmir.

In the mid - 1980s while Pakistan was a frontline state in the US - backed Mujahedeen's campaign against Soviet forces in Afghanistan, the Indian government was dealing with the secessionists' movement for an independent 'Khalistan.' India claims that Pakistan took the advantage of the circumstance and supported insurgency in Punjab (Ganguly and Kapur 2010, 38). Highlighting the Pakistani policy, Ganguly asserts, "Indeed it was India's growing frustrations with Pakistani involvement in the Punjab that in part, led India to embark on the Operation Brasstacks military exercise in 1987 (Ganguly and Kapur 2010)." In response fearing that it would end in an all - out war against Pakistan in the guise of exercise, Pakistan also mobilized its armed forces on the frontiers. Extensive diplomatic manoeuvre finally de - escalated the conflict.

However, the alleged Pakistani support to Jammu and Kashmir insurgency resulted in another round of military crises between India and Pakistan, officially known as the '1990 crisis.' Ganguly cites Chari, Cheema and Cohen who claimed that, "The 1990 crisis arose primarily out of an Indian attempt to intimidate Pakistan and coerce it into ceasing its support for the Kashmir insurgency (Ganguly and Kapur 2010, 40)." The crisis kept alive the chance of war between the two with reciprocated mobilization and counter mobilization along the Line of Control. The Pakistani military conducted its large Zarb - i - Momim military exercise in December 1989 and did not demobilize after the end of the exercise. India on the other hand deployed three military divisions into Kashmir and one division in Punjab (Hersh 1993, 56 - 73). At the height of the tension approximately two hundred thousand Indian forces were fielded against roughly a hundred thousand troops across the Line of Control in Kashmir. Finally, American diplomatic manoeuvres, including that of US foreign Secretary 'Robert Gates mission', deescalated the crisis (Basrur 2008, 57). For nuclear analysts, the crisis holds importance because it was at this time that both were believed to have acquired incipient nuclear capability.

Many believed that Indo - Pakistani nuclear capability will bring about harmony and tranquillity in the subcontinent. However, Pakistani support to Kashmir insurgency continued even after 1990s. At the height of Pakistani support in the immediate wake of Indo - Pakistani nuclear tests in May 1998, Pakistani intruders penetrated up to twelve kilometres into Indian Territory and occupied key heights on the Indian side of the LOC (Basrur 2008, 57 - 58). Essentially, this ended the longest period of tranquillity in the sub - continent since independence from Great Britain in 1947 (Ganguly and Kapur 2010, 47). The Indian military counter attacked the intruders to maintain the sanctity of LOC. Despite greater possibility of the confrontation escalating into full fledged war and potentially the nuclear war, Indian counter offensive was largely restricted to the Indian side of the border. Finally, Pakistan withdrew following American pressure (Basrur 2008, 58).

India's two prong strategy to compel Pakistan helped to de-escalate the conflict temporarily. India directly threatened Pakistan with war if Pakistan did not concede to Indian demands. On the diplomatic front, India put American pressure on Pakistan (Basrur 2008, 62). Responding to the pressure, the Pakistani President publicly denounced terrorism, outlawed several Jihadist groups and arrested several members of the terrorist groups, and pledged to prevent Pakistani territory from being used to encourage terrorism in Kashmir. On top of that, the diplomatic tour of the US Secretary of State Colin Powell in January 2002 assured both India and Pakistan toward normalization of the relations (Sood and Sawhney 2003, 80). However this did not encourage Indian de-mobilization from the Jammu and Kashmir sector. With the killings of 32 people at the Indian Army camp at Kaluchak Kashmir on May 14, 2002, the crisis re-erupted. War rhetoric on the Indian side indicated intent to strike Pakistan. At the height of the tensions, another American diplomatic intervention forced Musharraf to promise a permanent end to infiltration. This brought to the end of the Indian Operation Parakram and subsequent withdrawal of the forces to the peacetime locations (Ganguly and Kapur 2010, 56-57).

In the decade that followed the 2001-02 crisis, there was not any major militarized crisis between India and Pakistan; Indo-Pakistani relations witnessed a notable improvement (Swami 2011). In arguing for improvements in relations Basrur points out that,

> With each episode (crisis) it was becoming clearer that the use of force was not a viable option ... These attempts heightened the risk of unintended war breaking out. With each crisis, the experience of interdependence became sharper, bringing into question existing ways of approaching the larger political conflict (Kashmir) between the two countries (Basrur 2008, 63).

However, it should not be understood that the period since 2002 was tension - free. There was a significant number of terrorist activities in India supported by Pakistan. Most threatening aspect of the newest development was that the Pakistan - backed terrorist activities expanded beyond Kashmir. Notable examples include the 2005 Diwali bombing in Delhi, the 2006 railway station bombing in Mumbai, and the 2008 Mumbai terrorist attack. In all the cases, terrorists were linked to Pakistan. However quite distinctively from its strategic culture, India did not initiate any provocative military measures like on similar previous occasions. Instead, India embarked on a diplomatic campaign against Pakistan (Ganguly and Kapur 2010, 72 - 73). India who resorted to military measures during the Kargil War and the 2001 - 02 crisis despite a nuclear background surprisingly chose to avoid war rhetoric despite tremendous popular pressure on the leadership to act (Ramesh 2008).

Analysis of the post 2001 - 02 crisis suggests a major strategic development as being the reason for improvement on Indo - Pakistani relations: since 2003 Pakistan became the most important non - NATO ally in the US - led war on terror in Afghanistan. The Pakistani military became involved in counter terrorist operations in Pakistan but not to the US satisfaction, while simultaneously Pakistan became dissatisfied with American drone attacks in Pakistani territory and incursions such as to acquire Osama Bin Laden. This change in the US - Pakistani relationship would influence how India could most effectively engage Pakistan knowing that the US has consistently acted as the balancing force. Both India and the US would now apply diplomatic pressure to seek Pakistani support in dismantling sources international terrorism.

The prospect of improving Indo - Pakistani relationships was evident up until the 2016 Pathankot attack. Terror attacks had significantly dropped. Since the 2016 attack, subsequent attacks have significantly increased in frequency and contributed to a major deterioration in relations. Nonetheless, the most important attribute of their present relationship is the absence of war rhetoric even in the event of provoking incidents. With nuclear issues far from the centre of discourse and military operations being conducted despite their presence, the present relations between India and Pakistan are linked to strategic considerations more than to nuclear deterrence. Arguably, Pakistani policy in Kashmir is proactive to which Indian strategy has been responsive thus far. Therefore, one can argue that whether the present relations continue to endure depends on Pakistani foreign policy towards India and many other complicated Pakistani domestic considerations. On the other hand the deeper analysis of their motives to go nuclear also suggests a link to their conflict behaviour in the past, at present as well as in the foreseeable future.

Confirming to the realist model, both India and Pakistan claimed security imperatives of their nuclear tests. India's first Atomic Energy Act was enacted in 1948 (two years after that of the US) leading to the establishment of Indian Atomic Energy Commission. Later in the year 1954 Indian Department of Atomic Energy was established (Weiss 2010). Despite nuclear test in 1974, Indian Nuclear Program was claimed as peaceful until 1998. Ganguly argues that, "India's crushing defeat in the 1962 Sino - Indian War, China's 1964 nuclear test, Chinese threats to intervene in the 1965 Indo - Pakistani War, and the existing nuclear powers refusal to grant security guarantee" ultimately led the Indians to adopt the nuclear option openly. Similarly, Pakistani nuclear desire was first seen in 1957 with the establishment of Atomic Energy Commission in 1957. On the Pakistani motives, the Pakistani nuclear program was basically driven by the stalemated 1965 Indo - Pakistani War, US refusal to supply arms to Pakistan, the crushing defeat to India in the 1971 Indo - Pakistani War, India's growing conventional superiority and Indian nuclear test in 1974 (Ganguly and Kapur 2010, 18).

India has often cited the Chinese threat as the main rationale for their nuclear aspirations. Indian Defence Minister George Fernandez claimed that, "China, not Pakistan was India's potential threat No. 1 (Carranza 2009, 46)." Though India decided to remain non - nuclear during 1960s, the government decided to keep the nuclear option open in 1970s. India cited the Chinese threat being central in its decision not to become a party to Comprehensive Nuclear - Test - Ban Treaty in 1996 (Carranza 2009, 46 - 47). However, the notable improvement in the conflict - ridden

Sino - Indian relations in the 1990s did not hamonize with such Indian claims. Carranza notes that,

> After Prime Minister Rajiv Gandhi's visit to China in December 1988 both countries agreed to refrain from the use of 'military capabilities' in bilateral relations and signed four significant confidence - building border agreements in September 1993, including mutual troops withdrawals from the border. A final settlement of a of the border dispute was a real possibility after Chinese President Jiang Zemin's visit to New Delhi in late 1996, when a fifth border agreement was signed (Carranza 2009, 47 - 48).

Furthermore it is also evident that, "unresolved Indo - Pakistani conflict over Kashmir was more likely to result in war than the Sino - Indian border dispute (Carranza 2009, 48)." Therefore, the realist security model does not fully satisfy India's decision to 'go nuclear'. Had this been the case, India would have tested nuclear weapons after the Chinese test of 1964 instead of waiting until May 1998. This proposition has further support from Frey who raised the following questions: "Why did India develop a nuclear - weapons - capable infrastructure before 1964 in the absence of any nuclear threat? Why did India wait 34 years before it responded to the Chinese nuclear threat that emerged in 1964? Why did India develop the bomb first and only afterwards contemplate how to deploy it? Why did India accept the equalizing effects of nuclear weapons vis - à - vis Pakistan which, in doing so, voided much of its conventional superiority? (Carranza 2009, 46; Frey 2006, 17)" This suggests status and prestige models as more convincing than the security model of their nuclear motivations.

For Pakistan, the Indian threat has always been clear in strategic thinking. As Carranza notes, "Pakistan has a strong security rationale for openly 'going nuclear': to deter a conventional Indian attack and to achieve nuclear parity with India (Carranza 2009, 51)." The lack of American support to Pakistan in the Indo - Pakistani War of 1965, Indian refusal to sign the NPT in 1968, the humiliating defeat in the Bangladesh War in 1971, and the Indian nuclear test in 1974 clearly incentivized Pakistani nuclear aspirations (Carranza 2009, 16 - 21). (See Chakma 9 - 38 for detail analysis of Pakistani nuclear motivations) Here the realist security model largely amplifies President Zulfikar Ali Bhutto's public statement, "If India developed an atomic bomb, we too develop one even if we have to eat grass ... because there is no alternative to (the) atomic bomb (Jalal and Hasan 1970, 20)" and that Pakistani nuclear motivation is solely Indo - centric.

Apart from sub - continental dynamics of nuclear proliferation, the nuclear motivations of India and Pakistan are to a larger extent a consequence of the security dilemma that is in play in the region. According to Hagerty, a "Security dilemma arises when a state's mechanisms for increasing its security negatively impact the security and threat perceptions of the other state (Hagerty 1998, 67)." The historical dimension of Indo - Pakistani rivalry coupled with their geographic contiguity complicates security dilemmas of both India and Pakistan. While China's primary threat perception stems from the United States role in the Asia Pacific region (Chari 2003, 16). The Chinese security dilemma at the higher end instigates the South Asian security dilemma. In this context, Hersh asserts,

> China's desire to catch up with the United States would oblige India to prevent an adverse strategic balance. India's need for a secure nuclear deterrent against China involves expanding Indian nuclear weapons and delivery capabilities (Hersh 1993, 65).

The relentless Indian pursuit of nuclear development was in part to bridge the strategic balance as a consequence of Indian security dilemma. Hersh further asserts India's China specific nuclear direction that naturally impacts the Indo - Pakistani equation because it increases Indian capability vis - à - vis Pakistan (Hersh 1993, 65). Therefore the Indo - Pakistani nuclear dynamic is inherently linked with Sino - Indian nuclear dynamic. From this perspective, Pakistani nuclear policy can be clearly understood as a response to the perceived threat from India (Cohen, Chari, and Cheema 2000). Therefore, in order to maintain the strategic balance Pakistan will further seeks to advance its nuclear capability.

In reality, this poses a serious challenge in establishing stable deterrence in South Asia. Khan and Lavoy assert that,

The conventional wisdom that nuclear weapon capabilities raise caution in bilateral relations is proved wrong in South Asian nuclear regime. India blames Pakistan for raising nuclear dangers by harbouring asymmetric strategies against India, while Pakistan counters it saying Indian nuclear doctrine and increasing military capability has left Pakistan with no other option. This illuminates the locus of instability in the region (Khan and Lavoy 2008, 234 - 37).

On top of that the historical animosity between India and China and India and Pakistan, and the longstanding alliance between Pakistan and China reinforces the 'enemy's enemy is my friend' analogy for China and Pakistan in the South Asian security framework. This adds to Indian security dilemma. On the other hand, this underscores significance of 'China factor' in South Asian security.

3. DOCTRINAL APPROACHES IN A NUCLEAR CONTEXT

Given the asymmetric Indian military superiority over Pakistan, Indian motivation is more of status and prestige than security, while Pakistan's motivation is solely based on Kenneth Waltz's 'military logic of self-help systems (Sagan and Waltz 2003, 2).' As noted above, Indian content and Pakistani discontent on the status quo of Kashmir suggests the possibility of Pakistan initiating war with India is more likely than vice versa. Therefore, the security and stability of the region depends on how Pakistan uses its nuclear arsenal. Apart from that advancement of Pakistan's foreign policy toward India and to what extent Pakistan will link its nuclear weapons in Kashmir issue largely configures Pakistani strategic behaviour.

In February 2000, Pakistan declared the setting up of a National Command Authority (NCA). Thus far Pakistan has pursued a policy of ambiguity in its nuclear strategy. Chakma asserts that, "nuclear ambiguity could be a part of Pakistan's nuclear strategy as long as it serves their strategic objectives (Chakma 2011, 76 - 77)." As discerned from policy and application, Pakistani nuclear strategy has remained consistent since the inception of its nuclear weapons program in 1970s. According to Chakma, "Pakistan's nuclear doctrine seeks to deter both nuclear and conventional threats from India (Chakma 2009, 48)." This necessitates Pakistan's nuclear 'first use policy' given Pakistan's conventional inferiority. Pakistan's decision to decline India's 'no first use' offer made that first use policy even more definite (Izuyama and Ogawa 2003). Indian strategic reluctance to use force against Pakistan in the wake of Mumbai terror attack 2008 and subsequent improvement in Indo - Pakistani nuclear relationship can also be argued to be a result of nuclear stability. This until 2016 evidently had reinforced Pakistan's Low Intensity Conflict strategy in Kashmir because of the absence of Indian military strikes against Pakistan.

The scope of the Kargil War gave India a strategic position which evolved as a Pakistan specific Indian 'Cold Start Strategy'. Arguing that 'Indian nuclear doctrine retains the scope for conventional war - fighting' Khursid Khan claims that the "Indian aim to fight and win a conventional war with Pakistan exploiting the strategic space beneath the nuclear threshold, is highly risky, given the geographical contiguity (Khan 2012)." From this doctrinal perspective therefore, there is every reason to believe that despite having the intention to establish credible nuclear deterrence, there are inherently dangerous prospects for an arms race with the escalation of crises to much larger conflicts.

The Pakistani conception that the nuclear capability gave them a 'strategic equalizer' to Indian conventional superiority significantly dictates Pakistani strategic behaviour toward India. When extra regional alliances in favour of Pakistan are not possible due to other global considerations, and when keeping alive the arms race is impossible due to Pakistan's lesser economic capacity; proxies remain, the only alternative.

The Kargil conflict and 2001 - 02 military stand - off are two ideal examples of as to how the acquisition of nuclear capability in 1998 aggravated the underlying tensions between them. In the mean time the context in which these crises were resolved illuminates caution that nuclear weapons were developed to limit the crisis from turning into a full scale war. Arguing that the 'Soviet - Chinese clashes of 1969, the US - North Korean confrontation in 1990s and Indo - Pakistani crisis in 1999 and 2001 - 02 did not end in a full scale war is the demonstration of the nuclear power,' Basrur claims "nuclear rivals avoid not only nuclear war, but conventional war as well (Khan 2012)." The credible nuclear deterrence that the US and the USSR established in global nuclear regime engendered caution during crisis situations, thereby establishing nuclear peace theory by avoiding war. Scott D. Sagan argues that the 'Indo - Pakistani nuclear rivalry differs from the US - Soviet rivalry in three main ways: first, the South Asian nuclear arsenal is much smaller in size and less sophisticated; second, civil - military relations in Pakistan where the military has complete control over nuclear weapons, this is in contrast to assertive civilian control in both the US and Soviet Union; and third, the differences in mutual understanding, proximity, and hostility between the two nuclear rivals. India and Pakistan share a common history, territorial dispute, geographical proximity and more than six decades of enduring hostility which was entirely absent in the US - Soviet nuclear rivalry (Sagan and Waltz 2003, 91 - 92).' This is where the problem lies in establishing credible nuclear deterrence in Indo - Pakistani nuclear relations and that is what the security and stability of the region depends on.

Both Indian and Pakistani nuclear doctrine aspires to achieve minimum credible deterrence. Deterrence becomes credible when "threat of punishment is believed by the aggressor and left at him (Kilgour and Zagare 1991, 305)," and minimum deterrence is defined as "assured survivability against attacks (Rais 2007, 111 - 25).' Pakistani nuclear 'first use policy' in policy terms enhances the credibility of their deterrence. Since the inception of the nuclear program, Pakistan has consistently maintained ambiguity in its nuclear policy. Non - declaration of formal nuclear policy also forms a part of the policy. This keeps India guessing about Pakistani nuclear threshold and hence makes Pakistan's nuclear deterrence more credible. The Pakistani proxy war is the result of Pakistani understanding that it will avert Indian conventional aggression. The counter strategy to Pakistani proxy war is Indian 'Cold Start Strategy' which envisages the possibility of 'limited war' under the nuclear umbrella. Indian reluctance to escalate crises during the Kargil War and the 2001 - 02 crisis proves the robustness of nuclear credibility in South Asia. Nonetheless the irrationality of the decision - makers is often considered a cause for potential nuclear danger. Therefore, the sub - continental nuclear deterrence remains problematic because of the possibility of escalation of conflict into nuclear war between the nuclear powers.

In the mean time, the moratorium of further nuclear testing is a positive sign. In addition, Basrur argues: "the most remarkable feature of the Indo - Pakistani nuclear relationship is the non - deployment of nuclear forces which have provided a measure of stability to an otherwise fractious and unsteady relationship (Basrur 2008, 68 - 69)." These efforts indicate that India and Pakistan understand the 'nuclear weapon' and will act rationally. In reality, the recent escalations in tensions since 2016 have been characterized by heated discourse but the threat of nuclear weapons has not been a major feature. Accordingly, it can be argued that the existing nuclear doctrine and posture makes South Asian nuclear regime essentially stable and secure.

4. BRASSTACKS AND THE APPLICATION OF NUCLEAR THINKING

In regard to the Brasstacks crisis, the pessimists argue nuclear weapons played a part in erupting the 1987 and 1990 crisis. They argue the 'Brasstacks Exercise' was an Indian military manoeuvre designed to provoke Pakistani aggression, in a guise of which to launch preventive strike against Pakistani nuclear facilities so as to cap the incipient Pakistani nuclear program (Sagan and Waltz 2003, 93 - 94), whereas the 1990 crisis is the result of Pakistani asymmetric warfare against India, emboldened by the potential acquisition of a nuclear capability. In addition, it is the Pakistani conclusion that it could cause catastrophic damage to India without huge political and material costs (Ganguly and Kapur 2010, 38 - 39). In addition, the Pakistani thought process that this could provide an opportunity to attract international attention to the Kashmir issue and gave impetus to the Pakistani asymmetric strategy. Further analysis suggests that the crises did not escalate to full - scale war because of an awareness of both the parties to the dangers of nuclear escalation. Ganguly argues "this can be attributed to the mutual possession of nuclear weapons (Ganguly and Kapur 2010, 42)." Although optimists challenge the pessimists view on role of nuclear weapons in the escalation of the crises, they maintain that in overall it had stabilizing effects in Indo - Pakistani relations. To further reinforce, Ganguly quotes K. Subhramanyam's argument on the stabilizing role of the nuclear weapons,

> In 1965 when Pakistan carried out operation Gibraltar and sent in infiltrators, India sent its army across the cease fire line ... escalated into a full - scale war. In 1990 when Pakistan once again carried out a massive infiltration of terrorists trained in Pakistan, India chose not to resort to military action against Pakistan during 1990 crisis, ... stemmed from India's knowledge of the existence of an incipient Pakistani nuclear weapons program (Ganguly and Kapur 2010, 42).

Both the arguments are equally true. The Brasstacks crisis and 1990 crisis is the impact of nuclear weapons, in the mean time it is also true that possession of nuclear capability prevented them from going to full - scale war unlike in previous occasions. Therefore, evidently nuclear weapons can have duel stabilizing and destabilizing effects on South Asian security.

The post - May 1998 unfolding made the pessimists argument more powerful as a consequence of Kargil War and the 2001 - 02 military stand - off. South Asian security analysts are strongly divided on the impact of overt nuclearisation for the outbreak and resolution of Kargil War. The nuclear optimists argue that Kargil War was a consequence of shift in Pakistani strategic thinking and not necessarily an outcome of nuclear weapons. Rather it erupted more due to structural causes than any more immediate cause. Ganguly asserts that the Kargil War had its origin in "Pakistan's interest in jump-starting the Kashmir insurgency (Ganguly and Kapur 2010, 47)." India's extraordinarily restraint behaviour in the conflict supports this. Waltz draws a lesson from Kargil that "the presence of nuclear weapons prevented escalation ... to a full-scale war. This contrasts with the 1965 war, in which both were armed only with conventional weapons (Sagan and Waltz 2003, 115)." In support of Waltz's position, arguing that India would not have limited the scope of their operations in the absence of nuclear weapons Ganguly asserts,

> Despite the hostility of the BJP government toward Pakistan, its profound sense of betrayal about the Lahore peace process, the significant reserve forces at hand, and electoral pressures, the regime kept the entire conflict limited in scope and dimensions. It refused to open a second front [unlike in earlier circumstances] to alleviate pressures in Kashmir; it instructed the Indian Air Force (IAF) not to carry out sorties across the line of control; and it sought to terminate the conflict as soon as the last intruders had been evicted from the Indian side of LOC (Ganguly and Kapur 2010, 49).

Nonetheless, the timing means that pessimists maintain that the Kargil War essentially is the confirmation of the destabilizing effects of nuclear weapons. Even if this was to be the case, while the Indian government considered escalation of the conflict, it did not do so to the point of deploying the nuclear capability (Ganguly and Kapur 2010, 98-99). Former Indian Prime Minister Atal Bihari Vajpayee's statement supports this assessment:

> ... Nothing was ruled out. If ground realities had had required military operations beyond the LoC, we would have seriously considered it. We never thought atomic weapons would be used, even if we had decided to cross the LoC (Ganguly and Kapur 2010, 52).

Nuclear weapons therefore facilitated Pakistani conflict behaviour in precipitating the conflict and then prevented the same conflict from escalation as a result of Indian fear of nuclear war. This confirms the continuous relevance of Glenn Snyder's stability/instability paradox: "the greater the stability of the 'strategic' balance of terror, the lower the stability of the overall balance at its lower levels of violence (Snyder 1961, 198 - 99)" in South Asian nuclear regime.

As a consequence another much dangerous crisis was erupted only two years after the Kargil War when Pakistan backed terrorists attacked Indian Parliament in 2001. The 2001 - 02 military stand - off further supported the pessimists' view point that there would be a real danger of a nuclear Armageddon in South Asia (Sagan and Waltz 2003). The Indian adoption of 'Cold Start Doctrine' on 28 April 2004 to counter Pakistani asymmetric strategy in Kashmir underpins Sagan's fright of nuclear fall out in South Asia (Chakma 2011, 67). In actuality, this doctrine allows India "to mobilize quickly and undertake multiple retaliatory attacks in response to specific challenges posed by Pakistan's proxy wars in Kashmir (Ladwig III 2007/08, 158)." Such a shift in Indian strategy is most threatening of all. Even if the leaders act rationally there remains a possible escalation of conflict into nuclear war in the Indo - Pakistani realm. The deep - rooted mutual animosity, geographic contiguity, and enduring security dilemma amongst others challenge nuclear optimism.

As a part of the international system, the South Asian sub - system always had impacts on the international system. Following the 9/11 terror attacks, the global strategic environment hugely altered. Accordingly, the regional strategic context also changed when the United States undertook the Global War on Terror in Afghanistan. This put Pakistani asymmetric strategy towards India (that had become an established foreign policy tool for more than a decade) in peril. President Bush's warning post 9/11 to Pakistan that 'Pakistan would either side with the United States in the (new) war against terrorism or else be treated as a terrorist state ... forced President Musharraf to abandon support for the Taliban regime in Afghanistan (Ladwig III 2007/08, 99).' India, on the other hand as the victim from state sponsored terrorism from Pakistan enjoyed diplomatic high ground not only in the region but also in the wider international system.

In reality, this meant that 'Indian military action against terrorist threats became completely justified after terrorist attacks on the Jammu and Kashmir legislature on 1 October 2001, and a similar attack on the Indian parliament on 13 December (Basrur 2008, 60 - 61).' Primarily, it was the Indian fear that by opening up the Indo - Pakistani war, it could anger its newly - made strategic ally, the United States (Ganguly and Kapur 2010, 58). In addition, India's failure to quickly mobilize forces prevented conflict escalation in the immediate wake of Parliament terror attack and subsequently the American intervention facilitated end of Operation Parakram (Ganguly and Kapur 2010, 55 - 58). Another argument is that, 'President Musharraf's public assertion not to allow Pakistani territory to be used for any terrorist activities' satisfied, at least on paper, the Indian objective of operation Parakram to curb terrorism emanating from Pakistan (Ganguly and Kapur 2010, 58).' Nonetheless, there exists also the argument that America intervened during the crisis precisely because of the nuclear showdown (Ganguly and Kapur 2010).

Therefore, analysis of the 2001 - 02 crisis provides a mixed picture of the role of nuclear weapons in security and stability in the region. At this point of time, Carranza's argument holds value:

Nuclear weapons are great equalizer. India can only ignore this basic fact of international relations at its own peril. India's ...May 1998 nuclear tests pushed Pakistan further into nuclear club. By testing three nuclear - capable ballistic missiles at the peak of the May - June 2002 crisis, Pakistan made the point that India's comparative advantage in conventional weapons has been nullified since the May 1998 nuclear tests (Carranza 2009, 89).

The relative decline of terrorist incidents in the immediate aftermath of 2001 - 02 crisis invited arguments and counter arguments as to what extent nuclear deterrence has played a part to improve Indo - Pakistani relations. Ganguly argues that,

The post crisis cold peace in South Asia was because of the three non - nuclear factors: first, fear of the Pakistani military regime of undermining the invaluable US - Pakistani relationships; second, Indian coercive diplomacy that exacted a significant material price on Pakistan and third, reconciliatory approach of the Congress - led government of India (Ganguly and Kapur 2010, 65).

Kapur further argues that the improvement is primarily the result of Pakistani policy shift towards Kashmir and not necessarily from nuclear deterrence. Arguably, this is a consequence of the shifting regional strategic environment and domestic security situation in Pakistan in the aftermath of September 11, 2001, that thereby impeded Pakistan's ability to pursue its asymmetric strategy. Pakistani involvement in counter insurgency/counter terrorism campaign at home diverted Pakistani attention and resources from Kashmir conflict (Ganguly and Kapur 2010, 68). Notably, after the American pivot away from the Middle East and the drawdown of forces in Afghanistan the America pressure on Pakistan has subsided and conflict has remerged between the two regional rivals.

From the Indian perspective, India's cost - benefit analysis prompted India to avoid conflict with Pakistan. Ganguly's assessment provides sufficient evidence on the same. Evidence of this is the Indian restraint to militant attacks from Pakistan in the Indian Territory: the Diwali bombing in New Delhi in October 2005, the railway station bombing in Mumbai in July 2006, the Mumbai terror attack 2008, and the Pathankot attack in 2016. Under other circumstances, each of these could have easily led to Indo - Pakistani confrontation. Nevertheless, India took no rhetorical or military steps to threaten Pakistan as they have done in the past (Ganguly and Kapur 2010, 72 - 73).

5. PRECEDENTS FOR THE FUTURE

The above assessment of the implications of nuclear weapons on the South Asian security environment in the past and at present offers to some degree a prospect to extrapolate their likely effects on the region's future. The nuclear weapons have motivated new strategic developments in South Asia by facilitating the outbreak of Indo - Pakistani crises. Growing conventional asymmetry between India and Pakistan and the Indian pursuit of 'Cold Start Doctrine' against any Pakistan - backed militant activities in India fundamentally decreased Pakistani nuclear threshold. Such a disorder in the regional balance of power increases the possibility of arms race, thereby increasing the likelihood of a serious Indo - Pakistani conflict in the years to come.

The ending of Operation Enduring Freedom in Afghanistan in 2014 meant a decrease in strategic significance for Pakistan. The unpredictability of its internal politics is likely to affect the regional security dynamics along with its increasing international alienation. Threats from the Trump administration to withhold aid to Pakistan further jeopardise this position even if they have not manifested to date. Global concern will continue to restrain Indian and Pakistani decision makers from taking irrational decisions. Therefore extrapolating from the decade of Indo - Pakistani relations, it can be argued that in the near short term – Indo - Pakistani relation is likely to be stable, even though unfriendly, and that the two would not likely resort to major war. The evaluation of their past nuclear behaviour, suggests that future Indo - Pakistani conflict behaviour will be continuously dictated by the developing of the strategic environment in the region in which they operate.

The strategic environment hugely changed after nuclearisation: first, prospects for Indian economic growth have underlined increases in Indian military spending; the introduction of Indian 'Cold start Doctrine' facilitated by the post - nuclearization crises; Pakistan's domestic problems, the US war on terror in Afghanistan and Pakistan's strategic significance to the US.

The terrorist attacks against the United States and the following US - led war on terrorism significantly affected Indo - Pakistani strategic interactions. Pakistan's opportunity to 'mend fences' with its erstwhile (often unreliable) ally, the United States by abandoning its support to the Taliban regime in Afghanistan and conducting anti - militant operations in Pakistan dramatically altered the strategic landscape in South Asia. However, siding with the US in the war on terrorism cost Pakistan the domestic support gained from opposition to pro - US policy from fundamental Islamic groups, and potentially the loss of Afghanistan as the strategic buffer in any future military confrontation with India (Carranza 2009, 164 - 65).

The nuclear factor has added a new dimension to the persisting irritants between India and Pakistan. They are engaged in a nuclear arms race to modernize update and strengthen their nuclear - deterrent capabilities (Jain 2010, 76). Accordingly, traditional theories are inapplicable to India and Pakistan, including for instance Kenneth Waltz's argument that there is 'zero probability' of a major war among nuclear weapons states.

The Indo - Pakistan peace process hinges on the ability of Pakistan's political establishment to control terrorist groups from wreaking havoc in India. It is doubtful how much control the civilian government in Islamabad can exert, given that various terrorist outfits have vowed to continue their jihad in Kashmir (Jain 2010, 78). Deterioration since 2016 has created a situation that now appears heavily entrenched and will likely persevere for several years even if major diplomatic successes are achieved.

6. CONCLUSION

South Asian security, albeit complex to define, depends more on the Indo - Pakistani relationships than any other single factor. Arguably, since their independence, India and Pakistan have shared a hostile past; a legacy that cripples any possibility of conflict resolution underpinning the intractability of the conflict. The territorial dispute over Kashmir amongst others has kept the prospects for conflict active in their bilateral relationship.

Evidently, the South Asian conflict dynamics are situation - dependent. That said, any unfolding strategic environment in the regional security framework contributes toward a development of a new policy and strategy on the part of the major stakeholders, either India or Pakistan. Pakistan the weaker of the two, in particular attempted to achieve regional balance of power through equipping with qualitatively superior weapon systems, alliance with the extra - regional actors, proxy war tactics, and finally the nuclear weapons and its strategic application to outwit the asymmetric power disadvantage vis - à - vis India. The deep entrenched mutual animosity continues to revolve around the Kashmir issue. Sagan and Waltz argues, "The Indian government never accepted the United Nations mandate calling for a plebiscite to determine the fate of Kashmir. ... Pakistan, in turn, has never accepted Indian control over Kashmir (Sagan and Waltz 2003, 89 - 90)."

In the decade that followed the 2001 - 02 crisis relatively calm Indo - Pakistani relations were observed despite the continuation of minor and occasional incidents. If we consider the length of Indo - Pakistani relations starting from 1947 (independence), in the first 24 years until 1971 they fought three wars, in the 46 years since then, they have fought only one war in 1999 (the Kargil War) (Sagan and Waltz 2003, 115). This highlights the state of relative security and stability in the region. By 1971, India had already embarked into the nuclear program and conducted peaceful nuclear tests in 1974. Pakistan on its part decided to embark upon a nuclear path in 1972. By the late 1980s both had reportedly achieved the nuclear capability before they demonstrated in May 1998. Therefore the question 'Is south Asia more or less secured with nuclear weapons?' becomes relevant. It is because of the hostile past of the two with triggers of conflict remaining in place and the experience of Cold War nuclear peace.

However, during the nuclearization process and post - nuclearization period the frequent crisis situations developed between the two. The assessment of the eruption of crises and their resolution has been linked to the nuclear weapons in one way or other. The 1988 Brasstacks crisis was a result of Indian motive to launch preventive strike against

Pakistani nuclear facilities, while the 1990 crisis was the result of the Pakistani proxy war in Kashmir emboldened by the newly acquired nuclear capability. The role played by nuclear weapons cannot therefore only be attributed to conflict resolution.

The post May - 1998 crises; the Kargil War and the 2001 - 02 military stand - off, like in earlier crises had roots connected to nuclear weapons. Most importantly, the declared nuclear capability for Pakistan was an incentive to strike India using its proxy war tactic in Kashmir and wider India without fearing the retaliatory counter attacks from powerful India. Despite the potential to escalate into full - scale wars, both crises ended on a limited note. Indian strategic patience during the Kashmir episode and the 2001 - 02 crisis, and the global concerns of escalation of crises into a nuclear war all point toward implications of the nuclear weapons for conflict resolution. Be it the fear demonstrated by either of the parties to conflict during crisis and the US diplomatic manoeuvres. These clearly demonstrate the role of nuclear weapons as both the stimulus of insecurity and instability as well as the sponsor of security and stability in the world's most volatile zone of conflict.

Devin Hagerty argues that "Nuclear states do not fight wars with each other (Hagerty 1998, 184)", a logic that is based upon the Cold War nuclear experience. The thesis has been challenged by India and Pakistan who after acquiring nuclear capabilities in 1999 immediately resorted to war. Despite that, the South Asian unfolding nuclear dynamics added another theory of possibility of limited conventional wars between the nuclear rivals, reasons being the Kargil War and the evolution of Indian Cold Start doctrine. However, this inherently possesses the nuclear dangers. The changes in the nuclear thinking in South Asian security have had clear implications on the nuclear behaviour of India and Pakistan; the acceptance of nuclear dangers by both during the two post May - 1998 crises.

The elemental causes related to the national integrity such as fear for survival, self - interest and values/ideologies will continue dominating the Indo - Pakistani relationship. The religious imperatives in their relations as well as the political of the leadership intensify the momentum for conflict. Augmenting that, the structural causes such as the status/hold of the government in Pakistan, poor governance, inequality and social exclusion would continue to act as triggers. The Indo - Pakistani relationship embeds conflict as primary element of their interactions. Therefore possibility of war is real between the two.

The growing asymmetry of conventional forces leads many observers to focus on Pakistan as the regional source of nuclear threat but nuclear weapons are no longer the main asymmetrical strategy of Pakistan, this is demonstrated most clearly by its approaches to disrupting the Kashmir status quo. The major risks in going nuclear have, for better or worse, been overcome and the reality of an international rivalry in a nuclear context is the primary concern. The role of nuclear weapons is here most clearly defined as modifying the frame in which the conflict interaction takes place. The presence of nuclear weapons is limiting some sources of conflict but it is not muting them. The conflict between the states remains incredibly intense and thus serious escalation despite the nuclear context could lead rational leaders into irrational situations. Nuclear weapons ultimately are instruments of war, and there is no guarantee that they will not be used in a future Indo - Pakistani conflict.

REFERENCES

Basrur, Rajesh M. 2008. *South Asia's Cold War: Nuclear Weapons and Conflict in Comparative Perspective.* Oxford: Routledge.

Carranza, Mario Esteban. 2009. *South Asian Security and International Nuclear Order: Creating a Robust Indo-Pakistani Nuclear Arms Control Regime.* Abingdon: Ashgate.

Chakma, Bhumitra. 2009. *Pakistan's Nuclear Weapon.* Oxford: Routledge.

———. 2011. *The Politics of Nuclear Weapons in South Asia.* Abingdon: Ashgate.

Chari, P. R. 2003. *Nuclear Crisis, Escalation Control, and Deterrence in South Asia.* Washington D. C.: The Henry L. Stimson Center.

Cohen, Stephen P., P. R. Chari, and Parvaiz Iqbal Cheema. 2000. *The Compound Crisis of 1990: Perception, Politics, and Insecurity.* ACDIS Research Report. Urbana Champaign: University of Illinois.

Frey, K. 2006. *India's Nuclear Bomb and National Security.* London: Routledge.

Ganguly, Sumit, and S. Paul Kapur. 2010. *India, Pakistan, and the Bomb: Debating Nuclear Stability in South Asia.* New York: Columbia University Press.

Hagerty, Devin T. 1998. *The Consequences of Nuclear Proliferation: Lessons from South Asia.* London: The MIT Press.

Hersh, Seymour M. 1993. "On the Nuclear Edge." *The New Yorker,* March 29, 1993.

Izuyama, Marie, and Shinichi Ogawa. 2003. "The Nuclear Policy of Inida and Pakistan." NIDS Security Reports, no. 4 (March): 59 - 89.

Jain, B. M. 2010. *India in the New South Asia: Strategic, Military and Economic Concerns in the Age of Nuclear Diplomacy.* London: Tauris Publishers.

Jalal, Hamid, and Khalid Hasan. 1970. *Awakening the people: Speeches of Zulfikar Ali Bhutto, 1966 - 1969.* Rawalpindi: Pakistan Publications.

Khan, Feroz Hassan, and Peter R. Lavoy. 2008. "Pakistan: The Dilemma of Nuclear Deterrence." In *The Long Shadow: Nuclear Weapons and Security in 21st Century Asia,* edited by Muthiah Alagappa. California: Stanford University Press.

Khan, Khursid. 2012. "Limited War under Nuclear Umbrella and Its Implications for South Asia." http://www.stimson.org/images/uploads/research - pdfs/khursidkhan.pdf.

Kilgour, D. Marc, and Frank C. Zagare. 1991. "Credibility, Uncertainty, and Deterrence." *American Journal of Political Science* 35, no. 2 (May): 305 - 34.

Ladwig III, Walter C. 2007/08. "A Cold Start for Hot Wars: The Indian Army's New Limited War Doctrine." *International Security* (MIT) 32, no. 3 (Winter).

Rais, Rasul Bakhsh. 2007. "*Identity Politics and Minorities in Pakistan.*" *Journal of South Asian Studies* 30, no. 1(April): 111 - 25.

Ramesh, Randeep. 2008. "India Calls on UN to Ban Charity It Claims Is Front for Terror group." *Guardian*, December 11, 2008. Accesed January 25, 2018. http://www.guardian.co.uk/world/2008/dec/11/mumbai - terror - attacks - india.

SAARC Secretariat, Kathmandu, Nepal. n.d. "South Asian Association for Regional Cooperation." *SAARC.* Accessed January 25, 2018. http://www.saarc - sec.org/.

Sagan, Scott D. 2001. "The Perils of Proliferation in South Asia." *Asia Survey* 41, no. 6 (November/December).

Sagan, Scott D., and Kenneth N. Waltz. 2003. *The Spread of Nuclear Weapons: A Debate Renewed.* New York: W. W. Norton & Company.

Snyder, Glenn H. 1961. *Deterrence and Defence: Toward a Theory of National Security.* Princeton, N. J.: Princeton University Press.

Sood, V.K., and Pravin Sawhney. 2003. *Operation Parakram: The War Unfinished.* New Delhi: Sage Publication.

Swami, Praveen. 2011. "Figures Back Case for Army Rollback in Kashmir." *The Hindu*, October 28, 2011. Accessed January 25, 2018. http://www.thehindu.com/news/national/figures - back - case - for - army - rollback - in - kashmir/article2574588.ece.

Weiss, Leonard. 2010. "India and the NPT." *Strategic Analysis* 34, no. 2 (March): 255 - 271.

V

NUCLEAR SECURITY DYNAMICS IN SOUTH ASIA:
India and Pakistan Nuclearisation and Its Implications

1. INTRODUCTION

The aim of this paper is to analyse the security implications of nuclearisation for ongoing regional stability in South Asia. Nuclear weapons have taken prominence in the strategic considerations of many countries following the end of World War II. The four decade long US-Soviet nuclear struggle realized a nuclear war can not be won and must never be fought. Iccho Itoh, Mayor of Nagasaki claimed (during the Nagasaki Peace Declaration, 1995) that the human race cannot co-exist with nuclear weapons. Itoh's claim reflected the hellish Japanese experience of 9 August 1945 (ICNND 2009). The end of Cold War to some degree removed the immediate nuclear fear. However, it did nothing to unravel the Asian conundrum. India and Pakistan, the two powerful next-door neighbours share a deeply entrenched enmity in their bilateral relations. The Indo-Pakistani acquisition of nuclear capability in the late 1990s brought to the fore, the continued nuclear danger. Both repeatedly threatened to use nuclear weapons in combat in contrast to the Cold War US-Soviet rivalry and this has ignited global debates on the role of nuclear weapons in Asian security.

The introduction of nuclear weapons with the backdrop of Indo-Pakistani animosity subsequently altered regional strategic environment, making South Asia one of the most dangerous places on earth. Home to over one-fifth of the world's population including the largest portion of the world's poor, the Indian sub-continent has long been in a vicious circle of conflict. In recent years, the sustained economic growth of India, and Pakistan's pivotal role in the US led War on Terror have made the Asian security framework a subset of the global security complex.

The regional antagonists share a war - ridden past; however since 1971, there has not been state - on - state war between the two (Sagan and Waltz 2003). In this sense, Indo - Pakistani relations have improved. Both have displayed restrained conflict behaviour in crises both before and after May 1998 nuclear tests. Superficially, activity appears to show a thawing in relations; however deeper analysis of the situation is not so optimistic. 14 years since nuclearisation, the triggers of conflict between them still remain. War rhetoric continually threatens the security and stability of the region. Ganguly and Kapur acknowledging the criticality of Indo - Pakistani relations assert: Such a violent relationship, when combined with nuclear weapons, could prove to be a combustible mix (Ganguly and Kapur 2010, 2).

As many had believed, the existence of nuclear weapons couldn't ensure security and stability in the region. Confirmation is found in wider analysis of the Kargil War 1998 and the 2001 - 02 crises. Arguably there was relative peace during their covert nuclearisation until late 1990s which was marred by a number of conflicts. The scale of attacks that terrorists have become able to mount (evident since 9/11) and the concern that Pakistan could be a hub of international proliferation has only compounded the Asian security environment. However, the security - insecurity complex became more puzzling when series of Pakistan - backed militant attacks in India did not end in full - scale war as had previously been the case.

The security dilemma in South Asia is developing further. India's sustained economic growth and its strategic considerations would augment its military modernization; thereby further increasing Indo - Pakistani asymmetry in favour of India. Thus, Pakistan is more reliant its nuclear deterrent in order to maintain the regional balance of power.

South Asia as a region is a recent phenomenon and its definition varies. The South Asian Association for Regional Cooperation (SAARC) includes eight member countries: Afghanistan, Bangladesh, Bhutan, India, Pakistan, Nepal, Maldives, and Sri Lanka. The United Nations Population Information Network (POPIN) includes Afghanistan, Bangladesh, Burma, India, Iran, Nepal, Pakistan and Sri Lanka as part of South Asia. South Asian Studies Programs in University of California, Michigan, and Virginia amongst others have included different countries as South Asia. For clarity in this paper, South Asia includes the eight SAARC members.

Given the regional security complex and evolving definitions of security, it is difficult to establish what exactly security and stability in the region would mean. Primarily, this paper will consider the military security aspect to gauge the stability in the region. The term 'security and stability' will be used to define the state of relationship between India and Pakistan (Sagan and Waltz 2003).

The paper is divided in two main sections: the first section will appraise the South Asian security perspectives, while the second section will assess the implications of nuclear weapons on security and stability in the region. Following a brief introduction of the historical rivalry between India and Pakistan, it will evaluate the security situation spanning from the 1980s through to 2013. In doing so, the evolving strategic context will be put into perspective and nuclear weapons will be central within the wider thesis of nuclear deterrence and the associated dilemmas. The conclusion will postulate the future of nuclear South Asia.

2. THE HISTORY OF RIVALRY AND AN EVOLVING STRATEGIC ENVIRONMENT

Since partition, Indo-Pakistani relations have been shaped by three key factors: a religious dimension, internal political dynamics of both countries and the influences of external actors on their behaviour. Although the Hindu-Muslim conflict was not a twentieth century phenomenon in the South Asian history, and the episodes of communal violence leading up to the independence in August 1947 resulted in the cross border migration of about fifteen million people and the killings of approximately 500,000 Hindus, Muslims and Sikhs (Hagerty 1998, 64 - 65). This bloody process of partition embedded in their common historical legacy exerts a persistent negative influence on their relations. As a result, mutual mistrust threatens the regional security and stability that has become dependent on the development of internal and external political dynamics in both India and Pakistan.

The roots of the South Asian security situation can be traced back through history. Over the last six decades there were four military conflicts in South Asia; fought between India and Pakistan in 1948, 1965, 1971 and a low intensity conflict in 1998 (Kargil War). In addition, China and India fought in 1962 over border disputes. With this backdrop, the Stockholm International Peace Research Institute analysis shows:

> War, disputes over territories and borders, cross border involvement, and access to nuclear – all point to the fact that South Asia could become a major flash point where the actors resort to the use of weapons of mass destruction in case of war or conflict (Axelsson, Jonsson, Lindblad, Norlander, Norqvist, Unge, and Wigg 2002, 1).

The process of post - colonial state building and nation building was problematic in both the countries as they sought to establish national identities while facing internal turmoil: extremely segmented societies, divided by language, religious affiliation, class, tribe, and caste. Therefore history can be said to have made the Indo - Pakistani relationship fundamentally problematic. Benazir Bhutto's view speaks volumes, "It's our history. …three wars with a larger neighbour. …five times larger in military strength. In 1971, our country was disintegrated (Sagan and Waltz 2003, 111)." Highlighting further, Hasnat explains that Pakistani national strategy will be "derived from the tensions and unresolved conflicts with India, emerging from the legacy of historic experience... compounded by hostile relations about each other (Hasnat 2011, 13)."

Today India is the largest democracy with a secular identity augmented by steady economic rise. India over the years consolidated its control over Kashmir, despite Pakistani wars, crises, insurgencies, proxies, terrorism and international pressure. For Pakistan, Kashmir is still central in Pakistan's national identity without which the partition remains incomplete. While India attaches Kashmir to its secular identity. Basrur's assessment underpins the criticality of Kashmir from the Pakistani perspective:

> Pakistan's unremitting desire to wrest Kashmir has been repeatedly thwarted. Every stratagem - political alliance with the united States and China, multilateral pressure through the United Nations, the Islamic card via the Organization of Islamic Conference (OIC) and its individual members, war, proxy war -has failed to achieve the objective (Basrur 2008, 43).

Basrur's argument that India is in practice (though not formally) content with the longstanding division of Kashmir, and Pakistan remains unhappy about Indian control of Kashmir (Basrur 2008, 39). Even the nuclear reality did not help Pakistan. It is evident from the past that Pakistan is more likely to go to war with India over Kashmir than India might be. As Pakistani identity remains indeterminate and while Pakistan is deeply engulfed in fighting religious extremism at home, the 'global war on terror' in Afghanistan also exerts international pressure on Pakistani leadership. The criticality attached to identity and its linkage with Kashmir are problematic in Indo - Pakistani relations continually threatens conflict.

Another significant aspect in Indo - Pakistani relations is the asymmetric power distribution in South Asia. Structurally India enjoys overwhelming superiority over Pakistan in all dimensions; be it territory, population, economy, military power and GDP. Such an asymmetry historically has contributed to a complicated Pakistani security dilemma, consequently provoking dangerous Pakistani strategies towards India. Outlining six major dissimilarities between the Cold War and contemporary South Asia, Shaun Gregory argues that asymmetries will prevent contemporary South Asia from expecting the Cold War prescriptions for strategic stability to play.

Arguably, control over Kashmir was primary cause in past conflicts. Partition [in 1947] left a legacy of animosity between India and Pakistan. India and Pakistan fought over the control over Kashmir in 1947 - 48 and in 1965. The third war dismembered the Pakistani state in 1971, while the Kargil War 1999 ended in a stalemate. The consequences of these only serve the intractability of the conflict. Therefore the territorial contention over Kashmir continues to constitute a danger of another war between the two (Chun 2013, 93).

The 1947 war left India and Pakistan with possession of two - thirds and one - third of Kashmir respectively. Despite wars (to alter the status quo in Kashmir), the Line of Control still holds. The second war over Kashmir in 1965 officially ended under the Soviet - brokered Tashkent Agreement. The 1971 war did not change the situation with Kashmir despite disintegration of Bangladesh. The legacy of this catastrophic defeat would underpin Pakistani strategic behaviour and greatly reduce Indian security dilemmas.

After 1971, India and Pakistan enjoyed relative stability in their bilateral relations despite number of near - war situations. Diplomatic ties were re - established under the 1972 Simla Agreement. However, Pakistani discontent was clearly seen through their embarkation into a nuclear program in the aftermath of major military defeat in 1971. In part this was also a consequence of India's ambitious nuclear program. Pakistan reportedly achieved de facto nuclear capability by the late 1980s. During this period, the Indo - Pakistani rivalry was marginalized because of non - nuclear considerations such as Pakistan's unfavourable military position. The covert nature of nuclearisation may also have played a part (Chun 2013, 95 - 97).

Despite uneasy relations, historical analysis of the past Indo - Pakistani conflicts demonstrates that changes in the strategic environment always had implications on their conflict behaviour. General illustrations are the past developments and the ongoing war on terror in Afghanistan. That said, it should be noted that a number of confidence building measures along with continued international pressure on both India and Pakistan have made the present security situation far better than it used to be. However, as variables of conflict remain in the region, the likelihood of the conflict has not yet eroded. Today both are developing their operational nuclear forces and the conventional arms race hasn't stopped either. Military conflagration with a background of historical animosity and developing religious extremism underscores the potential for escalation of a larger conflict.

3. INDO-PAKISTANI SECURITY IN A NUCLEAR PERSPECTIVE

The nuclear aspirations of India and Pakistan were not a 1990s evolution. The nuclear ambitions of India and Pakistan date back to the 1950s and 1960s respectively though they acquired a de jure nuclear capability in May 1998 (Alam 2002, 8). It is widely believed that by the late 1980s both had acquired a de facto nuclear capability. Therefore, Indo - Pakistani nuclear relationships can be accounted in two distinct periods: pre - 1998 and post - 1998 periods. The former period is characterized by a relatively peaceful relationship, while the latter again constituted two distinct periods: an immediate post - 1998 period marred with two near - war situations and a period of much improved relations that continues to the present day.

In the mid - 1980s while Pakistan was a frontline state in the US - backed Mujahedeen campaign against Soviet forces in Afghanistan, the Indian government was dealing with a secessionist movement for an independent 'Khalistan.' India claims that Pakistan took the advantage of the circumstance and supported insurgency in Punjab. Highlighting the Pakistani policy Ganguly asserts, Indeed it was India's growing frustrations with Pakistani involvement in the Punjab that in part, led India to embark on the Operation Brasstacks military exercise in 1987.[1]

1 Brasstacks military exercise was undertaken by the Indian Army in Rajasthan region of India during November 1986 and March 1987. It was one of the largest mobilizations of Indian Armed Forces in the Indian subcontinent; larger than any NATO exercise and the biggest land exercise since World War

In response, Pakistan also mobilized its armed forces on the frontiers; however, extensive diplomatic manoeuvring finally de-escalated the conflict.

The alleged Pakistani support to the Jammu and Kashmir insurgencies resulted in another military crisis between India and Pakistan, known as the '1990 Crisis'. During 1990 Crisis, Indian attempt to intimidate Pakistan and coerce it into ceasing its support for the Kashmir insurgency. The crisis kept alive the chance of war between the two with mobilization and counter mobilization along the Line of Control. The Pakistani military conducted its large Zarb-i-Momim military exercise in December 1989 and did not demobilize after the end of the exercise. India on the other hand deployed three Divisions into Kashmir and one Division in Punjab.

At the height of the tension approximately two hundred thousand Indian forces were fielded against roughly a hundred thousand troops across the Line of Control in Kashmir. Finally, American diplomatic manoeuvres, including that of US foreign Secretary 'Robert Gates mission', deescalated the crisis. For nuclear analysts the crisis holds importance because it was at this time that both were believed to have acquired incipient nuclear capability.

Many believed that Indo-Pakistani nuclear capability will bring about harmony and tranquillity in the subcontinent. However, Pakistani support to Kashmir insurgency continued even after 1990s. At the height of Pakistani support and in the wake of nuclear tests in May 1998, Pakistani intruders penetrated up to twelve kilometres into Indian Territory and occupied key heights on the Indian side of the LOC. Essentially, this ended the longest period of tranquillity in the sub-continent since independence from Great Britain in 1947. The Indian military counter-attacked to maintain the sanctity of LOC and despite the possibility of the confrontation escalating into full-fledged war and the potential for nuclear war, the Indian counter offensive was largely

II. Many regard this as one of the most critical points in the relationships between India and Pakistan with regard to nuclear war.

restricted to the Indian side of the border. Ultimately, Pakistan withdrew following American pressure.

Kargil had been militarily and politically damaging to Pakistan. However, terrorist attacks in India possibly backed by Pakistan did not cease to exist. Examples being the hijacking of Indian Airlines aircraft in December 1999, terrorist attack on Jammu and Kashmir legislature on 1 October 2001, and attack on Indian Parliament on 13 December 2001. Consequently, India blamed Pakistan for backing the attackers and initiated Operation Parakram.

On the diplomatic fronts, India used American pressure on Pakistan. This resulted in the Pakistani President publicly denouncing terrorism, outlawing several Jihadist groups, arresting several members of terrorist groups, and pledging to prevent Pakistani territory from being used to foment terrorism in Kashmir. On top of that the diplomatic tour by US Secretary of State Colin Powell in January 2002 assured both India and Pakistan were working towards normalization of relations (Sood and Sawhney 2003, 80).

However with the killings of 32 people at the Indian Army camp at Kaluchak, Kashmir on May 14, 2002, the crisis re-erupted. War rhetoric on the Indian side indicated intent to strike Pakistan. At the height of tensions, another American diplomatic intervention forced Musharraf to promise a permanent end to infiltration. This brought an end to the Indian Operation Parakram and led to the subsequent withdrawal of forces to peacetime locations.

Since the 2001-02 crises, there have not been any major militarized crises between India and Pakistan. Indo-Pakistani relations have notably improved with a 'Composite Peace Dialogue' that started in 2004 in order to resolve the Kashmir dispute (Ahmed 2005, 138).

However, it should not be understood that the period since 2002 was tension-free. There were a significant number of terrorist activities in India supported by Pakistan. Notable examples include the 2005 Diwali bombing in Delhi, 2006 railway station bombing in Mumbai, and 2008 Mumbai terrorist attack. In all cases, terrorists were linked to Pakistan. However quite distinctively from their strategic culture, India did not initiate any provocative military measures like on similar previous occasions. Instead India embarked into a diplomatic campaign against Pakistan. Most significant of the terror attacks was the 2008 Mumbai terror attack, which could have easily taken them to full-fledged war. But India in response used its diplomatic tools to alienate Pakistan, and only discontinued 'composite dialogue.' India surprisingly chose to avoid war rhetoric despite tremendous popular pressure on the leadership to act. This was puzzling for many: Was this the result of existential nuclear deterrence or the result of Indian diplomatic, economic and strategic calculations?

In-depth analysis of the post 2001-02 crisis suggests several strategic considerations as the reasons for improvement on Indo-Pakistani relations: first, since 2003 Pakistan became the most important non-NATO ally in the US-led war on terror in Afghanistan. In the words of the US president Barrack Obama, as outlined in his Afghan-Pak strategy (in 2010), the success in Afghanistan depends Pakistan's ability to quell support from Pakistani soil to the Taliban in Afghanistan. Second; India saw no diplomatic advantage in resorting to military response.

Confirming to the realist model, both India and Pakistan claimed the security imperatives of their nuclear tests. However, evidence illustrates more than merely the security motivations. Analysis of their path to May 1998 indicates the Indian and Pakistani nuclear desire to develop immediately after independence. India's first Atomic Energy Act was enacted in 1948 (two years after that of the US) leading to the establishment of Indian Atomic Energy Commission. Later in the year 1954 Indian Department of Atomic Energy was established. Despite a nuclear test in 1974, the Indian Nuclear Program was claimed as peaceful until 1998. Ganguly argues that, India's crushing defeat in the 1962 Sino-Indian War, China's 1964 nuclear test, Chinese threats to intervene in the 1965 Indo-Pakistani War, and the existing nuclear powers' refusal to grant a security guarantee ultimately led the India's adoption of the nuclear option. Similarly, Pakistani nuclear desire was seen in 1957 with the establishment of the Atomic Energy Commission. The Pakistani nuclear program was basically driven by the stalemated 1965 Indo - Pakistani War, US refusal to supply arms to Pakistan, the crushing defeat to India in the 1971 Indo - Pakistani War, India's growing conventional superiority and Indian nuclear test in 1974.

India on their part has often cited the Chinese threat as the main rationale for their nuclear aspirations. Indian Defence Minister George Fernandez claimed that, China, not Pakistan was India's potential threat No. 1 (Carranza 2009, 46). India signed in PTBT in 1963. Though India decided to remain non - nuclear during 1960s, the Congressional government decided to keep the nuclear option open in 1970s. India cited the Chinese threat being central in its decision not to be the party to CTBT in 1996. However, a notable improvement in conflict - ridden Sino - Indian relations in the 1990s did not such such Indian claims.

Furthermore it is also evident that, unresolved Indo - Pakistani conflict over Kashmir was more likely to result in war than the Sino - Indian border dispute. Therefore, the realist security model does not fully satisfy India's decision to 'go nuclear'. Had this been the case, India would have tested nuclear weapons after the Chinese test of 1964 instead of waiting until May 1998. This proposition has further support from Frey who raised the following questions: why did India develop a nuclear - weapons - capable infrastructure before 1964 in the absence of any nuclear threat? Why did India wait 34 years before it responded to the Chinese nuclear threat that emerged in 1964? Why did India develop the bomb first and only afterwards contemplate how to deploy it? Why did India accept the equalizing effects of nuclear weapons vis - à - vis Pakistan which, in doing so, voided much of its conventional superiority? (Carranza 2009, 17) This suggests status and prestige models may be more convincing than the security model for their nuclear motivations.

For Pakistan, the Indian threat has always been primary in Pakistan's strategic thinking. Pakistan has a strong security rationale for openly 'going nuclear': to deter a conventional Indian attack and to achieve nuclear parity with India. Pakistan's nuclearisation process is clearly transformed out of India's nuclear program, and is fundamentally Indo - centric. Some significant events having a profound impact on Pakistan's perception of India's nuclear intentions: the assertion of Bhabha, the first chairman of Indian Atomic Energy Commission as India's reaction to a Chinese nuclear test in 1964 was that India could detonate a nuclear device in 18 months; India's commissioning of a Plutonium Reprocessing Plant in 1965; continuation of the US and Canadian assistance in Indian nuclear program despite Pakistani concerns. Chakma's further analysis of the Pakistani nuclear thinking suggests the 'India factor' as both the rationale and catalyst for openly going nuclear. The lack of American support to Pakistan in Indo - Pakistani War 1965, Indian refusal to sign a NPT in 1968, humiliating defeat in Bangladesh War in 1971, and Indian nuclear test in 1974 clearly incentivized Pakistani nuclear aspirations (Chakma 2009, 9 - 38). Here the realist security model largely amplifies President Zulfikar Ali Bhutto's public statement, "If India developed an atomic bomb, we too [will] develop one even if we have to eat grass ... because there is no alternative to [the] atomic bomb (Jalal and Hasan 1970, 20)."

Another important explanation of Pakistani nuclear tests is what Carranza noted, "nuclearism is more pronounced in Pakistan than in India and nuclear movement is weaker in Pakistan than in India (Carranza 2009, 52)." This also underpins the thesis that a nuclear weapon is a viable defence for weak state to ensure its security against strong states in the international system.

While China's primary threat perception stems from the United States role in the Asia Pacific region. Understandably, the Chinese security dilemma at the higher end will instigate South Asian security dilemma.

In reality, this poses a serious challenge in establishing stable deterrence in South Asia. On top of that the historical animosity between India and China and India and Pakistan, and the longstanding alliance between Pakistan and China reinforces the 'enemy of my enemy is my friend' analogy for China and Pakistan in the South Asian security framework. This adds to Indian security dilemma. On the other hand, this underscores significance of the 'China factor' in South Asian security.

The discussion above highlights the relative security implications of nuclear motivations on the regional security dynamics in South Asia. Given the asymmetric Indian military superiority over Pakistan, Indian motivation is more of status and prestige than security (in the region), while Pakistan's motivation is solely based on Kenneth Waltz's military logic of self-help systems (Sagan and Waltz 2003, 2). As noted above, Indian content and Pakistani discontent on the status quo of Kashmir suggests the possibility of Pakistan initiating war with India is more likely than vice versa. Therefore, the security and stability of the region depends on how Pakistan uses its nuclear arsenal, as India is less interested in becoming involved in conflict with Pakistan.

Pakistan declared the setting up of a National Command Authority (NCA) in February 2000 though it has not yet announced a formal nuclear doctrine. Thus far, Pakistan has pursued a policy of ambiguity in its nuclear strategy. Nuclear ambiguity could be a part of Pakistan's nuclear strategy as long as it serves their strategic objectives. As discerned from their policy and application, Pakistani nuclear policy has been consistent since the inception of nuclear weapons program in 1970s. It is clearly India-specific. Pakistan's nuclear doctrine seeks to deter both nuclear and conventional threats from India.

The fundamental tenet of Pakistani nuclear policy is to maintain and develop a credible nuclear deterrence. However, achieving this against India's nuclear build up and increasing conventional asymmetry poses the contradiction of a nuclear arms race.

India's first nuclear doctrine was released by India's first National Security Advisory Board (NSA) on 17 August 1999 as a Draft Nuclear Doctrine (DND). Later the Cabinet Committee on Security reviewed India's nuclear doctrine and set up the Indian National Command Authority (NCA) on 4 January 2003. The renewed DND represents

India's formal nuclear doctrine which aspires to maintain and develop a 'credible minimum deterrent', and adopt 'no first use' nuclear posture.

The DND states that India will not resort to the use or threat of use of nuclear weapons against states which do not possess nuclear weapons, or are not aligned with nuclear weapon powers. Critics point out that such an ambiguity in 'no first - use policy' keeps the possibility of Indian nuclear use against any Pakistani aggression. The scope of Kargil War gave India a strategic position which evolved as a Pakistan specific Indian 'Cold Start Strategy'. Arguing that Indian nuclear doctrine retains the scope for conventional war - fighting Khursid Khan claims that the Indian aim to fight and win a conventional war with Pakistan exploiting the strategic space beneath the nuclear threshold, is highly risky, given the geographical contiguity (Khan 2012).

4. IMPLICATIONS OF NUCLEAR WEAPONS ON SECURITY AND STABILITY IN SOUTH ASIA

Arguably, war has transformed a strategic culture for both India and Pakistan in their bilateral relationship. As a result the possibility of war is always a reality in the Indo - Pakistani rivalry even in the non - nuclear environment. The asymmetric power relation between India and Pakistan provides two options for Pakistan: first match the asymmetry either through an arms race or through the extra - regional alliance and second maintain the balance by resorting to asymmetric warfare. Such has been the case thus far. The Pakistani conception that nuclear capability gave them a 'strategic equalizer' to Indian conventional superiority significantly dictates Pakistani strategic behaviour toward India (Chun 2013, 99 - 102). When extra regional alliance in favour of Pakistan is not possible due to global considerations and when keeping alive the arms race is impossible due to Pakistan's domestic considerations; proxies remain, their only alternative.

Advocates of the nuclear South Asia refer to the US - Soviet Cold War relationships to explain security and stability in South Asia. The credible nuclear deterrence that the US and the USSR established in a global nuclear regime engendered caution during crisis situations, thereby establishing 'nuclear peace'. Scott D. Sagan makes his point that Indo-Pakistani nuclear rivalry differs from the US-Soviet rivalry in three prospects: first the South Asian nuclear arsenal is much smaller in size and less sophisticated; second civil-military relations in Pakistan where military have complete control over nuclear weapons in comparison to the assertive civilian control in both the US and Soviet Union; and third the differences in mutual understanding, proximity, and hostility between the two nuclear rivals. India and Pakistan share a common history, territorial dispute, geographical proximity and more than six decades of enduring hostility which was entirely absent in the US-Soviet nuclear rivalry. This is where the problem lies in establishing credible nuclear deterrence in Indo-Pakistani nuclear relations and that is what the security and stability of the region depends on. Whether Pakistan and India also could exhibit the similar nuclear behaviour requires an examination of their understandings of deterrence and the extent to which their nuclear doctrines and postures are consistent towards achieving deterrence.

In the meantime, the moratorium of further nuclear testing is a positive sign. In addition, Basrur argues: the most remarkable feature of the Indo-Pakistani nuclear relationship is the non-deployment of nuclear forces which have provided a measure of stability to an otherwise fractious and unsteady relationship (Basrur 2008, 68-69). These efforts indicate that India and Pakistan understand the 'nuclear weapon' and will act rationally.

In regard to the Brasstacks crisis, pessimists argue nuclear weapons played a part to erupt Brasstacks crisis 1987 and 1990 crisis. They argue 'Brasstacks Exercise' was an Indian military manoeuvre designed to provoke Pakistani aggression, in a guise of which to launch preventive strike against Pakistani nuclear facilities so as to cap the incipient Pakistani nuclear program, whereas the 1990 crisis is the result of Pakistani asymmetric warfare against India, emboldened by the potential acquisition of a nuclear capability. In addition it is the Pakistani conclusion that they could cause catastrophic damage to India without huge political and material costs.

The post-May 1998 unfolding made the pessimists argument more powerful as a consequence of Kargil War 1998 and 2001-02 military standoff. Both could have taken them to the nuclear brinkmanship. South Asian security analysts are strongly divided on the impact of overt nuclearisation for the outbreak and resolution of Kargil War. The optimists argue that Kargil War in 1999 was obvious in hostile Indo-Pakistani relations and was by no means triggered by de facto nuclear capability. Whilst the pessimists maintain that Kargil War essentially is the confirmation of destabilizing effects of nuclear weapons.

Distinguishably, pessimists uphold that the Pakistani acquisition of deliverable nuclear weapons is both a cause and effect of the end of 28-years of 'long peace' between India and Pakistan. De facto nuclear capability encouraged Pakistani conflict behaviour as a consequence of robustness of the nuclear deterrence. In this premise, such a nuclear complacency swayed Pakistan that full scale Indian retaliation could be more convincingly averted than it did in the 1990 crisis.

With regards to the resolution of Kargil War, pessimists challenge the optimists' position that, nuclear weapons' deterrent effects have prevented conflict escalation and thereby made the region safer (Basrur 2008, 73-74). They argue conflict resolution in this case is more to do with non-nuclear factors than the nuclear factor. They believe that Pakistan withdrew its forces from Kargil under pressure due to President Bill Clinton's pledge 'to withdraw forces to the Pakistani side of the LoC (Sagan and Waltz 2003, 96).' However, it was not in line with the ground reality because capture of the last major Indian military objective 'Tiger Hill' took place a good ten hours before Prime Minister Nawaz Sharif met with President Bill Clinton on 4 July, 1999 (Ganguly and Hagerty 2005, 161).

Though nuclear danger may have prevented the escalation of the Kargil skirmish, Sagan claims the disturbing legacy of the Kargil conflict which demonstrated a possibility of war between nuclear states and organizational biases of Pakistani military to exist, and play a role in triggering future conflicts. Both were cautious in using conventional military during Kargil conflict; however Indian government also considered the escalation of the conflict.

As a consequence another much dangerous crisis was erupted only two years after the Kargil War when Pakistan backed terrorists attacked Indian Parliament in 2001. The 2001 - 02 military stand - off further supported the pessimists' view point that there would be a real danger of a nuclear Armageddon in South Asia. The Indian adoption of 'Cold Start Doctrine' on 28 April 2004 to counter Pakistani asymmetric strategy in Kashmir underpins Sagan's fright of nuclear fall - out in South Asia. In actuality, this doctrine allows India to mobilize quickly and undertake multiple retaliatory attacks in response to specific challenges posed by Pakistan's proxy wars in Kashmir (Ladwig III 2007/08, 158). Such a shift in Indian strategy is most threatening of all. Even if the leaders act rationally there remains a possible escalation of conflict into nuclear war in the Indo - Pakistani realm.

Nuclear weapons were clearly in the background of the 2001 - 02 crisis. Truly if the terrorists involved in the parliament attack are backed by the Pakistani government, it could be argued that an Indian retaliatory attack is justifiable. Linking every incursion from Pakistani territory in such terrorist attack would be difficult to blame Pakistan. However, India's pressure for the handover of terrorists based in Pakistan fully satisfies the dilemma of origin. Though it complicates India's decision making to attack Pakistan for any terrorist attacks in India, essentially it constitutes another danger that a crisis could spiral to the nuclear level.

As a part of the international system, the South Asian sub - system always had impacts on the international system. Following the 9/11 terror attacks, the global strategic environment hugely altered. Accordingly, the regional strategic context also changed as the United States plunged into a global war on terror in Afghanistan. This put Pakistani asymmetric strategy towards India in peril. President Bush's warning post 9/11 to Pakistan that 'Pakistan would either side with the United States in the war against terrorism or else be treated as a terrorist state ... forced President Musharraf to abandon support for the Taliban regime in Afghanistan (Ladwig III 2007/08, 99).' India, as a result of this, enjoyed the diplomatic high ground not only in the region but also in the wider international system.

The possibility of nuclear weapons reaching the hands of the extremists looks slim in reality. However, with increasing extremist action against the establishment and the number of Al Queda operatives and supporters that live in Pakistan, nuclear dangers persist because of the organizational bias in Pakistan.

India's failure to resort to force in the wake of the 2002 Kaluchak massacre presents a critical puzzle despite their having all the capabilities to punish Pakistan. At this point of time, Carranza's argument holds value:

> Nuclear weapons are great equalizer. India can only ignore this basic fact of international relations at its own peril. India's ...May 1998 nuclear tests pushed Pakistan further into nuclear club. By testing three nuclear-capable ballistic missile at the peak of the May-June 2002 crisis, Pakistan made the point that India's comparative advantage in conventional weapons has conventional weapons has been nullified by the May 1998 nuclear tests (Carranza 2009, 89).

The much improved Indo - Pakistani relations after 2001 - 02 crisis and Indian strategic patience toward terror attack thereafter also underpins the stabilizing effects on their otherwise hostile relations.

Since 2004, India and Pakistan are engaged in a 'composite dialogue' evolved from the Lahore Memorandum of Understanding (MOU) signed in 1999. This was stalled after the Kargil War. In the following years, India and Pakistan made several agreements aimed at avoiding the risks of an outbreak of nuclear war: the hotline agreement in 2005; the launch notification agreement; and an Agreement on Reducing the Risk from Accidents Relating to Nuclear Weapons signed in 2007. Even the number of terrorist incidents also significantly declined. These stabilizing efforts testify to Indo - Pakistani awareness of interdependence by the way of mutual deterrence and the risks of accidental war. Nevertheless, there has been no such substantive progress on the critical issue of Kashmir.

Relative decline of terrorist incidents in the immediate aftermath of the 2001 - 02 crisis invited arguments and counter arguments as to what extent nuclear deterrence has played a part in improving Indo - Pakistani relations.

Others believed that improvement in the broader Indo - Pakistani relationship is the result of the pacifying effects of the nuclear deterrence. However, the improvement is primarily the result of Pakistani policy shift towards Kashmir and not necessarily from nuclear deterrence. Arguably this is a consequence of shifting regional strategic environment and domestic security situation in Pakistan in the aftermath of September 11, 2001, thereby impeding Pakistan's ability to pursue its asymmetric strategy. Pakistani involvement in the counter insurgency/ counter terrorism campaign at home diverted Pakistani attention and resources from Kashmir conflict (Chakma 2011, 68).

From the Indian perspective, India's cost - benefit analysis prompted India to avoid conflict with Pakistan. Ganguly's assessment provides sufficient evidence on the same. With economic rise at hindsight, India could not afford any conflict with Pakistan that would be financially costly. Evidence of these are the Indian restraints to militants attacks from across Pakistan in the Indian territory; Diwali bombing in New Delhi in October 2005, railway station bombing in Mumbai in July 2006 and Mumbai terror attack 2008. Under other circumstances each of these could have easily led to Indo - Pakistani confrontation. Nevertheless, India took no rhetorical or military steps to threaten Pakistan as they have done in the past (Chakma 2011, 72 - 73).

The assessment of the implications of nuclear weapons on the South Asian security environment in the past and at present offers to some degree an opportunity to extrapolate their likely effects on the region's future. The nuclear weapons have motivated new strategic developments in South Asia by facilitating the outbreak of Indo - Pakistani crises. Growing conventional asymmetry between India and Pakistan and the Indian pursuit of a 'Cold Start Doctrine' against any Pakistan - backed militant activities in India fundamentally decreases Pakistani nuclear threshold. Such disorder in the regional balance of power increases the possibility of arms race, thereby increasing the likelihood of serious Indo - Pakistani conflict in the years to come.

In the wider global strategic context, Pakistan today is a frontline strategic ally in the US led global war on terror. In the post 9/11 scenario, the importance of Pakistan in the US counter terrorism strategy requires stability in Pakistan, for it to take action against Islamist extremists. It is worth noting that the increasing willingness of the US to instigate surgical strikes on thought terrorist groups on Pakistani sovereign territory over recent months may indicate that the US is becoming impatient with Pakistani responses. With this in mind, the threat of US military capabilities further hampers the Pakistani security environment and as such will limit its desires to engage in boarder conflicts. Any increase in Indo - Pakistani conflicts in the region would jeopardize US led global war on terror in Afghanistan. Therefore, the arguments made above that the restraint shown by India during 2005, 2006 and 2008 terrorists attack in India is due to the fear from America makes sense. The delicate regional balance of power in South Asia after 9/11 is somehow maintained by the global focus in war on terror in Afghanistan, thus relative stability. For the time being the US is playing a starkly stabilising role in the region, though this may be expected to change in coming years given its withdrawal from Afghanistan.

As the end date for the NATO campaign in Afghanistan is set for 2014, Pakistani worries grow as its strategic significance decline. Unpredictability of its internal politics is likely to affect the regional security dynamics along - with Pakistan's increasing international alienation. This global concern would continue to restrain Indian and Pakistani decision makers from taking irrational decisions. Therefore extrapolating from the decade of Indo - Pakistani relations, it can be argued that in the near short term – Indo - Pakistani relation is likely to be stable and would not resort to major war until the end of US - led global war on terror in Afghanistan. The evaluation of their past nuclear behaviour, extrapolating suggests that future Indo - Pakistani conflict behaviour will be continuously dictated by the developing strategic environment in the region in which they operate though a return to the primary stabilizing factor of nuclearisation seems inevitable.

The nuclear factor has added a new dimension to the persisting irritants between India and Pakistan. They are engaged in a nuclear arms race to modernize update and strengthen their nuclear - deterrent capabilities (Jain 2010, 76). The historic understanding of a bilateral nuclear deterrent, which stems from the lessons of the cold war, does not allow for the complexity of the multilateral South Asian environment. Western scholars' theoretical writings are inapplicable to India and Pakistan, including for instance Kenneth Waltz's argument that there is 'zero probability' of a major war among nuclear weapons states.

The Indo - Pakistan peace process hinges on the ability of Pakistan's political establishment to control terrorist groups from wreaking havoc in India. It is doubtful how much control the civilian government in Islamabad can exert, given that various terrorist outfits have vowed to continue their jihad in Kashmir.

The US - India nuclear pact in 2008 initiated another debate on stability in South Asia. Many argue that the pact not only destabilizes the nuclear non - proliferation regime, but also offers incentives to other nuclear states to transfer nuclear technology to Pakistan and other threshold countries. China's decision to supply new nuclear reactors to Pakistan in 2010 and the Chinese National Nuclear Corporation's agreement with Pakistan for two nuclear reactors at the Chasma site justifies the consequences of US - India nuclear deal. This will give pace to nuclear arms race in the region and beyond.

5. CONCLUSION

South Asian security, albeit complex to define, depends more on Indo - Pakistani relationships than any other single factor. Purely in military terms, only Pakistan and India are the major state actors involved in conflicts historically. Arguably, since their independence India and Pakistan have shared a hostile past; a legacy that cripples any possibility of conflict resolution underpinning the intractability of the conflict. The territorial dispute over Kashmir amongst others has kept the prospects for conflict active in their bilateral relationship.

Evidently, South Asian conflict dynamics are situation - dependent. That said any unfolding strategic environment in the regional security framework contributes toward a development of a new policy and strategy on the part of the major stakeholders, either India or Pakistan. Pakistan, the weaker of the two, in particular attempted to achieve a regional balance of power through the equipment of qualitatively superior weapon systems, alliance with the extra - regional actors, proxy war tactics, nuclear weapons and its strategic application outwitting the asymmetric power disadvantage vis - à - vis India.

We have observed relatively calm Indo - Pakistani relationships in the last decade despite some minor and occasional incidents. If we consider the length of Indo - Pakistani relations starting from 1947 (since independence) for the early 24 years, they fought three wars until 1971, in the last 42 years since then, they fought only one war in 1999 (Kargil War) (Sagan and Waltz 2003, 115). This highlights the state of relative security and stability in the region. Interestingly, this constitutes the period of Indo - Pakistani nuclearisation. By 1971, India had already embarked into the nuclear program and conducted peaceful nuclear tests in 1974. Pakistan on its part decided to embark upon a nuclear path in 1972. By the late 1980s both had reportedly achieved the nuclear capability before they demonstrated in May 1998. Therefore the question 'Is south Asia more or less secured with nuclear weapons?' becomes relevant.

During the nuclearisation process and post-nuclearisation period, frequently crisis situations developed between the two. Assessment of the eruption of crises and their resolution has been linked to nuclear weapons in complex ways. The1988 Brasstacks crisis was a result of Indian motive to launch preventive strike against Pakistani nuclear facilities, while the 1990 crisis being the result of Pakistani proxy war in Kashmir emboldened by the newly acquired nuclear capability. The role played by nuclear weapons could not only be attributed toward conflict resolution.

The nuclear doctrine and policy of both the rivals have security imperatives. Both intended to establish credible minimum deterrence against potential aggressor. However, they have adopted differing nuclear use policy; 'No First Use' policy for India and 'First Use' policy for Pakistan. In essence this intends to establish stable mutual deterrence. The ambiguity as to what level of attack by Pakistani extremists within India would terminate Indian patience and what would trigger the Pakistani use of nuclear arsenal put both India and Pakistan into another layer of security dilemma. The dilemma then in turn would have both stabilizing and destabilizing effects – stability/instability paradox; hence keeping alive the prospect of continued conflict.

In case of post May-1998 crises; the Kargil War and the 2001-02 military stand-off, like in the earlier crisis had roots to the nuclear weapons. Most importantly the declared nuclear capability for Pakistan was an incentive to strike India using its proxy war tactic in Kashmir and wider India without fearing the retaliatory counter attacks from powerful India. Despite potential for escalation into full-scale war the crisis ended on a limited note. Indian strategic patience during the Kashmir episode and the 2001-02 crisis points toward implications of nuclear weapons as conflict-deterrents. These incidents clearly demonstrate the role of nuclear weapons as both the stimulus of insecurity and instability as well as the sponsor of security and stability in the world's most volatile zone of conflict.

Having faced the critical situation in these crises, indeed both may have realized the real impacts of the nuclear fall out. Other first generation nuclear powers were equally concerned about the possibility of crisis developing into nuclear carnage. Consequently, India and Pakistan opted not to fight the unwinnable war facilitated by the United States. The US concerns were also connected to the role of Pakistan in the US led 'War on Terror' in Afghanistan. Therefore, the regional strategic environment configured by global concerns of war on terror that continues to endure into 2014 and the regional balance of power will keep peace between two regional nuclear rivals in the short term. However, medium and long terms dynamics are likely to shift as the US withdraws from Afghanistan and the two rivals fall back on their nuclear deterrent.

Augmenting that, the structural causes such as the status/hold of the government in Pakistan, poor governance, inequality and social exclusion would continue to act as triggers. The Indo - Pakistani relationship embeds conflict as primary element of their interactions. Therefore the possibility of war is real between the two. However, the threat of nuclear war and international engagement would keep crises between the two limited in scale and scope.

Overall this paper has argued that nuclear weapons ultimately are instruments of war, and there is no guarantee that they will not be used in a future Indo - Pakistani conflict. As nuclear possessors, the two states understand the havoc that nuclear weapons can create in the event of any nuclear show down between them. This has forced them to be rational actors in any crisis situation amidst the stability/instability paradox. In the mean time both have developed operational nuclear forces with relative degree of survivability and credible delivery capability; thus instituting robust nuclear deterrence. Therefore, it is believed that the optimists' final result view point will continue to stand in future conflicts between India and Pakistan. That said the possibility of crisis situations unravelling to the nuclear level cannot be ignored given the variety and complexity of the non - nuclear factors that remain the real threat.

REFERENCES

Ahmed, Samina. 2005. "Nuclear Weapons and the Kargil Crisis." In *South Asia's Nuclear Security Dilemma: India, Pakistan, and China*, edited by Lowell Dittmer. London: East Gate.

Alam, Mohammed B. 2002. "India's Nuclear Doctrine: Context and Constraints." Heidelberg Papers in South Asian and Comparative Politics, Working Paper no. 11 (October 2002).

Axelsson, A., P. Jonsson, A. Lindblad, L. Norlander, A. Norqvist, W. Unge, and L. Wigg. 2002. "Indian and Pakistani Weapons of Mass Destruction in a Security Policy Context: A Comparative Analysis of Capabilities, Objectives and Consequences." *Swedish Defense Research Agency.*

Basrur, Rajesh M. 2008. *South Asia's Cold War: Nuclear Weapons and Conflict in Comparative Perspective.* Oxford: Routledge.

Carranza, Mario Esteban. 2009. *South Asian Security and International Nuclear Order: Creating a Robust Indo-Pakistani Nuclear Arms Control Regime.* Abingdon: Ashgate.

Chakma, Bhumitra. 2009. *Pakistan's Nuclear Weapon.* Oxford: Routledge.

———. 2011. *The Politics of Nuclear Weapons in South Asia.* Abingdon: Ashgate.

Chun, Kwang Ho. 2013. *The BRICs Superpower Challenge: Foreign and Security Policy Analysis.* Abingdon: Ashgate.

Ganguly, S., and Devin T. Hagerty. 2005. *Fearful Symmetry: India-Pakistan Crises in the Shadow of Nuclear Weapons.* Seattle: University of Washington Press.

Ganguly, Sumit, and S. Paul Kapur. 2010. *India, Pakistan, and the Bomb: Debating Nuclear Stability in South Asia.* New York: Columbia University Press.

Hagerty, Devin T. 1998. *The Consequences of Nuclear Proliferation: Lessons from South Asia.* London: The MIT Press.

Hasnat, Syed Farooq. 2011. *Global Security Watch: Pakistan.* Oxford: Praeger.

ICNND. 2009. "The Pace is Too Slow: Implementation Must Be Accelerated." ICNND Report: Civil Society Response. International

Commission on Nuclear Non-proliferation and Disarmament (ICNND). December 15, 2009.

Jain, B. M. 2010. *India in the New South Asia: Strategic, Military and Economic Concerns in the Age of Nuclear Diplomacy.* London: Tauris Publishers.

Jalal, Hamid, and Khalid Hasan. 1970. *Awakening the people: Speeches of Zulfikar Ali Bhutto*, 1966 - 1969. Rawalpindi: Pakistan Publications.

Khan, Khursid. 2012. "Limited War under Nuclear Umbrella and Its Implications for South Asia." Accessed February 22, 2013. http://www.stimson.org/images/uploads/research-pdfs/khursidkhan.pdf.

Ladwig III, Walter C. 2007/08. "A Cold Start for Hot Wars: The Indian Army's New Limited War Doctrine." *International Security* (MIT) 32, no. 3 (Winter).

Sagan, Scott D., and Kenneth N. Waltz. 2003. *The Spread of Nuclear Weapons: A Debate Renewed.* New York: W. W. Norton & Company.

Sood, V. K., and Pravin Sawhney. 2003. *Operation Parakram: The War Unfinished.* New Delhi: Sage Publication.

VI

TRANSFORMATION OF THE INDIA - PAKISTAN CONFLICT: Learning Lessons and Avoiding a 5th War

1. INTRODUCTION

After six decades of war the relationship between India and Pakistan is at a crossroads. The states have a choice: continue the stalemate, with both governments poised for nuclear exchange, or, take advantage of the numerous opportunities for cooperation and prosperity that positive bilateral relationships can offer. However, the choice is not easy given the emotion that the world's most enduring conflict has generated. The conflict is the UNs longest standing peace keeping mission; in effect since January 1949 (United Nations n.d.). The casualty statistics since the partition of Indio on the 14th of August 1947 are morose: millions have died and millions more have been displaced from their homes. The violence that ensued from the division alone caused between '100,000 and one million deaths and approximately 15 million people were forced to leave their homes to re-settle in the new states (Ganguly and Kapur 2012, 115)'. More sobering is the fact that since the 1947-48, the First Kashmir War, millions more have died in the following conflicts: the Second Kashmir War of 1965, the Bangladesh War of 1971, and the Kargil War of 1999. Furthermore, there have been a number of armed conflicts that stopped just short of all-out war: the 'Punjab War Scare (1951), Runn of Kutch (1965), the Brasstacks Crisis (1987), the Kashmir Nuclear Crisis (1990), the India-Pakistan Nuclear Test Crisis (1998), the New Delhi Parliament attack crisis, (2001), the Kaluchack attack crisis (2002), the Mumbai terrorist attacks (2008)' and the attack on the Indian Army brigade headquarters at Uri (2016) (Mohan 2013, 55). These crises constitute a legacy of inhumane treatment of belligerents, not to mention innocent civilians.

Given their history of conflict, what hope is there for India and Pakistan to resolve their long-standing dispute? Perhaps the noticeable transformations that have taken place since partition will provide an answer. Once considered as a 'minor-power' confrontation based on ideological divergences, the Indo-Pakistan conflict now has serious implications for the entire international system. The ramifications of terrorist networks in Pakistan and Kashmir have demanded that leading world powers focus on the Indo-Pakistan dialogue. Furthermore, where realist perceptions appear to have once dominated the thoughts of the opponents in this dyadic confrontation; the pure *realpolitik* pursuits have been altered by both sides' possession of nuclear weapons. It is therefore necessary to identify whether the present forces of that realpolitik have had the effect of stabilising the region or promoting further conflict. Furthermore, has colonial association with the European 'Westphalian' state system failed to adequately consider important socio-political aspects of these South-Asian states? These are interconnected and complex issues that are too often taken in isolation in the search of proposals for a simple conflict resolution strategy. Yet, they must be unwoven through a thorough understanding of the steps on both sides that have repeatedly brought India and Pakistan to the precipice of yet more violent conflict if any meaningful approach is to be forged.

Emerging from this transformation are a number of core issues that constitute the crux of the enduring Indo-Pakistan confrontation. Some of these are intractable, however, some are opportunities for peace. This paper will identify the core obstacles impeding peace and determine whether these obstacles can be successfully untangled or transformed. In doing so, the primary question concerning the prospect of further conflict between India and Pakistan can be answered. This paper has particular importance now because it highlights the current fledgling emergence of cooperation and how rare that is in the long history of hedging and competition. A critique of the realist approach that has characterized the conflict's management to date leads the paper to conclude that the realist approach has deepened the conflict and contributed directly to its intractability. Nonetheless, analysis of the conflict's trajectory leads to observations that the conflict is now showing indications of ripeness for transformation. As such, this paper argues that presently there is a unique opportunity for Conflict Transformation initiatives, but also cautions that this opportunity is also fragile in the face of the continued abundance of distrust and the many potential conflagration points that remain unchanged.

This paper will begin by looking at the historical context of the first Kashmir war and analyse whether the causes of the conflict contain enduring issues for the future. Where necessary this paper will make use of Waltz's three levels of analysis for causes of war: the State, the Individual and the International System, in order to distil the origins of the enduring conflict. The aim of the part is to demonstrate that the issues concerning the territory of Kashmir constitute the main cause of friction between India and Pakistan. Waltz's structural realism, which it will be argued offers a particularly strong explanation for many of the forces at play in this conflict, provides this essay with the springboard for understanding the potential role of more liberalist approaches to the conflict by which it is intended that the conflict can be moved from historical enmity at the state level to human - centred cooperation. Additionally, the historical analysis will show that the two states have failed to acknowledge the need to adequately consider Kashmiri and the socio - religious elements of friction, and instead pursued realist principles that threw the opponents into a perpetual cycle of conflict.

In the subsequent part, additional causal factors that have emerged since partition will be identified and for their effect on the Indo - Pakistan relationship, these include a brief examination of the effect of globalisation in the South Asian context. Part three will briefly look at Pakistan and India's external alliances in order to provide a geo - political context to the Indo - Pakistan relationship. Part four will then examine past peace process initiatives and current Confidence Building Measures (CBMs), including the composite dialogue initiatives to determine their effect on placating tension. The peace process initiatives will be examined under the analytical framework of 'Conflict Transformation' (CT) which is a modern theoretical approach for brokering peace by transforming the underlying causes of a given conflict. The CT framework has been chosen instead of the 'Track - Diplomacy' method as CT best explains the theory behind, and themes of, recent peace - building measures that exist between the two governments. Given the underlying causes of tension, the aim of this part will be to determine whether potential for peace within Kashmir exists through the people - centric benefits of cross - Line of Control interactions framed within the Conflict Transformation model. Furthermore, could such outcomes 'spill - over' and assuage the regional level, peace - inhibiting conflict causes outlined in the initial sections of this paper. The final part of the paper will conclude by summarising the themes brought out in the analysis of the preceding sections and determine the prospects for a fifth Indo - Pakistan war.

2. HISTORICAL CONTEXT

In order to understand why Kashmir is the predominant source of friction between India and Pakistan, it is salient to understand how the partition of the two states originated.

When the British drew up their plans for the independence of India, solidarity through secularism was never a priority for the colonialists who were hurriedly forming an exit strategy from a country that they had exploited for over a hundred years. In fact, during the early part of the 19th century British rulers found it more propitious to invoke communal unrest among the different ethnicities in India. This tactic was designed to ensure the colonial masters were never outmatched politically or physically. The overall British strategy at this time of colonial rule was best described by an officer who wrote under the assumed name of 'Carnaticus'. In the *Asiatic Review* he wrote: 'Divide et impera should be the motto of our Indian administration, whether political, civil or military (Chander 2003a, 11)'. This form of rule was enhanced by the sheer number of 'princely states'[1] that were

1 There were 562 Princely States in India, the largest of which were Jammu and Kashmir. Together these 'statelets' made up 45% of the land mass of the sub-continent.

'administered by a host of different Hindu, Sikh and Muslim rulers, all proclaiming subservience to British Imperial rule (Bose 2003, 14).' The validity of the divide - and - rule ploy was justified as the Muslim and Hindu communities joined together to fight against 'indiscriminate British annexation in the Great Rebellion of 1857 (Mohan 1992, 286).'

The point to highlight here is that Muslims and Hindu's have not always fought against each other in South Asia. This trend of cooperation between the religions is recorded as early as the '16th century when Emperor Akbar, a Muslim, forged a 200 year alliance with the Hindu Rajputs of Biknaer and Jaipur (Chander 2003a, 4).' The political boundaries between the two leaders' dominions were 'linked more closely to language and cultural boundaries (Chander 2003a, 6)' rather than purely economic, territorial or religious grounds. This latter point is worthy of note as it points to the relevance of modern realpolitik handling of Indo - Pakistani relations in the sub - continent: a point to which this paper will return to later when the potential for recent confidence building and peace - promotion measures are analysed.

When the All India Muslim League (AIML) formed in 1906, British patronage incited communal cleavages between Muslims and Hindus, 'heralding the first time that Hindu's and Muslims were formally separated in political terms (Chander 2003a, 14).' Many of the views of this group pointed towards providing greater equality for Muslims living under the oppressive rule of the Hindus in the princely states; a point of contention the British were able to exploit to great effect. The AIMLs objectives were not 'solely based on religious demography or against the 100 year Singh[2] regime in Kashmir, the objectives were largely steeped in the preservation of the culture and traditions associated with the Kashmir valley (Bose 2003, 24)' which points towards an important factor in the Indo - Pakistani relations that was never regarded with appropriate significance in the political wrangling over the territory during partition.

---

2 The Singh were ethnic Dogra's, upper-caste Hindu's from the Jammu region.

The India National Congress (INC) party, on the other hand, was vying for political independence from Britain and secular rights on behalf of both Muslims and Hindus. The point to highlight here is that the popular view of a complete division between Hindus and Muslims is incorrect. In the first instance, Muslim and Hindu elites did not foster the idea of a two - nation state. The cleavages between the socio - religious groups were in part fashioned by British colonials and the oppressive rule of the Dogra regime in the Jammu and Kashmir territory.

In terms of overall leadership, Mohammad Ali Jinnah, the leader of the AIML was, as late as 1946, prepared to accept autonomy of rule by whichever party gained the popular vote, however 'his acceptance of unity between Muslim and Hindus was predicated on undemocratic and unacceptable demands (Bose 2003, 18).' He demanded that he was to become the first Prime Minister despite the fact that his popularity paled in comparison to the charismatic Sheikh Abdullah, the leader of the INC, and a Kashmiri. Importantly for this analysis, Jinnah 'twice rejected the territorial contours of Pakistan as it emerged, describing them as "mutilated, truncated and moth - eaten (Jalal 2011, 10)." His aim was an arrangement that gave Muslims more equality in a 'partnership between two essentially sovereign states: Pakistan, representing Muslim majority province states and Hindustan, representing the Hindu - majority states'. This division of 'nations' along religiously - oriented lines was rejected by the INC, and moreover, was 'criticised by many important Muslim theologians (Chander 2003a, 19).' as Chander contends, 'the wishes of the Muslims in states where they were not a majority was never put to a vote (Chander 2003a, 19).'

When the British 'paramountcy' over the princely states and India lapsed by 14 August 1947 the two dominions of India and Pakistan came into existence. The partition did not occur without a terrible loss of life brought about by the embittered rivalry between the AIML and the INC over the authority of the princely states, particularly Kashmir, one of the largest states in the sub - continent.

The princely states were a peculiar case in the post - colonial transition. 'The states were effectively free to accede to either 'dominion', or to proclaim their own independence (Bose 2003, 30).' However, the choice was not simple for the state of Kashmir: contention over it was as much of a prominent feature in the partition of Pakistan and India as it is today. At that time the British census indicates that the population of Kashmir comprised 77 percent Muslim, 20 percent Hindu and three percent other (Bose 2003, 16).' The poverty of the Muslim masses was described as appalling and this point is made to impart the fact that not only has Kashmir always been a poor region 'but the friction between Hindu ruling elite and the impoverished Muslims in the region has always been present (Bose 2003, 25 - 29).'

As deliberations over the accession of Kashmir continued, the dominions of India and Pakistan were forming their national identities. In Pakistan, Jinnah was espousing views of impartiality and equality for all religions. He was acutely aware of the heterogeneous composition of his new state and that of India and of the need 'to separate issues of caste, creed or religion from the business of the state. His tolerant ideology was expressed clearly in numerous speeches he gave during the time of partition, expressing the fundamental principle of equality in Pakistan (Ahmed 2011, 23 - 24).' This is an important distinction to make as it contravenes the general two - nation state ideological views prevalent today, which mark a key source of friction between India and Pakistan.

Unfortunately, the secular ideologies of both nascent states' leaders were not reflected in the actions of murderous gangs throughout India and Pakistan who took part in bloodthirsty rampages against minority groups (Chander 2003a, 20). These tensions spilled into Kashmir in the form of 'an uprising against the maharajah with a distinctive pro - Pakistan character as 60,000 tribesman from the NWFP swept into Kashmir putting villages along the way to Srinagar to sword and fire (Mohan 1992, 290).' It was not until the maharaja sent for urgent assistance to the Indian government that the bloody revolt was supressed. The call to assist was not answered until the Indian government had secured an agreement that, once peace was restored, Kashmir would accede to Indian rule. The formal 'Instrument to Accession' document was signed on October 26, 1947 and further cemented tension between India and Pakistan.

Fighting continued following the coerced accession and in January 1948 the United Nations (UN) established the UN Commission for India and Pakistan (UNCIP) as a mediating force to resolve the aggression. The following Spring the Security Council put in place a resolution ordering the withdrawal of Pakistani forces. Once the withdrawal was complete the UNCIP urged the Indian forces to leave only the minimum force necessary to maintain security in the region and further directed that 'the Indian government should hold a plebiscite to determine accession of the state to Pakistan or India in accordance with the will of the people (Bose 2003, 39).'

Ultimately, the plebiscite never took place. 'India cites the reason is due to Pakistan not withdrawing its forces and upholding the pre-requisite UN resolution – to this day the two UNCIP resolutions have not been carried out (Mohan 1992, 295).' 'Pakistan blames India for perfidy (Bose 2003, 40).' The concluding action in the first Kashmir War was a drive by the Pakistani regular army that was repulsed by the Indian army. The subsequent truce in January 1949 would see the majority of Kashmir left in Indian hands, including the coveted Kashmir valley. The areas became Indian Jammu and Kashmir (IJK) and Azad (free) Jammu and Kashmir (AJK) on the Pakistani side. 'The dividing line was renamed the Line of Control (LoC) in 1972 (Bose 2003, 42).'

Thus ends the first part in the saga of Indo-Pakistan relations. Kashmir would go on to become the symbol of hatred between the two states and would be the focal point for two further wars between the states and a number of more minor crises. There are a number of factors that can be elicited from analysing the causes of the first war as they serve to illustrate some of the key nodes of friction between the states that endure today.

First, it is pertinent to note that 'official Pakistani nationalism ascribes the country's creation to the two-nation theory to which Indian Muslims were always a distinct community that had resisted assimilation into the South Asian, predominantly Hindu culture (Jalal 2011, 10).' Delving deeper into this misconception, some narratives indicate that many Pakistani's are accustomed to believe that their country's origins were inspired from a religious separatist movement against a Hindu controlled India. As described earlier, it was more the case that the AIML was not afforded an adequate share of power within a secular-inclusive India and found that they could not escape from the oppressive rule of the Hindu majority. This is why Kashmir has, for Pakistan, become the focal point of a riposte against Indian rule. The existence of a Muslim majority territory, ruled by Hindu elites is abhorrent to Pakistan, yet there is another dimension to consider, that of the strategic value of Kashmir. For Pakistan, it provides them with strategic depth and has proven beneficial during the Cold War and Global War on Terrorism for the US ally, giving Pakistan an element of international prestige.

The complicating factor in the peace process over Kashmir is made abundantly clear in Cohen's notion that:

> [T]here are two Kashmir's. Besides the physical territory, another Kashmir is found in the minds of politicians, strategists, soldiers and ideologues. This is a place where national and sub-national identities are ranged against each other (Cohen 2002, 45).

3. ENDURING CAUSES OF TENSION

3.1 The Nuclear Equation

The pivotal question is whether the 'nuclearisation' of both states has resulted in a more stable South Asia or a more volatile region. Given that two medium-intensity conventional conflicts have occurred following both nations' nuclear tests in 1998 it is evident that both states do not see the threat of nuclear strike as deterrence against all forms of conflict. In terms of determining whether Pakistan and India's security trajectories will meet in nuclear conflict, or total war, this paper will now provide a survey of the generation and policies of the dyadic nuclear capabilities since partition.

It wasn't until India's development programme became known that Pakistan pondered over the need for their own nuclear capability, however no firm steps were taken until the loss of East Pakistan and the state reverted to civilian rule under Zulfikar Ali Bhutto that 'Bhutto urged the Pakistan Atomic Energy Commission to begin preparing for a nuclear bomb program (Khan 2011, 269).

'In the 1980's Pakistan eventually obtained weapons - grade nuclear material and developed a rudimentary nuclear deterrence strategy (Khan 2011, 270).' China assisted by helping to 'fill critical technological gaps in bomb and missile production (Babu 2005, 254).' During the 1990's 'Pakistan's capability reached its zenith, the high point of which was the successful detonation of their first device that followed a few weeks after India's tests in May 1998. By the new millennium, the nuclear arms program was placed under tight military control and a National Command Authority was established which proved effective against India's Operation Parakaram in 2002 (Khan 2011, 270).' Today, Pakistan remains committed to the nuclear deterrent policy, a fact that has not changed since return to civilian rule in 2008.

The policy has had a paradoxical effect for Pakistan's bi - lateral relationship with India. Nuclear theorists such as Kenneth Waltz maintain that 'the prospects for peace increase with the spread of nuclear weapons (Waltz 1981, 30),' however, subscribers to the nuclear stability/instability paradox theory have not been vindicated as the opposite has occurred in South Asia. Since the overt testing of nuclear capabilities, India and Pakistan have engaged in conventional conflict a number of times, most critically in the Kargil war of 1999, when, were it not for the intervention of the US and the international community, a full nuclear exchange may have occurred. Following these actions, 'some theorists propose that Pakistan is now afforded the opportunity to provoke India over Kashmir secure in the knowledge that possession of nuclear weapons will limit any retaliation by India (Mohan 2013, 58)'. Furthermore, Pakistan has been able to continue clandestine attacks through proxy insurgents under this 'nuclear - umbrella' paradigm.

India's pursuit of nuclear weapons capability was prolonged given the nature of the threat around them, most notably from China, following the 1962 war, and China's nuclear capability program that matured following the 1964 tests. Logic might dictate that the non - alignment strategy of India might also have convinced India's leaders to develop a more robust security capability yet this was not the case. In part this can be attributed to the pacific nature of Nehru's leadership following partition and the hope that non - alignment meant India would not have to become embroiled in warfare on behalf of an alliance partner, as was common in the Cold War era.

As both India and Pakistan's nuclear capabilities, and importantly, policies, were developing, 'the opaque or perceived capabilities of the other was the main factor in checking all six crises from 1984 to 2002 (Ganguly and Hagerty 2005, 188 - 92)' thereby supporting standard logic on nuclear deterrence. The continued non - deployment status of both sides offers a unique view on the prospect of a further conflict. Furthermore, both sides have convened meetings aimed at articulating nuclear Confidence - Building Measures. Meetings for this purpose occurred in 1998, 1999 and 2004 and have gone a long way to assuring both sides of the 'rules' surrounding the two states' use of the weapons and dissipating any anxiety over a nuclear 'prisoner's dilemma'.

Viewed from a realist perspective, Pakistan's sensitivity to relative gains, i.e. grievance against India's relatively meteoric rise in strength and prosperity, has been ameliorated by the development of a nuclear - weapons capability. India has entered the nuclear arena reluctantly, coerced by the realisation of broader regional threats. However, India has been a 'responsible' nuclear user vis - à - vis Pakistan, given the latter's history of divulging nuclear weapon's technology to unstable regimes in the Middle East and North Asia, and furthermore, 'India continues to be an exemplar to other nations' on non - proliferation aims, so long as any disarmament process is non - discriminatory (Babu 2005, 256 - 57).' This consideration points towards a state that would adhere to 'responsible' use of weapons and an adherent of the 'non - first use' policy which is reflective of India's 'lack of anxiety over a conventional invasion by Pakistan (Ganguly and Hagerty 2005, 196).' However, as Ganguly and Hagerty go on to point out, 'the no first - use policy is likely purely rhetoric (Ganguly and Hagerty 2005, 197).' Faced with a mass conventional threat it is possible that India would make pre - emptive use of its nuclear weapons.

Pakistan has offset the risk of an Indian first - strike by achieving symmetry through the acquisition of its own nuclear weapons. As such 'first - strike' is unlikely given a number of factors outlined previously, namely: the uncertain nuclear strategies of each nation, non - deployed status, the geo - strategic factors, primarily the close proximity to each other and adjacent super - powers, and finally, the relationship with other powers in the international system. On the other hand, despite 'Pakistan's assurance that it has robust security protocols over her nuclear weapons (Khan 2011, 280 - 81)', the fear caused by insurgents and the history of conveying nuclear secrets to other nations is worrisome for India, 'particularly after it has voiced intention to provide nuclear weapons to a Muslim country in trouble (Waldron 2007, 23).' Most poignant of all is the apparent assumption by India that the military can instigate a successful limited war without escalating to a nuclear confrontation, as India did in 2002 when it mobilised forces in response to the Parliament attack by the Lashkar - e - Taiba (LeT). As will be shown later, Pakistan maintains a similar theory through use of proxy Islamic militants. This runs contrary to Waltz's theory, however, nuclear exchange remains unlikely. As Waltz correctly maintains, the 'cost of such an exchange is unbearable (Waltz 1981, 30)': particularly for neighbouring countries with economic woes and great potential for addressing such woes through cross - LoC interactions.

3.2 Islamism

> [T]he basic goal of Pakistan is a contest between a theocratic Islamic state and a pluralistic, multi-religious and democratic India. The contest is a regional replica of a global contest between the godless communism of the Soviet Union and pluralistic, god-fearing multi-ethnic and multi-religious US (Kamath 2005, 27).

Contemporary Pakistan emerged from an ideology shaped on the concept that religion would form the foundation of the nation: 'an ideal that was born of Ali Jinnah's fear that Muslim identity would be lost in a secular India (Johns and Lahoud 2005, 12).' Initially, this was a means of ameliorating social inequity between Hindus and Muslims in a unified India, and also as a means of 'promoting its strategic objectives with sympathetic Islamic nations in the Middle East (Kumar 2011, 482)', however, following partition, more fundamental Islamist influences took hold, most notably the 'strict Sharia'h laws were included within Pakistan's constitution, predominantly through the influential teachings of Abu'l - A - 'la Mawdudi who founded the fundamental religious group Jama'at - i - Islami in 1941 (Johns and Lahoud 2005, 12).' The role of religion became conflated with politics and took on more of a 'state - based' role rather than a 'community' role.

The role of Islam in Pakistan, and its effect on bi - lateral relations with India, has been profound and somewhat ambivalent, which in itself has caused tension and instability within Pakistan. When 'Ali Jinnah first proclaimed that Muslim's and Hindus not only subscribed to two different religious philosophies, but they fundamentally belonged to two different civilisations,' he set the vivisection of India into motion. However, he later provided contradictory messages to his people. In August 1947 he famously declared:

'You may belong to any religion or creed – that has nothing to do with the business of the state...You will find that in the course of time Hindus would cease to be Hindus and Muslims would cease to be Muslims, not in the religious sense, because that is the personal faith of each individual, but in the political sense as citizens of the State (Johns and Lahoud 2005, 110).'

The effect of this ambivalence was traumatic, and led to Pakistan struggling to foster a sense of national identity, ultimately; contributing the break - up of the nascent state in 1971, and independence of Bangladesh. The unification of Muslims within Pakistan has never been realised through Islam despite strong attempts, 'most notably by

General Zia-ul-Haq who used Islam to legitimise his rule, but this resulted in further sectarian tensions (Lodhi 2011, 48).' It is important to acknowledge the extent by which radical Islam, in the form of jihad, has been conflated with the military. By the late 1970's, an interpretation of the Holy Quran and its relevance to war was indoctrinated to the Army by General Zia. As Kumar proposes:

Jihad has been described as a continuous and never ending struggle waged on all fronts including political, economic, social psychological, domestic, moral and spiritual to attain the object of policy (Kumar 2011, 485).

However, a closer look indicates that the issues are not limited to the macro-level. The secular policy of India, (once the quixotic desire of Pakistan's leadership), and the ethnic tensions between tribes in Kashmir, the NWFP and castes within India, language and different cultural nuances within different regions have all had a marked effect on the relationship between the two states and domestic matters within the states. This ideological uncertainty is connected with a number of manifestations of Pakistan's instability and insecurity. Poverty, and radical Islamism and/or militant insurgency are correlated examples of Pakistan's instability paradigm that could be improved through CT measures.

3.3 Militant Insurgencies

Pakistan and India have faced numerous issues with domestic and exogenous insurgents. Pakistan has been widely criticised for using radicalised Islamists as proxy warriors to achieve political ends in the struggle against India. Examples are abound: during the initial invasion of Kashmir, 'Pakistan, under Operation Gibraltar, infiltrated a large force of guerrillas into the Kashmir valley to disrupt the state, with the expectation that it would be joined by a local insurrection, thereby culminating with Pakistan taking over the state (Nayar and Paul 2003, 166).' The insurrection did not occur; instead, India's conventional forces responded, and a full-scale war, the first of four, ensued. Another, more recent example of global notoriety was the supposed Pakistani Inter-Services

Intelligence (ISI) agency sponsorship of the LeT in the 2008 Mumbai terror attack. This attack undid much of the progress that had resulted from the 2004 Prime Ministerial level dialogue between the two nations.

Indian and Pakistani domestic insurgency is largely attributed to religious radical groups such as the Naxalites (a Maoist group), and Hindutva in India and the Jamaat–e - Islami (JI) and LeT in Pakistan. The origins of the grievances of these groups are worthy of examination as the themes continue to generate domestic unrest which, as will be shown, serves to de - stabilise both states, exacerbate Indo - Pakistan tension, and could lead to further conflict.

During the Cold War, the existence of radicalised Islamic groups served Pakistan's interests. 'Pakistan's contended border with Afghanistan divided a restive, ethnic, Pashtun population, and President Bhutto used the Islamic groups JI and Hizb - e - Islami to gain leverage over Kabul on the border issue (Haider 2011, 120).' The groups themselves saw an opportunity to address the social inequalities and immorality that pervaded throughout the border region, largely encapsulated within a political vacuum. Certainly, Zia - ul - Haq echoed that sentiment; in 1979 he stated: 'In the last thirty years…there has been a complete erosion of the moral values of our society…Islam from that point of view is the fundamental factor (Haider 2011, 122).' The US exploited these issues during the Afghan - Soviet war by supporting the recruitment and training of thousands of jihadists.

General Zia reaped the benefits from the rise of militants within Pakistan, seeing 'the militants as useful tools in achieving his aim of 'Islamising' all of Pakistan and perpetrating his foreign policy in defending Muslims against India. A prominent example is the Jammu - Kashmir Liberation Front (JKLF), a Pakistan based militant group who waged an '18 - month campaign of terror against India, supported by the ISI (Mohan 1992, 299).' These 'pursuits' were orchestrated hand - in - hand with General Zia's 'Islamisation' of the Pakistani army. The need for this proxy force grew during the 1990's when Soviet forces withdrew from Afghanistan and Pakistan felt the economic hardship brought about by US sanctions imposed in opposition to Pakistan's continued nuclear weapon development. Zia's focus shifted to Kashmir, and the militants waged their proxy war against India 'hijacking the nationalist movement that had emerged in IJK. Here, ISI support for the terrorists increased: at one stage the ISI were spending approximately USD $22 million per year on running their proxy war (Chander 2003b, 30).'

The rationale was to "bleed India by a thousand cuts" and force it to negotiate on Kashmir (Haider 2011, 124).' The proxy tactics have not been limited to activity within Kashmir: the Pakistani government are highly implicated in the 2001 terrorist attack on the Indian Parliament in New Delhi 'which resulted in the full mobilisation of Indian forces along the LoC in Kashmir. President Musharraf had assured the US that Pakistan's assistance to cross-border terrorism would end (Weinbaum 2005, 116)', and this largely appeared to be the case, until the dramatic Mumbai terrorist attack of 2008.

The narrative of the radical militant groups transformed over the 1990's and early 21st century, and this has had severe consequences for domestic stability in Pakistan. This is exemplified by the JKLF who stated 'that their aim was not only to liberate Kashmir from Indian occupation but also to liberate it from Pakistan occupation in the AJK area (Mohan 1992, 299).' Today, Pakistan's domestic concerns are centred on an existential militant threat. Some militant groups such as 'the Tehrik-i-Taliban Pakistan in the federally Administered Tribal Area (FATA) regard the Pakistani state as having sided with the US (Haider 2011, 126)' and were responsible for a '40,000 strong military assault on Islamabad's Red Mosque in December 2007 (Hussain 2011b, 138).' Moreover, there are numerous other concerns with militancy in Pakistan. One time opposing radical Islamic groups have joined forces against the state in a struggle against poverty, and in a drive to establish a new Islamic order, claiming territorial power in the FATA and Kashmir as well as redressing perceived social injustices.

The militant strife affecting India and Pakistan is not solely a domestic issue spawned from within the two states: considerable violence has emanated from nationalist movements from within Kashmir, such as the JKLF mentioned earlier. The progenitor of this insurgency dates back to the partition of India in 1947, when Kashmir nationalists harboured grievances against the impending Indian rule over fears of repression. The nationalist political ideology of Sheikh Abdullah, the 'Lion of Kashmir' still echoes around the mountains of Kashmir and is manifest in the anti - Indian militant activity seeking to redress the 'saddening and destructive process of New Delhi sponsored subversion of democratic rights and processes (Bose 2003, 47).'

4. THE CONTEMPORARY RELATIONS ENVIRONMENT: THE SOUTH ASIAN PARADIGM

In relation to Waltz's system level of analysis, the South Asian states' relations with other international actors provide a source of tension between them. As shown in the first part, it is clear that following partition, the two nascent dominions took on a Hobbesian attitude, resorting to conflict as the logical means of resolving their dispute. If viewing the relationship from one of Waltz's 'images', the system level (Nye and Welch 2011, 53 - 55), India and Pakistan initially practiced realpolitik within their own regional, and anarchic, bi - polar structure, exempt from the influences that alliances with other powerful states within the international system would have created. The non - alignment foreign policies of both states corroborate this notion.

Since partition India has largely maintained non - alignment trade and security policies and has attempted to resolve her conflict with Pakistan independently. This has served India well given that it is one of the fastest growing economies in the world. Furthermore, the majority of her wealth is derived from indigenous funds rather than from the export of goods and is therefore it is more resilient to economic shocks (Panda 2007, 95).' Although India continues to espouse political rhetoric concerning its non - aligned status, it is interesting to note that 'since 2000, when India had defence - related agreements with only eight nations, by 2008, the number of nations had increased to 26 (Hussain

2011a, 346).' This has implications for India's wider foreign policy and points towards her aspirations as a regional hegemon, particularly in the maritime domain of the Indian Ocean. Pakistan is wary of this increasing disparity between the two states and this causes ripples at the international system level.

4.1 U.S.-Pakistan · U.S.-India Alliances

It has been a somewhat mercurial relationship between the US and Pakistan with the South Asian state 'described by an American newspaper as "Paranoidistan": paranoid that every move the US makes in Pakistan is designed to benefit India (Jalal 2011, 7).' The relationship is one that has had a pronounced effect on the International system, and more recently, an ever increasing effect on India's aspirations as a regional hegemon. The episodic partnership between the West and Pakistan originated during the Cold War when the US sought assistance from Pakistan to curtail any spread of communism from the Soviet Union through Afghanistan. This burgeoning relationship faltered following the 1965 Kashmir War as the US ceased financial aid. This was not the last time the US would impose economic sanctions on Pakistan: they did so again in 1990, 1998 and 1999.

The well documented partnership between the US and Pakistan in the Global War on Terrorism (GWOT) has resulted in mixed fortunes for Pakistan. On the one hand, the US' revitalised interest in Pakistan following the 9/11 attack on America meant 'that Pakistan could seek to have the US imposed sanctions on them lifted (Weinbaum 2005, 103)', sanctions that were put in place following the military coup in 1999. On the other hand, the increase in terrorist activity within Pakistan's borders brought unwanted attention to the benefits of using these proxy forces against India. Additionally, Musharraf's support for the US fight against jihadists has brought severe domestic turmoil to Pakistan with radical Islamic militants causing thousands of deaths within its borders, and as described previously, across its borders. This instability has a direct bearing on the potential for further conflict with India.

Overall, the relationship could be described as one that has had narrow benefits for the two nations, and rarely have those benefits aligned. This has created an aura of distrust around the partners resulting in limited commitment between them. For example, 'the United States had no sense of obligation to directly assist Pakistan in the 1965 or 1971 wars against India and conversely Pakistan only assists the US as far as the good will of the elites in Pakistan are not unduly affected (Weinbaum 2005, 106).'

The early phase of the US relationship with India can be characterised as a necessary, but unwanted consequence of the US-Pakistan relationship. Its genesis dates back to the start of the Cold War when the US was striving for a foothold in South Asia as a means of curtailing Soviet encroachment onto the borders of the Middle East. Having been sympathetic to India's anti-colonial aspirations prior to partition, 'the US was initially optimistic that they would have a willing ally in the Cold War and favoured forging a strategic alliance with India over Pakistan. However, when India opposed any role in the Cold War, the US was forced to partner with Pakistan (Babu 2005, 242-44).'

The other, not inconsequential impact the US has had on India's relationship with Pakistan is the means by which the US has sought to balance the military strength between the two states. When Pakistan started using the weapons it gained possession of through their assistance in the Soviet-Afghan war against India, as it did in 1965, the US was forced to intervene so that the region did not degenerate into total war, which would have seriously complicated their efforts in Afghanistan. The balancing act was achieved by mollifying India with economic aid and technical assistance. Furthermore, the US has also indirectly assisted India by 'intervening twice more when the potential for full-scale war between India and Pakistan threatened (Weinbaum 2005, 114).' The 2002 diplomatic intervention halted the most serious potential for a nuclear war since the Cuban missile crisis.

Suffice to say, US presence in South Asia has had a marked effect on Indo-Pakistan relations due to a number of factors that can be summarised as follows: first, US financial aid has allowed Pakistan to become the twelfth largest military force in the world, thereby going some way to reducing asymmetry vis-à-vis India and, as a corollary, has emboldened Pakistan. Second, the aid, or partnership in the GWOT, has had the unintended consequence of instigating domestic instability through insurgency: the spill-over into India has similar effect and increases distrust between the nations. Finally, The US' policy of pacifying India through technical and economic assistance concomitant to their assistance to Pakistan has meant that the overall effect in the long-term has been a neutral one.

4.2 The Influence of China on Indo-Pakistani Relations

The relationship China has fostered with Pakistan has had a marked effect on India's global aspirations, and as a corollary, it has had an impact on the Indo-Pakistan relationship. The technical and military equipment assistance China has given to Pakistan has, from a realist perspective, closed the power-gap and allowed Pakistan to continue her proxy war under a 'nuclear umbrella'. The effect of this support should not be underestimated as it has allowed Pakistan to continue to stick a large thorn in the side of India's aspirations to rise as a regional hegemon. Over the past two decades India has, through diplomatic channels, demanded that Pakistan do its utmost to quell the cross-border terrorism. The success of Pakistan's counter-insurgency efforts has ebbed and flowed and has not met India's demands. As such, India has been forced to adopt a more offensive strategy in order to negate the potential for a nuclear response to India's more direct military action against Pakistani state-sponsored terrorism. The strategy would involve what is termed 'India's "Cold Start Doctrine" which involves mass mobilisation of approximately eight Indian Battle Groups in order to neutralise Pakistan's military, including nuclear, capability within 72 hours, that is, before it could be deployed and used against Indian territory (Malik 2013).'

It is not clear how China would react to such a move but what has become increasingly clear is China's strategy of encircling, or containing, India. China's 'String of Pearls' consists of 'maritime ports in a number of countries within the Indian Ocean, a region that India has axiomatic claims as the maritime guardian. Presently, China has developed port facilities in Sri Lanka, Bangladesh, Myanmar, and notably Gwadar in Pakistan (The Economist 2013).' Furthermore, 'China has developed much of the border region of the Sino - India disputed territory of Arunachal Pradesh, a disputed region China refers to as South Tibet (The Economist 2013).' It is axiomatic to say that China would not be against seeing India embroiled in further destabilising conflict with Pakistan. As one of India's main foreign policy matters, the Chinese dilemma needs to be factored into the Indo - Pakistan issues. A scenario whereby China uses Pakistan as a proxy force, supported by provision of armaments through the port of Gwadar is a situation India cannot afford to let materialise. To achieve this India has to overcome her well - documented lack of strategic culture in order to manage the complicated maritime threat axis. The fact that the 'seven tons of explosives used in the 1993 Mumbai attack were brought onto Indian soil by sea (The Economist 2013)' and the LeT terrorists that perpetrated the 2008 Mumbai terror attacks also arrived by sea was a salient reminder that maritime security plays a prominent part in the enduring conflict between India and Pakistan.

5. NEW STRATEGIES FOR PEACE

> Whenever things threatened to fall apart during our negotiations -and they did on many occasions- we would stand back and remind ourselves that if negotiations broke down the outcome would be a bloodbath of unimaginable proportions...The thought always sobered us up, and we persisted despite many setbacks. You negotiate with your enemies, not your friends (Bose 2003, 201).
>
> Nelson Mandela, 1997

Having outlined the complexity of the relationship between India and Pakistan a number of themes should now be evident: first, despite the gains in military power, and economic benefits to the two sides, Sino - US presence in South Asia has had a debilitating effect on Indo - Pakistani relations overall: this is more evident if viewed through a realist lens. Second, Pakistan's poverty has spawned the insidious use of insurgents in a proxy war under the shadow of a nuclear umbrella which has stymied any chances of conflict resolution. Third, the complicated territorial and socio - religious dynamic of the Kashmir territory is not limited to the two states, but includes the secessionist aspirations of the Kashmiri population. Furthermore, the ideological dimension of the 'two - state' philosophy that caused the partition of India and Pakistan in 1947 still exists in the leaders of both countries. The issues prevalent in Kashmir are a manifestation of Pakistan's Islamic ideology and India's secular ideals, and therefore from a socio - political viewpoint, demand a more liberal approach to conflict resolution. Finally, the nuclear security paradox, which rather than dissuading conflict, has facilitated limited - war between the states. Given this entrenched South Asian paradigm, how can Conflict Transformation be framed?

5.1 Learning from Previous Peace Initiatives

Cognisant of these impediments to peace, a number of attempts have been made to either eradicate the source of tension or ameliorate the consequences of intractable issues. Today this occurs through what is known as the 'Composite Dialogue' process, 'a framework for which was established in 1997 during the inaugural Joint Working Group for the Composite Dialogue (Hussain 2011a, 320).' Aside from this formalised process, other mediation has occurred, for example, the July 1972 Simla agreement that followed the 1971 war, the Lahore Declaration of 1998 and Agra Summit of 2001.

At first the Lahore declaration proved most promising, as it was more ambitious than the Simla agreement which was vague in most areas aside from the establishment, and 'sanctity', of the LoC. The Lahore agreement stated that 'an environment of peace and security is in the supreme national interest of both countries and the resolution of all outstanding issues, including Jammu and Kashmir is essential for this purpose (Bose 2003, 226).' It further recognised that 'the nuclear dimension of the security environment of both countries adds to their responsibility for avoidance of conflict...[and to] intensify their composite and integrated dialogue process (Bose 2003).'

Despite the declaration, and subsequent Memorandum of Understanding being detailed about some confidence - building measures; over the nuclear issue, the declaration was non - specific 'reflecting the agreement to discuss concepts and doctrines with a view to elaborating measures for confidence - building in the nuclear and conventional fields, aimed at prevention of conflict, and reaffirming their commitment to the economic goals and objectives of the South Asian Association for Regional Cooperation (SAARC) (Chander 2003b, 62).' The text does reflect the intention to generate some tangible confidence building measures, among them an increase in people - centric measures such as 'liberalizing the visa and travel regime and humanitarian issues such as POWs (Chander 2003b, 58 - 73).' Nevertheless, the Kargil War that closely followed the Lahore meeting spelt the end of further progress, with cries of Pakistani perfidy emanating from India. Of additional importance is the acknowledgement of the 'Mujahedeen elements that contributed to Pakistan's efforts in the secretive precursory operations in late 1998 (Nath 2003, 94 - 95)' and assisted in the continuing proxy war in Kashmir thereafter. Once again, radical Islamic elements are in part responsible for the deep cleavage between these states.

5.2 Indo - Pakistani Dialogue: People - Centric Peace Processes

More recently, the 'most promising attempt at initiating peaceful measures was made in January 2004 during the SAARC meeting (Tikekar 2005, 188).' At this meeting a number of initiatives were agreed upon by the two state's leaders, however, following the 2008 Mumbai terror attacks peace progression was once again halted. Fortunately, the composite dialogue process was quick to resume by February 2011. The progress of the dialogues indicates that 'both countries are moving towards a people - centric approach (Akhtar 2012, 2)' to conflict resolution which differs from earlier dialogue meetings.

Currently India and Pakistan each have one finger curled around the prong of the Kashmir 'wishbone', however, it is the Kashmiris that will determine which side, if any, gains the larger piece. Consequently, the issue of a territorial stalemate must be ignored by Pakistan and India:

both states need to be aware that the Kashmiri population's grievances play an integral part in the peace process and as such, people - centric, cross - LoC interactions are a vital cog in the mechanism for peace. Furthermore, any dialogue process concerning Kashmir must be a confluence of the multi - dimensional issues concerning India, Pakistan, Kashmiri's, and China, given its occupation of Indian Kashmir.

Rather than the traditional Pakistani narrative over Kashmir, i.e. the unfinished agenda of partition, Pakistan's leadership has been forthcoming in proposing more flexibility. 'In December 2006, General Musharraf envisioned greater freedom of movement of the population, self - governance, a staged demilitarisation of the region, increased trade, and a joint supervision mechanism established (Akhtar 2012, 11).' This provoked a positive response from India's government who, rather than rigidly adhering to their usual narrative, i.e. Kashmir is a legitimate and integral part of India, 'Prime Minister Singh showed readiness to turn the LoC into a "Line of Peace" with freer flow of goods, ideas, people and services, with the land and water resources divided for joint benefit for the people on both sides of the LoC (Akhtar 2012, 12).'

5.3 Emerging Initiatives: The Conflict Transformation Approach

Many emerging Indo - Pakistan peace initiatives are based on the application of the 'Conflict Transformation' (CT) approach to resolving the Kashmir issue.

As explained in the first section of this paper, the crux of the Indo - Pakistan relationship issue is Kashmir, and until recently, the leadership of both states have approached the issue with a realist view, focussing on territorial aspects rather than the multi - dimensional issues that pervade within Kashmir. This realist view has done well to explain the historical enmity but has done little to offer new ways to break the cycle that has become increasingly hostile. CT acknowledges those multi - dimensional aspects; as Miall proposes: 'it is a 'process of engaging with and transforming the relationships, interests, discourses, and if necessary, the very constitution of society that supports the violent conflict (Akhtar 2012, 3).'

The Global Centre for Conflict Transformation identifies five types of transformation that can promote the cessation of enduring conflicts. These include: 'context transformations, structural transformations, actor transformations, issue transformations, and rules transformations (Transfconflict n.d.).' In relation to the Indo - Pakistan conflict, as Akhtar points out, 'the Kashmir conflict is going through all five types of transformations one way or another (Akhtar 2012, 7).' Of paramount relevance to the analysis in this paper is 'structural transformation'. It is the view of this author, that structural transformation has the capacity to affect the fundamental causes of the enduring conflict. That is not to say that the other four transformation streams aren't relevant as they are all, to some degree, inter - related and 'phased' in that one normally occurs before another in order to set conditions for the feasibility of a subsequent transformation process.

As has been shown in previous sections of this paper, the epicentre of the Indo - Pakistan conflict is Kashmir, but the issues concerning this territory are far deeper than mere territorial lines on the map. The friction runs to the core of the people that reside not only in Kashmir, but throughout India and Pakistan, it is a people - centric, cultural, ideological, religious, ethnic and social matter that demands a people - centric approach for rapprochement between the governing states. The ethnic nexus between these two nations can facilitate a CT approach in that a degree of harmony is viable through economic initiatives. The logic of such an approach can be traced back to the pre - colonial era of the sub - continent. Before British colonialism, the 'relationship between a collective identity and the state was structured within the framework of a layered sovereignty (Behera 2008, 26).' Examining the epistemological foundation of South Asian states indicates that the notion of a Westphalian state structure in the South Asia context is flawed. As Mohan argues:

> 'the colonial demarcation of territorial borders...defined the sovereignty of a state...and opened a Pandora's Box of problems in a region where newly formed states were not well versed with Westphalian norms (Mohan 2013, 64).'

Furthermore, colonial imposition 'ruptured the old indigenous and creative, mechanisms of compromise and collaboration, creating wide, unbridled gaps (Behera 2008, 26).' It is suggested that regenerating an environment of collaborative, people - centric activities could promote peace in Kashmir and elsewhere on the Indo - Pakistan border. The CT theory meets this requirement, and there is evidence that measures arising from recent composite dialogue agreements support the validity of the CT theoretical framework. The relationship between conflict zones and development is further substantiated by the Secretary General of the UN, who, in 1992 pointed out 'the promotion of sustainable economic development is an essential aspect of conflict prevention or resolution (Mahapatra and Shekhawat 2008, 4)' yet as Collier and Hoffler argue 'the benefits of development decrease with the duration of conflict (Collier and Hoffler 1998, 565)', therefore New Delhi and Islamabad have tended to refrain from committing finances which would adequately re - develop the Kashmir region.

By collaborating on a number of mutually beneficial economic and social initiatives, a non - zero - sum game can be created and may transform the underlying issues, addressing the multi - dimensional, people - centric Kashmir dilemma. In modern conflict resolution theory, this sits within the framework of CT. Increased interdependence born out of trade and other people - centric cross - LoC activities may engender a spirit of reconciliation at the state level, in other words structural transformation at state level changes the asymmetric relationship to a symmetric one through economic interdependence. It is hoped that this positive change will result in better social conditions within Kashmir and ergo, a decrease in the instances of radical militancy within Kashmir. However, a key demand of the Kashmiri population is a concomitant reduction in state armed forces which has not yet occurred.

One of the most successful transformation initiatives is the proposals for increasing trade between the two states, akin to Track - Three diplomacy initiatives. In terms of 'context transformation', globalisation has changed the context of the South Asian socio - economic environment. Regions such as Kashmir, or for that matter, poor states, cannot afford to be marginalised as the relative gains gap between neighbouring states is likely to increase. One way of improving the resilience of Pakistan's economy is through greater trade and collaboration on mutually beneficial industrial projects with India. Trade with India in the few years immediately following partition was relatively large. In '1948 - 49, 56 percent of Pakistan's exports went to India and 80 percent of West Pakistan's imports were from India. However, by 1958 only four percent of Pakistan's exports went to India and both states actively disengaged from trade relations (Sridharan 2005, 327).' Since then, the trade between the states has been punctuated by a hiatus (1965 - 1974).

As mentioned earlier, increasing trade and consequently, economic interdependence, is part of the structural transformation line of CT and despite the lack of progress at the Islamabad - New Delhi level, CT theorists are buoyed by the considerable moves made in trade interactions within Kashmir. These have been initiated following the cross - LoC travel initiatives on - going since 2004. Significantly, 'on 21 October 2008, three years after the resumption of the cross - LoC bus service, a 61 year breakdown of trade ties across the LoC ceased when trucks moved between Srinagar and Muzaffarabad and Poonch - Rawalakot (Akhtar 2012, 16).' As a corollary to this new trade interaction, 'further trade enabling mechanisms were put in place: banking, communications networks, regulatory networks for trade dispute resolution, mutual acceptance of letters of credit (Akhtar 2012, 18)' are but some examples.

These have created further people - centric modalities between parties on both sides of the LoC and are expected to result in better prosperity and increased interdependence, thereby contributing to a decrease in ethnic or religiously motivated violence within Kashmir. This, it is hoped will transform the contradictions that form the focus of Pakistan's grievances.

6. CONCLUSION

The enduring issues in this conflict are purportedly intractable; however there is hope for rapprochement between the two nations. As shown, a composite dialogue process, increasingly focussed on a bottom - up, people - centric approach to transforming the very issues that impede peace constitutes the best hope for an enduring peace settlement. However, before such confidence building measures will work, the governments of both sides need to acknowledge the fundamental causes of conflict between them, and, moreover, incorporate them into the peace process. To summarise the issues, it is proposed that four factors should be considered in further composite dialogue.

First, previous adherence to realist, zero - sum policies has promoted conflict, rather than created stability in the sub - continent. The anarchic paradigm that characterised South Asia's foreign policy has been swept aside by globalisation. Furthermore, increasing cross - LoC interactions are marginalising the perception that the state is the exclusive power able to resolve, or perpetrate conflict. Individuals are having greater say in how the relationship between the two states will progress. Rather than stymie this interaction, the two governments should encourage the positive engagements that promote socio - political interdependence.

Second, the international system, particularly in the Asian region, has changed and continues to do so. Globalism, and a dynamic, thriving East and South Asian economy is driving major powers to focus their attention within India and Pakistan's strategic, geopolitical horizons. Pakistan's new democratic era engenders hope within the international community for a successful Indo - Pakistan dialogue. Furthermore, the value major powers hold on traditional alliances is changing. The withdrawal of US forces from Afghanistan may herald a decline of military and economic support for Pakistan, thereby increasing Indo - Pakistan interdependence. When considered against the recent development of Indo - US relations, Pakistan might seek to counter - balance this by invigorating relations with China.

Third, positive progress can be quickly impeded by the subversive radical militant elements still at large within the sub-continent. In acknowledging this the two leaders must cast aside the ideological barriers that have blinded their perspectives. Failure to do this will see the continued activity of cross-border terrorism, reliance on the nuclear deterrence, and a proclivity for tit-for-tat limited war in the epicentre of the Indo-Pakistan relationship: Jammu and Kashmir.

Fourth, Pakistan needs to see beyond the ideological element of the Kashmiri territorial dispute which 'India accuses Pakistan of being fixated upon (Bose 2003, 223).' Moreover, a constructivist might argue that the desire to (re)incorporate Kashmir within each state's boundaries would merely irrevocably upset the delicate balance of communal and socio-political relationships there. With such understanding it is proposed that India and Pakistan can channel their energy into more mutually beneficial political policies.

What are the prospects of a fifth Indo-Pakistan conflict? This paper concludes with the following proposition:

Given the characteristics of the fundamental causes of conflict between India and Pakistan, a fifth India-Pakistan war is unlikely if the two governments can reach an accord on the four factors summarised above, and continue with the people-centric conflict transformation initiatives generated by the composite dialogue process but this is a relatively young development in Indo-Pakistani relations. Conflict is much more probable if these conditions are not met, and if the two states reaffirm reliance on realist policies of hedging against the relative power rise of the other state. In this case, the current theme of limited war or 'sub-conventional' confrontations in Kashmir, fought by state-sponsored Pakistani terrorists, is the likely outcome for the foreseeable future.

REFERENCES

Ahmed, A. 2011. "Why Jinnah Matters?" In *Pakistan: Beyond the Crisis State*, edited by M. Lodhi, 21 - 34. Karachi: Oxford University Press.

Akhtar, S. 2012. "Expanding Cross - LOC Interactions: A Conflict Transformation Approach to Kashmir." *Spotlight on Regional Affairs* 31 (1&2): 1 - 48.

Babu, B. Ramesh. 2005. "US and the Indo - Pak Equation: Back to Square One and Beyond." In *India - Pakistan Relations: Courting Peace from the Corridors of War*, edited by P. M. Kamath, 239 - 68. New Delhi: Promilla & Co.

Behera, N. C., ed. 2008. *International Relations in South Asia: Searching for an Alternative Paradigm*. New Delhi: SAGE.

Bose, S. 2003. *Kashmir: Roots of Conflict, Paths to Peace*. Cambridge: Harvard University Press.

Chander, P. 2003a. *India and Pakistan: Unending Conflict*. Vol. 1. New Delhi: APH Publishing Corporation.

– – –. 2003b. *India and Pakistan: Unending Conflict*. Vol. 3. New Delhi: APH Publishing Limited.

Cohen, S. P. 2002. "India, Pakistan and Kashmir." *Journal of Strategic Studies* 25 (4): 32 - 60.

Collier, P., and A. Hoffler. 1998. "On Economic Causes of Civil War." *Oxford Economic Papers* 50 (4): 563 - 73.

Ganguly, S., and D. T. Hagerty. 2005. *Fearful Symmetry: India - Pakistan Crises in the Shadow of Nuclear Weapons*. New Delhi: Oxford University Press.

Ganguly, S., and S. P. Kapur. 2012. "The Jihad Paradox: Pakistan and Islamist Militancy in South Asia." *International Security* 37 (1): 111 - 41.

Haider, Z. 2011. "Ideologically Adrift." In *Pakistan: Beyond the Crisis State*, edited by M. Lodhi, 113 - 130. Karachi: Oxford University Press.

Hussain, S. R. 2011a. "The India Factor." In *Pakistan: Beyond the Crisis State*, edited by M. Lodhi, 319 - 48. Karachi: Oxford University Press.

Hussain, Z. 2011b. "Battling Militancy." In *Pakistan: Beyond the Crisis

State, edited by M. Lodhi, 131 - 48. Karachi: Oxford University Press.

Jalal, A. 2011. "The Past as Present." In *Pakistan: Beyond the Crisis State*, edited by M. Lodhi, 7 - 20. Karachi: Oxford University Press.

Johns, A. H., and N. Lahoud., eds. 2005. *Islam in World Politics*. Abingdon: Routledge.

Kamath, P. M. 2005. *India - Pakistan Relations: Courting Peace from the Corridors of War*. New Delhi: Promilla & Co.

Khan, F. H. 2011. "Pakistan as a Nuclear State." In *Pakistan: Beyond the Crisis State*, edited by M. Lodhi, 267 - 82. Karachi: Oxford University Press.

Kumar, S. 2011. "Pakistan's Strategic Thinking." *Strategic Analysis* 35 (3): 479 - 492.

Lodhi, M. 2011. "Beyond The Crisis State." In *Pakistan: Beyond the Crisis State*, edited by M. Lodhi, 45 - 78. Karachi: Oxford University Press.

Mahapatra, D. A., and S. Shekhawat. 2008. "The Peace Process and Prospects for Economic Reconstruction in Kashmir." *Peace & Conflict Review* 3 (1): 1 - 17.

Malik, Imran. 2013. "India's Cold Start Doctrine Madness." *The Nation*, January 27, 2013. https://nation.com.pk/27 - Jan - 2013/india - s - cold - start - doctrine - madness.

Mohan, A. 1992. "The Historical Roots of the Kashmir Conflict." *Studies in Conflict & Terrorism* 15 (4): 283 - 308.

Mohan, S. 2013. "Transforming the Line of Control: Bringing the Homeland Back In." *Asian Politics & Policy* 5 (1): 51 - 75.

Nath, R., ed. 2003. *Musharraf's War*. New Delhi: Lancer's Books.

Nayar B. R., and T. V. Paul. 2003. *India in the World Order: Searching for Major Power Status*. Cambridge: Cambridge University Press.

Nye, J. S., and D. A. Welch. 2011. *Understanding Global Conflict and Cooperation: An Introduction to Theory and History*, 8th Edition. Boston: Pearson.

Panda, R. 2007. "Evolving Power Equations in the Asia - Pacific Region." In *Rising India: Friends and Foes*, edited by P. Nanda, 89 - 117. New Delhi: Lancer Publishers.

Paul, T. V., ed. 2005. *The India - Pakistan Conflict: An Enduring Rivalry*. Cambridge: Cambridge University Press.

Sridharan, E. 2005. "Improving Indo - Pakistan Relations: International

Relations Theory, Nuclear Deterrence and Possibilities for Economic Cooperation." *Contemporary South Asia* 14 (3): 321 - 39.

The Economist. 2013. "India as a Great Power: Know Your Own Strength." *The Economist*, March 30, 2013. https://www.economist.com/news/briefing/21574458 - india - poised - become - one - four - largest - military - powers - world - end.

Tikekar, M. 2005. "Cultural Idiom in the Indo - Pak Conflict." In *India - Pakistan Relations: Courting Peace from the Corridors of War*, edited by P. M. Kamath, 187 - 238. New Delhi: Promilla & Co.

Transconflict. n.d. "Principles of Conflict Transformation." Accessed March 10, 2013. http://www.transconflict.com/gcct/principles - of - conflict - transformation/.

United Nations. n.d. "UNMOGIP: United Nations Military Observer Group in India and Pakistan." Accessed July 24, 2017. https://unmogip.unmissions.org/.

Waldron, A. 2007. "Viewing the Future Through History." In *Rising India: Friends and Foes*, edited by P. Nanda, 1 - 31. New Delhi: Lancer Publishers.

Waltz, K. N. 1981. "The Spread of Nuclear Weapons: More May Be Better." *The Adelphi Papers* 21 (171): 1 - 32.

Weinbaum, M. 2005. "Pakistan and the United States: A Partnership of Necessity." In *America and the World in the Age of Terror*, edited by D. Benjamin. Washington, D. C.: Center for Strategic & International Studies.

VII

AFTER THE KARGIL WAR:
Avoiding a 5th India - Pakistan War

1. INTRODUCTION

After seven decades of war the relationship between India and Pakistan is at a crossroads. The states have a choice: continue the stalemate, with both governments poised potentially for nuclear exchange, or, take advantage of the numerous opportunities for cooperation and prosperity that positive bilateral relationships can offer. However, the choice is not easy given the emotion that the world's most enduring conflict has generated. Moreover, it is the UNs longest standing peace keeping mission, having commenced in January 1949 (United Nations n.d.). The casualty statistics since the partition on 14 Aug 1947 are morose: millions have died and millions more have been displaced from their homes. The violence that ensued from the division alone caused between '100,000 and one million deaths and approximately 15 million people were forced to leave their homes to re - settle in the new states (Ganguly and Kapur 2012, 115).' More sobering is the fact that since the 1947 - 1948 First Kashmir War, millions more have died in the following conflicts: the Second Kashmir War of 1965, the Bangladesh War of 1971, and the Kargil War of 1999. Furthermore, there have been a number of armed conflicts that stopped just short of all - out war: the 'Punjab War Scare (1951), Runn of Kutch (1965), the Brasstacks Crisis (1987), the Kashmir Nuclear Crisis (1990), the India - Pakistan Nuclear Test Crisis (1998), the New Delhi Parliament attack crisis, (2001), the Kaluchack attack crisis (2002), and the Mumbai terrorist attacks (2008) (Mohan 2013, 55).' These crises constitute a legacy of inhumane treatment of belligerents, not to mention innocent civilians.

Given their history of conflict, what hope is there for India and Pakistan to resolve their long - standing dispute? Perhaps the noticeable transformations that have taken place since partition will provide an answer. The Indo - Pak conflict now has serious implications for the entire international system as the ramifications of terrorist networks in Pakistan and Kashmir have demanded that leading world powers focus on the Indo - Pak dialogue. Furthermore, where realist perceptions appear to have once dominated the thoughts of the opponents in this dyadic confrontation; the pure *realpolitik* pursuits have been altered by both sides' possession of nuclear weapons. Another international relations conundrum that is worthy of consideration in the South Asian context concerns the need to identify whether realist assumptions have had the effect of stabilizing the region or promoting further conflict. Furthermore, has colonial association with the European 'Westphalian' state system failed to adequately consider important socio - political aspects of these South - Asian states?

Emerging from this transformation, are a number of core issues that constitute the crux of the enduring Indo - Pak confrontation. Some of these are intractable; however, some are opportunities for peace. This paper will identify the core obstacles impeding peace and determine whether these obstacles can be successfully removed or transformed. In doing so, the primary question concerning the prospect of further conflict between India and Pakistan can be addressed.

The first section of this paper will explore a critical enduring cause of tension within the region. While many papers exist that explore how the territorial disputes and differing ideologies shape the nature of the Indo - Pak conflict, this paper will pay particular focus to the Stability - Instability Paradox as there are few precedents set in international relations theories that explain the nature of two nuclear states engaged in direct and on - going conflict. The Second Section will explore the position of these two states within the international system and how those positions reaffirm assumptions about the nature of the nuclear paradox. It will briefly look at Pakistan and India's external alliances in order to provide a geo - political context to the Indo - Pak relationship. Chapter three will then examine past peace process initiatives and current Confidence Building Measures (CBMs), including the composite dialogue initiatives to determine their effect on placating tension. The peace process initiatives will be examined under the analytical framework of 'Conflict Transformation' (CT) which is a modern theoretical approach for brokering peace by transforming the underlying causes of a given conflict.

2. AN ENDURING CAUSE OF TENSION: The Nuclear Equation and Stability-Instability Paradox

As the two sides were settling into their positions behind the Line of Control (LOC), a broad range of other factors came to exacerbate the Indo - Pak relationship. Whilst there are many issues that have caused friction between the two nations, this chapter will focus on one key topic that, in the view of this author, could be assuaged through a process of dialogue between India and Pakistan. It is anticipated that through dialogue, these enduring obstacles to peace can be transformed and therefore the potential for conflict can be reduced. Whether or not the dialogue process is entered into, analysts will be able to more accurately determine whether further conflict is probable. Before the states' positions in the international community are examined, the nuclear paradox will be scrutinised.

The pivotal question in understanding this conflict is whether the 'nuclearisation' of both states has resulted in a more stable or a more volatile South Asian region. Given that two medium - intensity conventional conflicts have occurred following both nations' nuclear tests in 1998 it is evident that both states do not see the threat of nuclear strike as deterrence against all forms of conflict. In terms of determining whether Pakistan and India's security trajectories will meet in nuclear conflict, or total war, this paper will now provide a survey of the generation and policies of the dyadic nuclear capabilities since partition.

It wasn't until India's development programme became known that Pakistan pondered over the need for their own nuclear capability, however no firm steps were taken until the loss of East Pakistan and the state reversion to civilian rule under Zulfikar Ali Bhutto that 'Bhutto urged the Pakistan Atomic Energy Commission to begin preparing for a nuclear weapons program.

Nevertheless, there was no urgency until India tested its first device in 1974 (Khan 2011, 269).' 'In the 1980's Pakistan eventually obtained weapon - grade nuclear material and developed a rudimentary nuclear deterrence strategy (Khan 2011, 270).' During the 1990's 'Pakistan's capability reached its zenith, the high point of which was the successful detonation of their first device that followed a few weeks after India's tests in May 1998. By the new millennium, the nuclear arms program was placed under tight military control and a National Command Authority was established which proved effective against India's Operation Parakaram in 2002 (Khan 2011, 270).' Today, Pakistan remains committed to the nuclear deterrent policy, a fact that has not changed since return to civilian rule in 2008.

The policy has had a paradoxical effect for Pakistan's bi - lateral relationship with India. Nuclear theorists such as Kenneth Waltz maintain that 'the prospects for peace increase with the spread of nuclear weapons (Waltz 1981, 30).' However, subscribers to the nuclear stability/instability paradox theory have been vindicated as the opposite has occurred in South Asia. Since the overt testing of nuclear capabilities India and Pakistan have engaged in conventional conflict a number of times, most critically in the Kargil war of 1999, when, were it not for the intervention of the US and the international community, a full nuclear exchange may have occurred. Following these actions, 'some theorists propose that Pakistan is now afforded the opportunity to provoke India over Kashmir secure in the knowledge that possession of nuclear weapons will limit any retaliation by India (Mohan 2013, 58).' Furthermore, Pakistan has been able to continue clandestine attacks through proxy insurgents under this 'nuclear - umbrella' paradigm.

India's pursuit of nuclear weapons capability was prolonged given the nature of the threat around them, most notably from China, following the 1962 war, and China's nuclear capability program that matured following the 1964 tests. Logic might dictate that the non-alignment strategy of India might also have convinced India's leaders to develop a more robust security capability yet this was not the case. In part this can be attributed to the pacific nature of Nehru's leadership following partition and the hope that non-alignment meant India would not have to become embroiled in warfare on behalf of an alliance partner, as was common in the Cold War era.

Nevertheless, by the mid 1960's, nuclear ambition featured in India's security policy however, Perkovich contends that 'India's nuclear weapon capability only vaguely responded to an ill-defined security threat (Perkovich 1999, 6)', further arguing that national security was not the paramount reason for generating nuclear capability, as 'no prior strategic doctrine was used, nor were the military involved in the decision-making (Perkovich 1999, 6).'

As both states' nuclear capabilities, and importantly, policies, were developing, 'the opaque or perceived capabilities of the other was the main factor in checking all six crises from 1984 to 2002 (Ganguly and Hagerty 2005, 188-92)' thereby supporting standard logic on nuclear deterrence. This is particularly the case for deterrence between nations with a history of conflict such as India and Pakistan. Notwithstanding the vague understanding of each nation's nuclear strategy, Pakistan and India have made certain arrangements such as 'the 1998 agreement not to target each other's nuclear facilities or the 1999 agreement to inform each other of impending nuclear tests and, significantly, the states have agreed not to actively deploy its nuclear weapons (Ganguly and Hagerty 2005, 188-92).'

The non-deployment status of both sides offers a unique view on the prospect of a further conflict. 'Weaponization can be thought of as the process of developing, testing, and integrating warhead components into a militarily usable weapon system. Deployment can be defined as the process of transferring bombs and/or warheads to military units for storage and rapid mating with delivery systems at military bases (Chari 2001, 25).' Although Chari posits that non-deployment and 'weaponization' offer some de-stabilising elements, this author agrees with Chari's final position that the 'non- deployment/weaponization is more stable due to the symmetrical reasons (Chari 2001, 28)' inherent in the sub- continental context. This is primarily due to potential for the bilateral Indo–Pak nuclear symmetry transforming into a three-party China–India–Pakistan asymmetry. If one of this triad increased its nuclear forces, 'anxiety in others would lead to a three-way arms race (Chari 2001, 27).' Considering India's history of responding to threats with conventional force and the lack of will to antagonise China, it is considered that the notion of symmetrical nuclear capabilities is valid.

Furthermore, both sides have convened meetings aimed at articulating nuclear Confidence- Building Measures. Meetings for this purpose occurred in 1998, 1999 and 2004 and have gone a long way to assuring both sides of the 'rules' surrounding the two states' use of the weapons and dissipating any anxiety over a nuclear 'prisoner's dilemma'. To date neither side has transgressed on the nuclear agreements although missile tests are ongoing, notably Pakistan's test of a Shaheen-1 missile on April 10, 2013 (Newland and Rehman 2013).

To summarise this section, Pakistan is of the perception that nuclear capability provides more security against conventional Indian threat. However, Pakistan is less able to use conventional force to resolve the Kashmir territorial dispute because of the certainty that India will respond militarily to an inter-state threat, as it has done previously. Moreover, attempts by Pakistan to do just that under the nuclear umbrella 'have been assuaged by intervention from the US, for example during the Kargil and 2002 (Operation Parakaram) confrontations (Sridharan 2005, 322).' Given the recent North and South Korean tensions it is envisaged that international community pressure will mount on the current nuclear states, therefore India and Pakistan may be further restrained from any bellicose action.

Viewed from a realist perspective, Pakistan's sensitivity to relative gains, i.e. grievance against India's relatively meteoric rise in strength and prosperity, has been ameliorated by the development of a nuclear-weapon capability. India has entered the nuclear arena reluctantly, coerced by the realisation of regional threats. However, India has been a 'responsible' nuclear user vis-à-vis Pakistan, given the latter's history of divulging nuclear weapon's technology to unstable regimes in the Middle East and North Asia, and furthermore, 'India continues to be an exemplar to other nations' on non-proliferation aims, so long as any disarmament process is non- discriminatory (Babu 2005, 256-57).' All of this points towards a state that would adhere to 'responsible' use of weapons and an adherent of the 'non-first use' policy which is reflective of India's 'lack of anxiety over a conventional invasion by Pakistan (Ganguly and Hagerty 2005, 196).' However, as Ganguly and Hagerty go on to point out, 'the no first-use policy is likely purely rhetoric (Ganguly and Hagerty 2005, 197).' Faced with a mass conventional threat it is possible that India would make pre-emptive use of its nuclear weapons.

International relations theory alludes to the relative gains equation that Pakistan has sought to achieve symmetry through the acquisition of nuclear weapons. As such 'first-strike' is unlikely given a number of factors outlined previously, namely: the uncertain nuclear strategies of each nation, non-deployed status, the geo-strategic factors, primarily the close proximity to each other and the presence of adjacent super-powers, and finally, the relationship with other powers in the international system. On the other hand, despite 'Pakistan's assurance that it has robust security protocols over her nuclear weapons (Khan 2011, 280-81)', the fear caused by insurgents and the history of conveying nuclear secrets to other nations is worrisome for India, 'particularly after it has voiced intention to provide nuclear weapons to a Muslim country in trouble (Waldron 2007, 23).' Most poignant of all is the apparent assumption by India that the military can instigate a successful limited war without escalating to a nuclear confrontation, as India did in 2002 when it mobilised forces in response to the Parliament attack by the Lashkar-e-Taiba (LeT). This runs contrary to Waltz's theory, however, nuclear exchange remains unlikely. As Waltz correctly maintains, the 'cost of such an exchange is unbearable (Waltz 1981, 30).'

3. THE SOUTH ASIAN PARADIGM

In relation to Waltz's system level of analysis, the South Asian states' relations with other international actors provide another source of tension between them. As shown in the first chapter, it is clear that following partition, the two nascent dominions took on a Hobbesian attitude, resorting to conflict as the logical means of resolving their dispute. If viewing the relationship from one of Waltz's 'images', the system level (Nye and Welch 2011, 53 - 55), India and Pakistan initially practiced realpolitik, taking a combative approach through the acquisition of nuclear capabilities that provide only a detraction from cooperation and dialogue, within their own regional, and anarchic, bi - polar structure, exempt from the influences that alliances with other powerful states within the international system would have created. The non - alignment foreign policies of both states corroborate this notion.

As conflict emerged between the two states, both began to acknowledge the need to forge external relationships, predominantly because of the changes to the international system, especially within the Asian region, that were effecting their geopolitical aspirations: examples being China's rise as a Communist nation, the Cold War, Pakistan's strategic value to the US, and the benefits of a globalised economy. Pakistan began the change from non - alignment by fostering enduring political and military relationships with two countries that have a profound effect on the Indo - Pak relationship. By 1953 Pakistan had forged an alliance with the US and 'by 1964 a strategic alliance with China through a commercial water and air agreement that paved the way for more military - based aid and infrastructure agreements (Datta 2003, 232).'

Since partition India has largely maintained non - alignment trade and security policies and has attempted to resolve her conflict with Pakistan independently. This has served India well given that it is one of the fastest growing economies in the world and, aside from the 2011 - 12 fall in GDP, has 'maintained a growth rate of 7.5 percent since 2002, far outstripping most economies in the world. Furthermore, the majority of her wealth is derived from indigenous funds rather than from the export of goods and is therefore more resilient to economic shocks (Panda 2007, 95).' Although India continues to espouse political rhetoric concerning its non-aligned status, it is interesting to note that 'since 2000, when India had defence-related agreements with only eight nations, by 2008, the number of nations had increased to 26 (Hussain 2011, 346).' This has implications for India's wider foreign policy and points towards her aspirations as a regional hegemon, particularly in the maritime domain of the Indian Ocean. Pakistan is wary of this increasing disparity between the two states and this causes ripples at the international system level.

In relation to this paper's analysis, the US-Pakistan and Sino-Pakistan alliances have had the most dramatic effect on Indo-Pak relations which will be explained shortly. However, it is worthy of note at this point that a new paradigm in the globalised context has emerged: interdependence is increasingly becoming a paramount factor. At the system level, increased interdependence would reduce incentives for conflict, although as Chun contends, the dyadic nuclear capability has engendered 'an interdependence derived from the mutual fear of nuclear attack, but paradoxically this has generated an increase of conventional and proxy conflict (Chun 2013, 64)' as shown in an earlier section of this paper.

3.1 US-Pakistan-US-India Alliances

It has been a somewhat mercurial relationship between the US and Pakistan with the South Asian state 'described by an American newspaper as "Paranoidistan": paranoid that every move the US makes in Pakistan is designed to benefit India (Jalal 2011, 7).' The relationship is one that has had a pronounced effect on the international system, and more recently, an ever increasing effect on India's aspirations as a regional hegemon. The episodic partnership between the West and Pakistan originated during the Cold War when the US sought assistance from Pakistan to curtail any spread of communism from the Soviet Union through Afghanistan. This burgeoning relationship faltered following the 1965 Kashmir War as the US ceased financial aid. This was not the last time the US would impose economic sanctions on Pakistan: they did so again in 1990, 1998 and 1999.

Overall, the relationship could be described as one that has had narrow benefits for the two nations, and rarely have those benefits aligned. This has created an aura of distrust around the partners resulting in limited commitment between them. For example, 'the United States had no sense of obligation to directly assist Pakistan in the 1965 or 1971 wars against India and conversely Pakistan only assists the US as far as the good will of the elites in Pakistan are not unduly affected (Jalal 2011).' Moreover, Pakistan perceived that the US had let them down when forced to withdraw their forces from Kargil in 1999.

The early phase of the US relationship with India can be characterised as a necessary, but unwanted consequence of the US - Pakistan relationship. Its genesis dates back to the start of the Cold War when the US was striving for a foothold in South Asia as a means of curtailing Soviet encroachment onto the borders of the Middle East. Having been sympathetic to India's anti - colonial aspirations prior to partition, 'the US was initially optimistic that they would have a willing ally in the Cold War and favoured forging a strategic alliance with India over Pakistan. However, when India opposed any role in the Cold War, the US was forced to partner with Pakistan (Babu 2005, 242 - 44)', as described earlier.

As a fervent campaigner against the spread of Weapons of Mass Destruction during the 1960's and 70's India was opposed to the US - Pakistan alliance and ultimately was forced to forge a relationship with the Soviet Union, against her best intentions of maintaining the policy of non - alignment. The aim of this alliance was to gain a measure of parity vis - à - vis Pakistan's military build - up courtesy of the US during the Afghan - Soviet war. The other factor that aggrieved India was the US' apparent ignorance of Pakistan's nuclear weapons programme. Whether the US was in fact oblivious to the programme or acting that it was, is uncertain, however the lack of awareness at the time was seen as convenient due to the presiding priority of defeating the Soviets in

Afghanistan. The eventual nuclear capability that Pakistan acquired has had a serious impact on Indo - Pak relations, as discussed earlier. Ironically, 'the US 'civil - nuclear' energy deal made between Prime Minister Singh and President G.W. Bush in July 2005 (Karnad 2007, 251)' has now swung animosity over US alliances back with Pakistan.

The other, not inconsequential impact the US has had on India's relationship with Pakistan is the means by which the US has sought to balance the military strength between the two states. When Pakistan started using the weapons it gained possession of through their assistance in the Soviet - Afghan war against India, as it did in 1965, the US was forced to intervene so that the region did not degenerate into total war, which would have seriously complicated their efforts in Afghanistan. The balancing act was achieved by mollifying India with economic aid and technical assistance.

Furthermore, the US has also indirectly assisted India by 'intervening twice more when the potential for full - scale war between India and Pakistan threatened (Weinbaum 2005, 114).' The 2002 diplomatic intervention halted the most serious potential for a nuclear war since the Cuban missile crisis.

Suffice to say, US presence in South Asia has had a marked effect on Indo - Pak relations due to a number of factors that can be summarised as follows: first, US financial aid has allowed Pakistan to become the twelfth largest military force in the world, thereby going some way to reducing asymmetry vis - à - vis India and, as a corollary, has emboldened Pakistan. Second, the aid, or partnership in the GWOT, has had the unintended consequence of instigating domestic instability through insurgency: the spill - over into India has similar effect and increases distrust between the nations. Finally, The US' policy of pacifying India through technical and economic assistance concomitant to their assistance to Pakistan has meant that the overall effect in the long - term has been a neutral one. In terms of its effect on predicting future conflict between India and Pakistan history may provide an indicator, and that has been one of a stalemate.

3.2 Indian Foreign Relations

The relationship China has fostered with Pakistan has a marked effect on India's global aspirations, and as a corollary, it has an impact on the Indo-Pak relationship. The technical and military equipment assistance China has given to Pakistan has, from a realist perspective, closed the power-gap and allowed Pakistan to continue her proxy war under a 'nuclear umbrella'. The effect of this support should not be underestimated as it has allowed Pakistan to continue to stick a large thorn in the side of India's aspirations to rise as a regional hegemon. Over the past three decades India has, through diplomatic channels, demanded that Pakistan do its utmost to quell the cross-border terrorism. This success of Pakistan's counter-insurgency efforts has ebbed and flowed and has not met India's justified demands. As such India has been forced to adopt a more offensive strategy in order to negate the potential for a nuclear response to India's more direct military action against Pakistani state-sponsored terrorism. The strategy would involve what is termed 'India's "Cold Start Doctrine" which involves mass mobilisation of approximately eight Indian Battle Groups in order to neutralise Pakistan's military, including nuclear, capability within 72 hours, that is, before it could be deployed and used against Indian territory (Malik 2013).'

It is not clear how China would react to such a move but what has become increasingly clear is China's strategy of encircling, or containing, India. China's 'String of Pearls' consists of 'maritime ports in a number of countries within the Indian Ocean, a region that India has axiomatic claims as the maritime guardian. Presently, China has developed port facilities in Sri Lanka, Bangladesh, Myanmar, and notably Gwadar in Pakistan (The Economist 2013).' Furthermore, 'China has developed much of the border region of the Sino-India disputed territory of Arunachal Pradesh, a disputed region China refers to as South Tibet (The Economist 2013).' It is axiomatic to say that China would not be against seeing India embroiled in further destabilising conflict with Pakistan.

India may choose to deal with China's encirclement at sea; indeed India has purported to articulate this intent within its 'non-alignment

2.0 policy'. As one of India's main foreign policy matters, the Chinese dilemma needs to be factored into the Indo - Pak issues. A scenario whereby China uses Pakistan as a proxy force, supported by provision of armaments through the port of Gwadar is a situation India cannot afford to let materialise. To achieve this, India has to overcome her well - documented lack of strategic culture in order to manage the complicated maritime threat axis.

Presently India does not have a coherent maritime policy, if Mahan's attributes of a maritime nation are considered then India lacks a proficient 'character of government (Till 2004, 41)' that effectively coordinates maritime activity in response to threats. According to Admiral Prakash 'there is no single government agency which has the span of responsibility or the authority to act as the focal point of India's maritime policies and interests (Prakash 2007, 144).' This is relevant to the Indo - Pak equation as it is not only the threat of Chinese containment that India needs an effective maritime policy for. The fact that the 'seven tons of explosives used in the 1993 Mumbai attack were brought onto Indian soil by sea (Prakash 2007, 138).' and the LeT terrorists that perpetrated the 2008 Mumbai terror attacks also arrived by sea is a salient reminder that maritime security plays a prominent part in the enduring conflict between India and Pakistan.

4. STRATEGY FOR PEACE: A Dialogue Process

Having outlined the complexity of the relationship between India and Pakistan a number of themes should now be evident: first, despite the gains in military power, and economic benefits to the two sides, Sino - US presence in South Asia has had a debilitating effect on Indo - Pak relations overall: this is more evident if viewed through a realist lens. Furthermore, the ideological dimension of the 'two - state' philosophy that caused the partition of India and Pakistan in 1947 still exists in the leaders of both countries. The issues prevalent in Kashmir are a manifestation of Pakistan's Islamic ideology and India's secular ideals, and therefore from a socio - political viewpoint, demand a more liberal approach to conflict resolution. Finally, the nuclear security paradox, which rather than dissuading conflict, has encouraged an increase in limited - war between the states.

In order to determine whether the trajectory of India and Pakistan's tempestuous relationship is veering toward rapprochement, or degeneration into further conflict, this paper will examine the potential for success of existing peace process initiatives and discuss whether they will directly, or indirectly, ameliorate or remove the aforementioned obstacle to peace.

4.1 Previous Peace Initiatives

Cognisant of these impediments to peace, a number of attempts have been made to either eradicate the source of tension or ameliorate the consequences of intractable issues. Today this occurs through what is known as the 'Composite Dialogue' process, 'a framework for which was established in 1997 during the inaugural Joint Working Group for the Composite Dialogue (Lodhi 2011).' Aside from this formalised process, other mediation has occurred, for example, the July 1972 Simla agreement that followed the 1971 war, the Lahore Declaration of 1998 and Agra Summit of 2001.

At first the Lahore declaration proved most promising, as it was more ambitious than the Simla agreement which was vague in most areas aside from the establishment, and 'sanctity', of the LoC. The Lahore agreement stated that 'an environment of peace and security is in the supreme national interest of both countries and the resolution of all outstanding issues, including Jammu and Kashmir is essential for this purpose (Bose 2003, 226).' It further recognised that 'the nuclear dimension of the security environment of both countries adds to their responsibility for avoidance of conflict...[and to] intensify their composite and integrated dialogue process (Bose 2003, 226).'

Despite the declaration, and subsequent Memorandum of Understanding being detailed about some confidence - building measures; over the nuclear issue, the declaration was non - specific 'reflecting the agreement to discuss concepts and doctrines with a view to elaborating measures for confidence - building in the nuclear and conventional fields, aimed at prevention of conflict, and reaffirming their commitment to the economic goals and objectives of the South Asian Association for Regional Cooperation (SAARC) (Chander 2003, 62).' The text does reflect the intention to generate some tangible confidence building measures, among them an increase in people - centric measures such as 'liberalizing the visa and travel regime and humanitarian issues such as POWs (Chander 2003, 58 - 73).' Nevertheless, the Kargil War that closely followed the Lahore meeting spelt the end of further progress, with cries of Pakistani perfidy emanating from India. Of additional importance is the acknowledgement of the 'Mujahedeen elements that contributed to Pakistan's efforts in the secretive precursory operations in late 1998 (Nath 2003, 94 - 95)' and assisted in the continuing proxy war in Kashmir thereafter.

More recently, the 'most promising attempt' at initiating peaceful measures was made in January 2004 during the SAARC meeting (Tikekar 2005, 188). At this meeting a number of initiatives were agreed upon by the two state's leaders, however, following the 2008 Mumbai terror attacks, radical Islamists are yet again blamed for halting peace progression. Fortunately, the composite dialogue process resumed in February 2011 and appears to be facilitating initiatives instigated during the 2004 dialogue. This indicates that 'both countries are moving towards a people - centric approach (Akhtar 2012, 2)' to conflict resolution which differs from earlier dialogue meetings.

4.2 Emerging Initiatives: The Conflict Transformation Approach

Many emerging Indo - Pak peace initiatives are based on the application of the 'Conflict Transformation' (CT) approach to resolving the Kashmir issue. As explained it the outset of this paper, the crux of the Indo - Pak relationship issue is Kashmir, and until recently, the leadership of both states have approached the issue with a realist view, focussing on territorial aspects rather than the multi - dimensional issues that pervade within Kashmir. CT acknowledges those latter aspects; as Miall proposes: 'it is a 'process of engaging with and transforming the relationships, interests, discourses, and if necessary, the very constitution of society that supports the violent conflict (Akhtar 2012, 3).'

The Global Centre for Conflict Transformation identifies five types of transformation that can promote the cessation of enduring conflicts. These include: 'context transformations, structural transformations, actor transformations, issue transformations, and rules transformations (Transconflict n.d.).' In relation to the Indo - Pak conflict, as Akhtar points out, 'the Kashmir conflict is going through all five types of transformations one way or another (Akhtar 2012, 7).' Of paramount relevance to the analysis in this paper is 'structural transformation'. It is the view of this author, that structural transformation has the capacity to affect the fundamental causes of the enduring conflict identified earlier in the paper. That is not to say that the other four transformation streams aren't relevant as they are all, to some degree, inter - related and 'phased' in that one normally occurs before another in order to set conditions for the feasibility of a subsequent transformation process.

A useful parallel to the Indo - Pak situation is to consider how the CT model applied to the Northern Ireland conflict, another enduring conflict that had socio - religious causes. In the case of Northern Ireland all five levels of CT were evident at different points. Three worthy of mention were 'context transformation' that occurred with the development of the European Union and end of the Cold War, 'actor transformation' that was ultimately successfully realised once the peace brokers understood that merely seeking consensus among the two governments, as attempted through the Anglo - Irish agreement, was not sufficient. 'The governments realised that the grievances of other actors, such as Sinn Fein, needed to be addressed (Bose 1999, 159).' The Good Friday agreement made allowances for all - party issues. Finally, 'structural transformation' occurred 'as the pan - Nationalist coalition developed sufficient alliances and confidence to balance the hitherto asymmetric relationship between the parties (Miall 2004).' This was a political - structural change opposed to an economic one that this paper is proposing for the Indo - Pak relationship. Whilst there are a number of contextual differences between the Northern Ireland and Indo - Pak conflict, there are thematic similarities that analysts can draw CT lessons from.

The friction runs to the core of the people that reside not only in Kashmir, but throughout India and Pakistan, it is a people - centric, cultural, ideological, religious, ethnic and social matter that demands a people - centric approach for rapprochement between the governing states. The ethnic nexus between these two nations can facilitate a CT approach in that a degree of harmony is viable through economic initiatives.

By collaborating on a number of mutually beneficial economic and social initiatives, a non - zero - sum game can be created and may transform the underlying issues, addressing the multi - dimensional, people - centric Kashmir dilemma. In modern conflict resolution theory, this sits within the framework of CT. Increased interdependence born out of trade and other people - centric cross - LoC activities may engender a spirit of reconciliation at the state level, in other words structural transformation at state level changes the asymmetric relationship to a symmetric one through economic interdependence. It is hoped that this positive change will result in better social conditions within Kashmir and ergo, a decrease in the instances of radical militancy within Kashmir. Indeed, a 2011 report highlights a 49 percent fall in militant activity over that year. However, a key demand of the Kashmiri population is a concomitant reduction in state armed forces which has not yet occurred.

One of the most successful transformation initiatives is the proposals for increasing trade between the two states, akin to Track - Three diplomacy initiatives. In terms of 'context transformation', globalisation has changed the context of the South Asian socio - economic environment. Regions such as Kashmir, or for that matter, poor states, cannot afford to be marginalised as the relative gains gap between neighbouring states is likely to increase. One way of improving the resilience of Pakistan's economy is through greater trade and collaboration on mutually beneficial industrial projects with India. Trade with India in the few years immediately following partition was relatively large. In '1948 - 49, 56 percent of Pakistan's exports went to India and 80 percent of West Pakistan's imports were from India. However, by 1958 only four percent of Pakistan's exports went to India and both states actively disengaged from trade relations (Sridharan 2005, 327).' Since then, the trade between the states has been punctuated by a hiatus (1965 - 1974). Furthermore, in the words of the Secretary General for the Consumer User and Trust Society in his 2012 report on India - Pakistan trade relations: current trade is 'almost negligible (Mehta 2012).'

As mentioned earlier, increasing trade and consequently, economic interdependence, is part of the structural transformation line of CT and despite the lack of progress at the Islamabad - New Delhi level, CT theorists are buoyed by the considerable moves made in trade interactions within Kashmir. These have been initiated following the cross - LoC travel initiatives on - going since 2004. Significantly, 'on 21 October 2008, three years after the resumption of the cross - LoC bus service, a 61 year breakdown of trade ties across the LoC ceased when trucks moved between Srinagar and Muzaffarabad and Poonch - Rawalakot (Akhtar 2012, 16).' As a corollary to this new trade interaction, 'further trade enabling mechanisms were put in place: banking, communications networks, regulatory networks for trade dispute resolution, mutual acceptance of letters of credit (Akhtar 2012, 18)' are but some examples.

These have created further people - centric modalities between parties on both sides of the LoC and are expected to result in better prosperity and increased interdependence, thereby contributing to a decrease in ethnic or religiously motivated violence within Kashmir. This, it is hoped will transform the contradictions that form the focus of Pakistan's grievances.

Structural transformation initiatives best occur when state - level actors make 'issue transformations' and the demand for trade in Kashmir put pressure on state politicians to create the bureaucratic mechanisms for facilitating the trade. The fourth round of Composite Dialogue held in March 2007 did just that. The removal of some cross-LoC travel hindrances has facilitated easier movement of the Kashmiri population and trade, yet there are still many infrastructural difficulties to overcome before the economy on both sides can realise the benefits of this initiative. It is the author's view that the increased interactions within Kashmir generated by cross-LoC trade and travel 'structural transformation' initiatives will spill-over and have a confidence–building effect within Islamabad and New Delhi. Most importantly, social benefits of the increased prosperity, such as better living conditions, education, civil-society institutions, will likely proliferate, and there is already evidence of this having occurred within Kashmir.

5. CONCLUSION

The enduring issues in this conflict are purportedly intractable; however there is hope for rapprochement between the two nations. As shown, a composite dialogue process, increasingly focussed on a bottom-up, people-centric approach to transforming the very issues that impede peace constitutes the best hope for an enduring peace settlement. However, before such confidence building measures will work, the governments of both sides need to acknowledge the fundamental causes of conflict between them, and, moreover, incorporate them into the peace process. To summarise the issues, it is proposed that two factors should be considered highly in further composite dialogue.

First, previous adherence to realist, zero-sum policies has promoted conflict, rather than created stability in the sub-continent. The anarchic paradigm that characterised South Asia's foreign policy has been swept aside by globalisation. Furthermore, increasing cross-LoC interactions are marginalising the perception that the state is the exclusive power able to resolve, or perpetrate conflict. Individuals are having greater say in how the relationship between the two states will progress. Rather than stymie this interaction, the two governments should encourage the positive engagements that promote socio-political interdependence.

Second: the international system, particularly in the Asian region, has changed and continues to do so. Globalism, and a dynamic, thriving East and South Asian economy is driving major powers to focus their attention within India and Pakistan's strategic, geopolitical horizons. Pakistan's new democratic era engenders hope within the international community for a successful Indo-Pak dialogue. Furthermore, the value major powers hold on traditional alliances is changing. The withdrawal of US forces from Afghanistan may herald a decline of military and economic support for Pakistan, thereby increasing Indo-Pak interdependence. When considered against the recent development of Indo-US relations, Pakistan might seek to counter-balance this by invigorating relations with China.

The final benefit to be understood as being afforded by this approach, which is unique to this case, is that the distrust and suspicion generated by nuclearisation may be best overcome by the re-establishment of cooperation and interdependency. The principle issue highlighted by the stability-instability theory is that multiple forces occur within this conflict and are multiplied to different degrees at different levels; while the mutually assured destruction logic may be responsible for restricting state-to-state war, it similarly encourages on-going limited violent exchanges which are also undesirable. Attempting to unravel this aspect of the conflict in isolation will prove fruitless for the unique paradox that it presents to the relationship. Similarly, attempting to solve this entrenched conflict at any one of the international, state, or individual level will be ineffective for the are all interconnected and is, in part, why efforts to date have failed. As such, this paper concludes that a broad Conflict Transformation approach offers the best hope to deescalating a regional conflict that continues to present a global challenge.

REFERENCES

Akhtar, S. 2012. "Expanding Cross - LOC Interactions: A Conflict Transformation Approach to Kashmir." *Spotlight on Regional Affairs* 31 (1&2): 1 - 48.

Babu, B. Ramesh. 2005. "US and the Indo - Pak Equation: Back to Square One and Beyond." In *India - Pakistan Relations: Courting Peace from the Corridors of War*, edited by P. M. Kamath, 239 - 68. New Delhi: Promilla & Co.

Bose, S. 1999. "Kashmir: Sources of Conflict, Dimensions of Peace." *Survival* 41 (3): 149–171.

———. 2003. *Kashmir: Roots of Conflict, Paths to Peace.* Cambridge: Harvard University Press.

Chander, P. 2003. *India and Pakistan: Unending Conflict.* Vol. 2. New Delhi: APH Publishing Corporation.

Chari, P. R. 2001. "Nuclear Restraint, Risk Reduction, and the Security - Insecurity Paradox in South Asia." In *The Stability - Instability Paradox: Nuclear Weapons and Brinkmanship*, edited by Michael Krepon and Chris Gagne. Washington, D. C.: Henry L. Stimson Center.

Chun, Kwang Ho. 2013. *The BRICs Superpower Challenge: Foreign and Security Policy Analysis.* London: Ashgate.

Datta, R. 2003. "The Kargil War: China Factor." In *Musharraf's War*, edited by R. Nath. New Delhi: Lancer's Books.

Ganguly, S., and D. T. Hagerty. 2005. *Fearful Symmetry: India - Pakistan Crises in the Shadow of Nuclear Weapons.* New Delhi: Oxford University Press.

Ganguly, S., and S. P. Kapur. 2012. "The Jihad Paradox: Pakistan and Islamist Militancy in South Asia." *International Security* 37 (1): 111 - 41.

Hussain, S. R. 2011. "The India Factor." In *Pakistan: Beyond the Crisis State*, edited by M. Lodhi, 319 - 48. Karachi: Oxford University Press.

Jalal, A. 2011. "The Past as Present." In *Pakistan: Beyond the Crisis State*, edited by M. Lodhi, 7 - 20. Karachi: Oxford University Press.

Karnad, B. 2007. "The India - United States Rapprochement, the Nuclear

Deal, and Indian National Interest." In *Rising India: Friends and Foes*, edited by Prakash Nanda, 242 - 263. New Delhi: Lancer Publishers.

Khan, F. H. 2011. "Pakistan as a Nuclear State." In *Pakistan: Beyond the Crisis State*, edited by M. Lodhi, 267 - 82. Karachi: Oxford University Press.

Lodhi, M. 2011. "Beyond The Crisis State." In *Pakistan: Beyond the Crisis State*, edited by M. Lodhi, 45 - 78. Karachi: Oxford University Press.

Malik, Imran. 2013. "India's Cold Start Doctrine Madness." *The Nation*, January 27, 2013. https://nation.com.pk/27 - Jan - 2013/india - s - cold - start - doctrine - madness.

Mehta, Pradeep S. 2012. "Trade Relations between Pakistan and India." *Pakistan Institute of Legislative Development and Transparency (PILDAT).*

Miall, H. 2004. "Conflict Transformation: A Multi - Dimensional Task." In *Transforming Ethnopolitical Conflict*, edited by A. Austin, M. Fischer, and N. Ropers, 67–90. Berlin: VS Verlag für Sozialwissenschaften.

Mohan, S. 2013. "Transforming the Line of Control: Bringing the Homeland Back In." *Asian Politics & Policy* 5 (1): 51 - 75.

Nath, R., ed. 2003. *Musharraf's War.* New Delhi: Lancer's Books.

Newland, J., and F. Rehman. 2013. "Pakistan Test - Fires Nuclear - Capable Missile that Could Hit Deep Within India." *NBC News*, April 10, 2013. Accessed October 20, 2016. http://worldnews.nbcnews.com/_news/2013/04/10/17685030 - pakistan - test - fires - nuclear - capable - missile - that - could - hit - deep - within - india.

Nye, J. S., and D. A. Welch. 2011. *Understanding Global Conflict and Cooperation: An Introduction to Theory and History*, 8th Edition. Boston: Pearson.

Panda, R. 2007. "Evolving Power Equations in the Asia - Pacific Region." In *Rising India: Friends and Foes*, edited by P. Nanda, 89 - 117. New Delhi: Lancer Publishers.

Perkovich, G. 1999. *India's Nuclear Bomb: The Impact on Global Proliferation.* Berkeley: University of California Press.

Prakash, A. A. 2007. "A Vision of Maritime India: 2020." In *Rising India: Friends and Foes*, edited by Prakash Nanda, 131 - 48. New Delhi: Lancer Publishers.

Sridharan, E. 2005. "Improving Indo - Pakistan Relations: International Relations Theory, Nuclear Deterrence and Possibilities for Economic Cooperation." *Contemporary South Asia* 14 (3): 321 - 39.

The Economist. 2013. "India as a Great Power: Know Your Own Strength." *The Economist*, March 30, 2013. https://www.economist.com/news/briefing/21574458 - india - poised - become - one - four - largest - military - powers - world - end.

Tikekar, M. 2005. "Cultural Idiom in the Indo - Pak Conflict." In ***India - Pakistan Relations: Courting Peace from the Corridors of War***, edited by P. M. Kamath, 187 - 238. New Delhi: Promilla & Co.

Till, G. 2004. *Seapower: A Guide for the Twenty - First Century*. London: Frank Cass.

Transconflict. n.d. "Principles of Conflict Transformation." Accessed March 10, 2013. http://www.transconflict.com/gcct/principles - of - conflict - transformation/.

United Nations. n.d. "UNMOGIP: United Nations Military Observer Group in India and Pakistan." Accessed July 24, 2017. https://unmogip.unmissions.org/.

Waldron, A. 2007. "Viewing the Future Through History." In *Rising India: Friends and Foes*, edited by P. Nanda, 1 - 31. New Delhi: Lancer Publishers.

Waltz, K. N. 1981. "The Spread of Nuclear Weapons: More May Be Better." *The Adelphi Papers* 21 (171): 1 - 32.

Weinbaum, M. 2005. "Pakistan and the United States: A Partnership of Necessity." In *America and the World in the Age of Terror*, edited by D. Benjamin. Washington, D. C.: Center for Strategic & International Studies.

VIII

BREAKING INDIA AND PAKISTAN'S ENDURING RIVALRY:
Pakistani Viewpoint

1. INTRODUCTION

> "There is no reason why these States should be antagonistic to each other. On the other hand, the rivalry and the natural desire and efforts on the part of one state to dominate the social order and establish political supremacy over other in the government of the country will disappear. It will lead more towards natural goodwill by international pacts between them, and they can live in complete harmony with their neighbours. This will lead further to a friendly settlement all the more easily with regard to minorities by reciprocal arrangements and adjustments between Muslim India and Hindu India..."
>
> - Muhammad Ali Jinnah: Lahore Declaration (1940) (Qureshi 1998, 94)

This declaration by the then leader of the minority Muslim League party in a pre-Independence British India can now be seen as, at best, aspirational or more negatively as unrealistic. The inter-state rivalry between India and Pakistan is one of the most long running conflicts in the modern era. It began with the violent mayhem of partition in 1947 that saw hundreds of thousands of deaths, followed by more than fifteen thousand dead in various inter-state wars and between forty to one hundred thousand dead in the extant Kashmir insurgency (The Economist 2011). The fact that these states have gone to war four times within a sixty year period without resolving their underlying issues remains of significant concern to the rest of the world. The Kashmir issue, seen by many observers as "one of the most hotly contested territorial disputes in the world today (Nye and Welch 2011, 228), should be seen as both a symptom and a cause of that enduring rivalry. Events such as the recent Kashmiri border confrontations between India and Pakistan in January 2013 ensure that the risk of miscalculation by either side is ever present. The concern of unintended military escalation, leading to further conflict in the near future, is magnified by these both South Asian antagonists having nuclear weapons at their disposal.

This paper will examine whether a future Indo - Pakistan war should it viewed as an inevitable conflict. Moreover, it will seek to explain the principal historical causes of India and Pakistan's troubled relationship. The domestic level factors that will be covered include how and why the territorial state of Kashmir has assumed such totemic importance to each nation. The history of respective religious and political groups' progress to independence has shaped both their views of their opponents but also themselves. Each state's narrative has been shaped by partition and the accession of Kashmir in 1947 and this becomes accentuated by each successive crisis. Within this domestic area are incompatible ideologies and common belief systems. Additionally, there is the issue of institutional mismatch that needs to be addressed; India's multi-party constitutional government existing in contrast with the Pakistani military led or militant influenced government.

At the regional level territorial allocation again is of critical importance. Relative regional power balance is critical and this research will support, via model choice, a practical explanation of Pakistan's ability to match or cancel out India's strengths (Paul 2006, 601). This approach links to Pakistan's acquisition of certain key weapon systems such as the nuclear capability which has yielded it different outcomes to that which would be expected from a European/Cold War model of deterrence. Similarly, Pakistan has adjusted its tactics to maximise advantage of its asymmetric capabilities that includes the use of guerrilla warfare in Kashmir.

Lastly, at the international level this paper will explore the relationships between the United States and China with Pakistan and India. Historically, this was a three - way international power triangle that included the Soviet Union but with the end of the Cold War this has morphed into that of support from the two superpowers above. Some research indicates their support contributes more to stasis than to resolution of the problem.

One significant complication to this study is in regards to the availability and historical reliability of the past records. As an example, Alastair Lamb noted that while there are copious amounts of literature on the origins of the Jammu and Kashmir dispute, most is 'permeated with propaganda favourable to either India or Pakistan (Lamb 1997, 299).' This understandable national bias makes it difficult to determine an objective middle ground if such a thing exists. Moreover, there are a range of factors that could act as emerging threats to the current volatile peace. These include the historical enmity created by the twin nations' births resulting from the partition of the British Indian sub - continent. An additional concern is their recognised history of mutual suspicions and miscalculations which have often lead to violent confrontation between the two nations (Nye and Welch 2011, 228 - 29). Due to the volatility of the complex relationship between India and Pakistan it would appear that external international actors are both essential to try to cap these tensions but also act inadvertently to further complicate any resolution.

Another literal issue to clarify is the whether the next violent confrontation will be a 'war' or a different level of level of conflict? The wars of 1947, 1965 and 1971 could be seen as classic examples of Rupert Smith's 'inter - state industrial war (Smith 2006, 29 - 63).' The last major military action between them was in 1999 and remained localized to Kargil; Smith defines it as more a strategic skirmish than war due to acquisition of nuclear weapons by the protagonists (Smith 2006, 249). The changing capabilities available to the Pakistan Army have impacted on and will continue to determine their willingness to engage their neighbour in hostilities. Each of these factors of territorial dispute; strategy shaped by national identity and political systems; capability from irregular to nuclear; and alliances will be examined.

Throughout the paper, the implications of this South Asian relationship and its impact on other international interests will be considered within each section. The conclusion will summarise whether the changes in the regional environment are enough to make India and Pakistan now more or less likely to go to war than at the outset of the serious conventional war between them in 1999. Changes in internal political systems and changing pressures of alliances are some of the key drivers but may contribute more to stabilising the situation than increasing volatility.

2. THEORETICAL MODEL

Joseph Nye wrote that "there is a certain logic of hostility, a dilemma about security that goes with interstate politics (Nye and Welch 2011, 2)." This section will look at a range of methods of understanding why states go to war and then apply that to the question of why the fractious relationship between India and Pakistan has endured. It is assumed that both states are rational actors who will go to war or are prepared to fight for logical self-interest.

At its simplest, international relations as a field of study is tied to a number of core labels such as realism and liberalism. Adherents of realism view the world as an anarchic place with no overarching control of the various self-centred nation states (Nye and Welch 2011, 4-9). This system relies upon the classic Westphalian sovereign state achieving a balance of power with is opponents through diplomacy or military power. In this case security and the allocation of resources are determined by the most powerful states and their allies (Nye and Welch 2011). It sees a constant zero-sum competition where the gain of one state must be at the expense of another. In this sense, hegemonic India, as the dominant nation, should be the one who determines the relationship between India and Pakistan. From a realist point of view, Pakistan should have no choice given its position of military weakness 'but to engage in security-seeking behaviour by any means necessary,' either through external pacts or by switching substantial domestic resources to defence spending (Narang 2009, 143).'

A liberal perspective in contrast sees that there are international institutions sitting above the states in a global society which enable a more complex inter-relationship that values trade, democracy and financial interests as much as security. The logic of this model has states tending towards peace as a result of the mutual benefits of economic cooperation, while simultaneously becoming adverse to war as opportunity costs rise (Nye and Welch 2011, 52). For liberalism, democratic states are less likely to fight another liberal democratic state but will fight against a tyranny as clearly this type of enemy will not cooperate with it or with the international institutions that enable the mutual benefits. A democratic India has been able to transform its position in international politics more through industrial development and industrial trade than developing strong military capabilities. As the world's largest democracy, it needs to ensure the interests of its population are met by the expansion of its economy and national prosperity.

These periodic conflicts continue due to one or both countries being dissatisfied with the status quo and that is constructed across multiple levels. Further work on the enduring rivalry between these South Asian powers has detailed the following issues or causes of on-going conflict: unresolved territorial issues, political incompatibility, incompatible positions on national identity and a lack of significant economic and trade links between the two states. When explaining why the smaller Pakistan has not given up the challenge, Thazha Varkey Paul refers to the unique 'power asymmetry (Paul 2006, 600-30).' This 'truncated power asymmetry' was a combination of Pakistani capability, strategy and tactics with the Kashmir region and alliance support. The size of the ground meant Indian was unable to deploy its forces in significant numbers to overmatch the Pakistani dispositions. The Indian superior strength was further reduced by the use of large numbers of irregular forces by Pakistan notably during the Kargil operations and those subsequent to that.

Despite a range of actions by both countries and by external actors to reduce the regional tensions this South Asian rivalry has lasted for more than sixty years and more importantly, as yet, it would appear to be no nearer to a resolution. Paul argues that the current impasse would require an appropriate internal or external shock to force a final termination of the enduring rivalry (Paul 2005, 251). It will require a massive game changing event, comparable to Partition's impact on the South Asian region and initiation of the India - Pakistan diarchy to resolve it. The factors above will now be explored in more detail below.

3. THE ENDURING RIVALRY MODEL AS AN ANALYTICAL FRAMWORK

In their 1993 paper Enduring Rivalries: Theoretical Constructs and Empirical Patterns Gary Goertz and Paul F. Diehl set out an analytical methodology in which due consideration is made to historical continuity so that protected conflicts may be better understood. In their work, they set out how 'a fundamental assumption of the concept of enduring rivalries is that conflicts between the same two protagonists are related to one another (Goertz and Diehl 1993, 150).' From this assumption the analysist of any given protracted conflict may take that historic events continue to shape future realities. The enduring rivalry model then, comes about as an extensive hysterography of relations where past relations are given no less deference than current affairs on which focus is typically placed. The aim of such an approach is to understand by what method a conflict developed and according identify potentially resolution approaches that may otherwise remain elusive.

For India and Pakistan, the enduring rivalry framework, that seeks to differentiate persistent interstate conflicts from those that exist within a limited time period and or that may have more readily defined causes, offers insight as to why improved relations have been so elusive. Despite its relative recent emergence as a regional conflict, the Indo - Pakistan conflict with four clearly defined wars and numerous additional incursions and cross-border attacks meets the criteria for being an enduring rivalry. This paper uses the enduring rivalry approach to explore the nature of and contributory factors to this conflict. In this way, it focuses its attention on the realities of these two principle state actors that have contributed to the persistent nature of the conflict. Nonetheless, the nature of the Indo-Pakistan rivalry goes beyond the Indian-subcontinent and is identified as being in many ways impactful at the regional level. The regional significance in both economic and security spheres means that the greater conflict encompasses a number of regional and international actors and impacts a range of national interests which in turn define regional cooperation and stability. This paper will focus its attention in this regard on China and the US, as being key actors in not just in containing but also in resolving this enduring rivalry.

The enduring rivalry model has been used successfully to greater understand the nature of other difficult to resolve conflicts such by Michael Grieg who in his 2001 article "Moments of Opportunity: Recognizing Conditions of Ripeness of International Mediation between Enduring Rivals" employed this approach in understanding the conflict in Northern Ireland. Moreover, the model itself has been used by T. V. Paul who first identified the India-Pakistan conflict as fitting within the definition of and enduring rivalry; "conflicts between two or more states the last more than two decade with several militarized inter-state disputes punctuating the relationship in between (Paul 2005, 3)." This paper looks to build on T.V. Paul's work with considerations for how recent developments have been shaped by historical animosity and conflict.

4. COLONIAL LEGACY

In August 1947, the British Empire conducted a hasty withdrawal from India that was followed by an eventual agreement to divide the federation on a duel basis of demography and geography. 'The two newly independent states, the Dominion of Pakistan and the Union of India, inherited significant linked and overlapping communal (Chander 1987,

303)[1] problems that had not been completely solved by the partition process (Chander 1987).' Partition, the exact meaning of which was disputed by both major political and religious groupings, was reluctantly conceded by the British due to increasing fears of civil in the face of large scale inter - communal violence (Talbot and Singh 2009, 2).

In many respects the violence of partition should have been no surprise to either of the new governments of India or Pakistan. The wide - ranging outbreaks of communal violence that occurred throughout the 1920s and early 1930s meant short term problems in containment but also fuelled further reaction and added to longer term deep - rooted animosity. The ostensibly all - inclusive Congress Party was unable to ensure that its secular and nationalist narrative and aims were not compromised by some of its members' involvement in Hindu communal parties (Chander 1987, 304). It was due to these increasingly intractable divisions that the Muslim League's 'two nation theory' gained ground amongst the Muslim population (Aziz 2005, 163). Fear of the numerically superior Hindu population grouping perpetually and dominating the minority Muslim population meant the single state model would be inherently dangerous. Jinnah believed that a single state of India was an artificial creation of the British Raj which led to the Hindu and Muslim peoples of India being held 'forcibly together by unnatural and artificial methods of a British Parliamentary statute (Aziz 2005, 164).'[2] The significant differences of religions, standards, societal customs and literature dictated, to his mind, the impossibility of a successful independent united India outside of a British Raj construct. This view that 'India has never been a true nation, it only looked that way on the map' was diametrically opposed by Congress (Collins and Lapierre 1997, 130). This argument, the 1940 Lahore Declaration, that India's future peace and happiness could only be served by allowing the 'major nations separate homelands' with both a Hindu state and a distinct Muslim state formed the basis for eventual partition.

---

1 Chander describes the word 'communal' in India as differing from the accepted English definition and instead meaning "the hatred by someone of a community following a religion different from their own."

2 Jinna's Lahore declaration.

The Hindu dominated Congress Party saw Muslim communalism or the requirement for a distinct Muslim political identity as a British ploy to weaken their all-India, anti-colonialist and nationalist cause. Given that they believed their vision would deliver a viable integrated secular state they saw no need to focus on minority issues. In their opinion, religious issues should be seen as irrelevant as Congress was supposed to support and advocate the interests of the whole Indian sub-continental population be they Hindu or Muslim. Any Muslims promoting such divisive policies were too regarded as parts of a British 'divide and rule' campaign.

The British took to the idea of partition initially as a means of leverage against Congress' demands and then grudgingly as a final method of avoiding massive bloodletting from a slide towards civil war. Jinnah's early reassurance to Mountbatten was that the "surgical operation" of partition could halt the inter-communal violence. His allegorical comparison of partition to a court case he once handled, where a familial shares dispute was resolved satisfactorily by court arbitration and the two brothers ultimately becoming the greatest of friends, was not to happen with separate independence (Collins and Lapierre 1997, 130).

It was the practical detailed division of India and most notably the dissection of Bengal and the Punjab that countered Jinnah's hopes of a peaceful separation. The division of these two large provinces along artificial fault-lines created in very short order by a British civil servant-led team ultimately led to massive inter-religious violence in August 1947 and necessitated a vast population exodus along religious lines. Sir Cyril Radcliffe and his team of Hindus and Muslims only had one month to complete their hugely complex task which was to have such ramifications for the future peace of the two nations. Whilst the religious mix of his team was supposed to ensure impartiality, accusations remained that differing influences were to have an impact, such as Viceroy Lord Mountbatten and his alleged Indian sympathies (Lamb 1997, 56). Estimates vary as to the exact scale of the resultant enforced migration but in the region of two million people crossed the new borders to align with their new nations avoid further violence. The communal violence that spread across a broad swathe of the sub-continent was to claim more up to two hundred and fifty thousand victims and reinforce negative communal resentments (Chapman 2000, 195).

As well as the ethnic strife created by the rushed mechanics of partition, the allocation of certain key economic resources such as the industrial centre of Calcutta was to have inevitable enduring and negative consequences. The division of Bengal and the Punjab without the retention of key industries only delivered a "moth-eaten Pakistan" as opposed to the economically viable state originally anticipated by Pakistan (Collins and Lapierre 1997, 131). The award of key tracts of land also meant the allocation of important headwaters to India rather than Pakistan and again this was to contribute to enduring tensions only resolved with eventual external arbitration; the 1960 Treaty of Indus Waters (Racine 2002, 117). It was the failings of the British Raj in anticipating the depth of the problems relating to Jammu-Kashmir that had grave consequences for the two newly independent states and created lasting enmity between the two rivals (Lamb 1997, 19).

The legitimacy of the transfer of one of the 565 separate Indian princely states at the time of independence is seen by many as a cause of the current-Pakistan rivalry but it should rather be seen as much as a symptom as a cause. As the August 1947 independence deadline for the Indian sub-continent approached, the Hindu Maharajah or ruler of the mostly Muslim Jammu-Kashmir state (78 per cent majority) (Ghosh 2003, 3) vacillated, unable to decide where to transfer the loyalties of his formally independent principality. At this point there were major internal tensions which boiled over into a revolt by a large grouping of the Poonch Muslims, many of whom were ex-British Indian Army soldiers. By September, this had developed into a near civil war and this strife was compounded by the arrival of fellow Muslim Pashtu tribesmen from Pakistan's North West Frontier Province.

By October 1947, the Maharajah, Hari Singh, now turned to India for military assistance but this could not be granted without a formal process of transferring the state to Indian control, known as accession.

The events that led to the signing of the Act of Accession remain controversial to this day, with recent British research indicating that India moved its forces to the state capital of Srinagar to support the Maharajah's forces prior to formally completing the legal process (Lamb 1997, 157). Thus Pakistan's immediate objections that the accession and India's subsequent (or more to the point, prior) military operations were illegal could be vindicated. India disputed their adversary's claims that the Maharaja was coerced into signing or that he acted under duress. Additionally, the Islamabad government was kept outside of any of these key discussions and decisions over the accession between the last British Viceroy and Nehru's Indian Government. The discrepancies over the timing, Jinnah and his government believed were enough to invalidate India's claim to legal jurisdiction over the state. Thus, Pakistan's two-nation concept was seen to be defeated by Indian aspirations to gain this multi-ethnic and divided territory and this reinforced the Pakistani fears of India's future intentions.

Whilst partition resulted in the two independent nations with freedoms to decide on political priorities and set the values within their respective social orders it did not lead to peace. Any hopes of natural goodwill between neighbours were dashed by the violence of the immediate aftermath of partition. As Talbot and Singh noted, partition was not merely a separation of territory it was "foremost accompanied by a division of minds (Talbot and Singh 2009, 8)." This division has endured.

5. NATIONAL IDENTITIES AND MUTUAL SUSPICION

The post partition government of Pakistan had exceedingly few resources and no structure or culture of government administration. Accordingly, the foreign policy aim of the fledgling state of Pakistan was quite easy to define; mere survival and that meant it was inclined to see its eastern neighbour as the principal threat to its well-being (Chapman 2000, 263). Even before partition was instigated the nascent Pakistani leadership was voicing its concerns to the outgoing British with Jinnah understood to have told Mountbatten that he was 'afraid of what the Congress government would do to Pakistan (Jalal 1994, 292).' Thus, the horrors of partition perpetuated this view of its more economically powerful rival as 'hegemonic, bellicose, threatening, underhand and stubborn amongst its leadership, whether military, civilian or religious (Racine 2002, 112).' The seizure of Kashmir by what Pakistan says was illegal action lent further support to suspicions.

Pakistan's leaders across the civil, military and religious spectrum are often predisposed to see the hand of India in damaging events and thus instinctively lay the blame at their adversary's door. This can be seen to be almost a psychological reaction to the nation's feeling of insecurity and lack of self-confidence. Pakistan's identity was based upon being different by virtue of religion but it became almost an ideology of difference rather than as strictly defined religious movement in the early years of the Pakistani nation (Racine 2002, 113). Islamic identity was a means of distinction from their Hindu opponents. The development of the Hindu nationalist political branch leading to the electoral victories and rise to power in Delhi of the Bharatiya Janata Party (BJP) was happily seized as evidence that the Pakistani nation and its Muslim League forebears were right all along. It appeared to vindicate all that had been articulated in the two-nation theory where: The Hindu-Muslim conflict was not merely religious. It was the clash of two civilizations, of two peoples who had different languages, different literary roots, different ideas of education... when this idea of cultural variance was combined with diversity in social customs and modes of livelihood the emergence of a united Indian nation was doomed without redemption (Aziz 2005, 143).

Indian suspicions of Pakistan's intentions became similarly negative following the horrors they had experienced of the Muslim slaughter of Hindus and Sikhs during partition. This was to be reflected in comments from the mid-sixties interview of the late Krishna Menon, Indian UN representative and former Defence Minister of the 1950s and early 60s. Menon stated that 'Pakistan is a danger to us: she claims our territories and she has taken them; she probes our frontiers and she carries on subversive activities inside India; she means no good to us... (Brecher 1968, 170)' India did not or could not sympathise with the Pakistan perspective while it saw itself at risk from Pakistan in its early days of existence. Instead it chose to see Pakistani actions as illegal or aggressive, particularly those in Kashmir. This in turn led to further cycles of suspicion and reaction.

The Pakistani national narrative chose to ignore all that indicated there was significant commonality between the two religious groupings and set the religious identity at the cornerstone of its national identity. As such, it deeply felt grief at the separation of the nation when its eastern wing broke away in 1971 to form Bangladesh. As if it were not enough that fellow Muslims felt Pakistan could not meet their needs, the secession was made worse by the aiding and abetting of their enemy next door, India. Pakistani former President Musharraf noted that during the Kargil crisis in 1979 "my troops were itching for a chance to avenge what had happened in 1971 in East Pakistan (Musharraf 2006, 72)."

A further psychological aspect of the Pakistani identity was the aggressive nature of its dealings with its neighbour and willingness to initiate conflict in 1947, 1965 and 1999. Given its perception that India is always threatening, it in time developed an attack first mentality of defence. This was aided at times by external actors supplying high grade weaponry in attempt to weaken an India which challenged the balance of power in the region. Here Pakistan was only too ready to exploit any perceived Indian military weaknesses that followed the 1962 Sino-Indian war. The old pre-independence culture of a large Muslim warrior-race that was represented in the British Army also added another level to the military's identity of the state; that of being militarily superior to the Indian armed forces (Racine 2002, 115). The formation of both armies in 1947 is used as a further example of bad faith on behalf of the Indian state where it appropriated significant amounts of equipment that was destined for Pakistan under the formal division of the former British Indian Army. The narrative of Indian victories was thus always to be explained by the underhand methods used to disadvantage Pakistan.

As the Pakistani state has developed it has had to alter its focus on the Muslim identity versus the national identity. The idea of Muslim separatism that was essential to galvanise a separatist movement in the mid-1940s has had to change to ensure the same argument is not used against it to further divide the remaining western half of the original Pakistan. This has had repercussions within the disparate nature of the Pakistani population where within the new nation differences have sometimes appeared greater than common linkages. The nature of some of the provinces that formed Pakistan, such as the former North West Frontier Province (NWFP), with its anti-centrist stance has created difficulties maintaining the national identity. Imposing a national language of Urdu on the wider population in absence of wide spread practice has, at best, been slowly embraced. This need to build a Pakistani civil society from narrow first principles has meant slow and incomplete progress towards the development of government structures and political leadership. Kashmir as the compelling narrative has been used by the military to seize key roles in society. At the same time, the Kashmir narrative has been used by Militant Islamists to form an alternative ascendancy within Pakistan.

6. CONTRASTING POLITICAL SYSTEMS

This section will examine the contrasting types of political regime that developed from a common background under the British Raj. For most of the period since independence these have been simplified under the labels of Indian democracy and Pakistani military authoritarianism. This is important in the context of what type of regime is predisposed to resort to the use of force; the evidence shows less democratic states are more likely to initiate and escalate disputes (Tremblay and Schofield 2005, 225).

The primary focus of this section will be to understand how and why the Pakistani regime has differed from India's and its resultant impact on its relations with its adversarial neighbour. Pakistan's nominal democratic rule has been limited by routine interventions by the military when the other state institutions are at loggerheads. The fledgling independent Pakistani state was neither envisaged as a theocracy or a military - led state, instead Jinnah intended it as 'only a popular, representative and democratic form of government (Jalal 1994, 276).' This aim was complicated by need to ensure central control of a divided patch - work of states, the lack of structures and the untimely death of its founder before a constitution could be imposed. The first democratic phase lasted until 1958 when President Mirza revoked the constitution allowing General Muhammad Ayub Khan in to power. The prime minister's office was undermined and, as president, Ayaub Khan imposed rule by decree until forced to step down in 1969 following serious unrest. A martial law period continued through until 1971 under General Agha Muhammad Yahya Khan. Following the defeat of West Pakistan forces in the civil war in 1971 he too resigned but this time allowing a return of democratic politics. As the new civilian president, Zulfikar Ali Bhutto, was a divisive figure and he faced increasing challenges after introducing a new constitution which altered the political power balance between executive, legislative and judicial arms of state. Widespread rioting broke out after his controversial re - election in 1977 and with the political parties unable or unwilling to rein in the violence the army stepped in again. This second military era was led by then Chief of the Army Staff (COAS), General Mohammed Zia ul - Haq, with martial law remaining in force until 1985. Zia, having amended the constitution, became both President and COAS in 1978 and set about his policy of increased state Islamization. This included changes to the legal system and saw that the military tribunals were tasked with ensuring concurrence with Shari'a law (Jaffrelot 2002, 78 - 79). During this period the army held the reins of a large number of civilian institutions with 10 per cent of posts held by military officers. Although political parties and associated meetings were banned he gained useful support from a number of Muslim League politicians who sat in his government.

A third democratic era came in with multi - party elections in 1988 resulting in the formation of a coalition government led by Benazir Bhutto's Pakistan Peoples' Party (PPP). Her time in office was marred by coalition in - fighting and the power wielded by the president under reforms brought in by Zia. Fractious political exchanges with the opposition coalition, the Islami Jamhuri Ittehad (IJI – Islamic Democratic Party) under Nawaz Sharif were divisive rather productive and in turn set off violent disruptions in Sind province. An increasing number within Pakistani leadership circles, particularly the military, saw this as a 'dreadful decade of democracy,' focussing on the instability of the political process and accusations of pointless politicking whilst not dealing with the mounting economic woes of the country (Musharraf 2006, 71). Having been dismissed by the president Bhutto's Pakistan Democratic Alliance, her PPP and others less the dissenting MQM, was to suffer a decisive defeat in the late 1990 election, as much a result of the first-past-the-post system as to overall popular dissatisfaction. Nawaz Sharif and his incoming IJI coalition was now the next to attempt genuine political and social improvements. Whilst he had some successes with the liberalisation of the previously nationalised industries his coalition did not have the two thirds majority sufficient to make changes to the constitution to reduce the limiting hand of the president.

There was increasing national frustration at a pattern of 'political floundering' under Benazir Bhutto and Nawaz Sharif who rotated through the prime ministerial office without improving the lot of the populace (Wolpert 2010, 75). In Musharraf's view 'the vulnerability to corruption of elected officials created conditions that led to an army takeover, while those in opposition and many from other walks of life, particularly the intelligentsia, frequently appealed to the army to take power or change the government (Musharraf 2006, 71).' The Pakistan army had become so intertwined with elements of the political system that it appeared it began to see itself as the sole arbiter of the political direction of the nation. Furthermore, elements of the army were now perhaps more focussed on political events in Islamabad than on their military role. Musharraf's later comments reflect this skewed role when noting the ISI's monitoring of the internal political system in 1998 as it "confirmed [to the Corp Commanders' Conference] that the president and the chief justice were in collusion to throw out the National Assembly and with it their real target. Prime Minister Nawaz Sharif (Musharraf 2006, 82)." The then President Farooq Leghari and the Chief

Justice, Sajjad Ali Shah, were attempting to use a range of means to limit the expanding powers of the Prime Minister, including a contempt of court case, intended to result in Sharif's disqualification from office (BBC News 1997). Whilst on this occasion the army sided with the prime minister against his opponents, Sharif was to then effectively seal his own political fate by the manner in which he effectively sacked the COAS. The military were incensed by the Prime Minister's perceived lack of respect for the institution of the armed forces in the way he forced the resignation of General Karamat, the incumbent COAS, and replaced him with Musharraf. Musharraf in particular was determined there should be no repetition of such an event and therefore was to act swiftly a little under a year later to carry out his own "counter-coup" when faced by a forced resignation attempt by Nawaz Sharif.

By 2008 there was a momentous change in the Pakistani political structure with relatively free presidential elections conducted; resulting in victory for Asif Zadari, widower of the recently murdered Benazir Bhutto and leader of PPP. Just as significantly the army attempted to withdraw from the open political arena as Musharraf's military successor as COAS, General Ashfaq Kayani, issued a decree reversing the previous policy of routine military involvement in national politics (Wilkinson 2008). Undoubtedly, there was an intent to arrest its declining popular image, tarnished by its meddling in politics, and return to its 'defender of the nation' role. This realignment to concentrate on military matters would also refocus army personnel given the difficult internal counter-insurgency campaign against Pakistani Islamic militants.

The army role was one of the few formed institutions inherited by Pakistan at independence and has therefore remained one of the country's most powerful institutions. Whilst it had traditionally been held in high esteem as one of the few stabilizing influences in the nation this has been weakened by an increasing blurring between the military, political and business spheres. It will take time for the military to re-learn its role, given that a significant amount of its officer corps will have some experience in this pre-eminent role over at least the last decade. Furthermore it will require the raising of the elected politicians' game to ensure this transition to democratic politics is maintained whilst dealing with growing polarisation between Islamist extremism and the reforming secular wing of Pakistani politics.

The concept of reform comes at a time when greater regional stability is of global concern. Al Qaeda has diminished in presence after the loss of Taliban protections in Afghanistan and this contributes directly to an increase in border security for Pakistan yet the rise of the Islamic State (ISIS) in Iraq and Syria, areas further west are a considerable concern. Pakistani domestic stability has long been questioned and tribal groups and extremists may not elude the attention of ISIS leaders that may see possibilities for radicalisation in a population deprived economically, disassociated from government and raised on a chiefly Islamic identity. Facing continued economic strife and domestic discord Pakistan must ensure that it can maintain the stability preferably without further military enforcement of governance that has proved to be a hurdle to longer term domestic peace. Should Pakistan fail as a state this is a grave security concern for all global actors. As a nuclear armed state, its on-going stability must be maintained in order that weapons of mass destruction or their technology are not acquired by groups that may use them.

The domestic political scene in Islamabad has recently had cause to celebrate the first elected civilian government able to complete its five year term, under Prime Minister Raja Pervez Ashraf, without the usual intervention from the military. Whether this returns the Pakistani state machinery to an optimal balance of executive, legislature and judiciary remains to be seen. The current prime minister returned to office having been removed by the military in 1999 and so much will depend on his leadership in restructuring and securing the state.

7. WARS BETWEEN THE NATIONS

Whilst Pakistan under Jinnah tried to avoid formally becoming involved in the Kashmir war, in 1948 it committed regular ground troops to the campaign but was unable to stop the Indian forces pushing back to what became the Cease - Fire Line (CFL). Eventually, under the UN mandated cease - fire of 1949 the fighting between Pakistani irregulars or 'raiders', as the Indians described them, regular Pakistani forces and Indian forces resulted the division of Kashmir. Two - thirds of the state was left under Indian control (Jammu and Kashmir) and consisted of Ladakh, Jammu and the Valley of Kashmir. The remaining one - third came under the control of Pakistan and was thus termed 'Azad' (free) Kashmir and the Northern Areas. As India had called for UN assistance, to counter what they termed Pakistani aggression, it had to accept UN recommendations. The UN's even handed approach alarmed India, with Nehru believed to feel that he had made an error of judgement by internationalising the Kashmir problem by calling for UN support (Lamb 1997, 279).

The second Indo - Pakistani war took place in 1965 as Pakistan looked to exploit perceived Indian military weaknesses following their defeat by Chinese forces in the 1962 Sino - Indian war over the disputed Aksai - Chin region. Following earlier Chinese intervention, approximately a fifth of Pakistan's Kashmiri territory was ceded to China, much to the irritation of India which disputed Pakistan's right to involve itself in what it viewed as internal Indian territorial business. This was to mean China now had a say in any final resolution of the land dispute between India and Pakistan. Islamabad's conventional attack across the 1949 cease - fire - line (CFL) resulted in a military impasse with her eastern neighbour. The Soviet Union sponsored the peace talks in Tashkent, following the UN directed ceasefire; this resulted in the exchange of captured land by both sides and a return to the CFL positions.

The third and largest conflict between the two South Asian opponents was the most devastating in impact to both of the nations. The 1971 war was unique as it started as a result of Indian support to East Pakistan secessionists. It resulted in the halving of the size of Pakistani population following the formation of Bangladesh and shattered the confidence of the nation whilst reinforcing prejudices and animosity with India (Wolpert 2010, 45). The resulting peace talks in Simla in 1973 saw the conversion of the CFL into a more permanent Line of Control (LOC) although not formally granting any ownership rights to Pakistan administered territory.

The 1999 Kargil conflict arose when the Pakistan military conducted a covert operation to occupy a series of strategic locations in the vicinity of the LOC. The Pakistani military has tried to frame the dispute as the result of provocative Indian over - reaction to limited cross - border incursions by 'Kashmiri freedom fighting mujahideen' along the Line of Control (LOC) (Musharraf 2006, 87). In contrast, the Indians saw the hand of the regular Pakistani military in the increasing border tensions; with the newly appointed General Musharraf, Pakistani COAS, being blamed for his 'aggressive ambitions (Sen 2002, 179).' The secret movement of regular Pakistani forces to forward defensive positions in the vicinity of the LOC was authorised by the military in January 1999 in anticipation of a perceived Indian build - up of offensive forces on their side of the LOC. It was not until early May 1999 that clashes occurred between Indian forces and both regular and irregular Pakistani forces with the "mujahideen" occupying over 500 square miles of Jammu - Kashmir or 'Indian - occupied territory'.

Whilst the then Prime Minister Nawaz Sharif was to claim that he had not authorised the operation there were reasons why he would have felt he would have gained from what the Pakistani media termed an adventurist war. First he might have felt that promoting what was a deeply felt national goal to international attention would distract domestic gaze from his difficult political battles at home. There is also a thought that it was also to appeal to the small but powerful Islamic orthodox body within the country (Schofield 2010, 214). International opinion, and particularly the US, saw Pakistan as the instigator of the conflict through its support for the infiltrators from across its borders (Schofield 2010, 217). At this point the US enjoyed significant influence with both Pakistan and India and was able to pressure them, notably Pakistan, into a ceasefire. The Army viewed Sharif as having buckled under US pressure and accepted an unconditional withdrawal; this frustration was to impact on the subsequent relations between the prime minister and COAS. Whilst other politicians saw this episode concluding with a 'complete diplomatic surrender,' others such as Benazir Bhutto were scathing in their analysis of the decision to allow or support the infiltrators in the first place. She saw it as 'the biggest blunder in Pakistan's history, which had cost Pakistan dearly (Schofield 2010).'

8. NUCLEAR BOMBS AND MILITANTS

India was the South Asian initiator with regard to nuclear weapons testing in both 1974 and 1998. To both the Pakistanis and many other observers there was only one route that Pakistan could follow and that was to hurriedly demonstrate its own nuclear capability. The logic for this was seen as far less complex than why the Indian government chose to start a regional nuclear race; Pakistan's national security was directly threatened by India raising the stakes. As the weaker nation that had been beaten in nearly all their conventional military confrontations and then been effectively torn in half following the East Pakistan defeat, it was clear that Pakistan felt genuine security fears over this escalation of capability (Narang 2009, 139).

Smith argues that from 1998 the threat of nuclear war precluded either country, although having the 'manpower, industrial base and ideological bent for old-fashioned industrial war,' from going beyond a strategic stand-off not unlike the Cold War (Smith 2006, 249). Following the May 1998 Indian detonation of five nuclear bombs and the responding six Pakistani nuclear explosions some analysts began to view nuclear weapons as the overriding factor determining crisis stability between India and Pakistan. That Pakistan still went ahead with the Kargil infiltration showed either a dangerous level of risk acceptance or that there were flaws in the analysis and weighting given to stability arising from nuclear weapons.

There was a rush by scholars to understand the implications of Kargil in the light of the nuclear risks. For the analysts who sat in the 'proliferation pessimists' camp, Kargil and the episodes that followed were confirmation that the enduring enmity between the two South Asian rivals had been further destabilised by the introduction of nuclear weapons and hence there was a significant chance of nuclear war in South Asia. In the other corner, the 'proliferation optimists', saw that these events not intensifying to major inter-state war was proof of the stabilising effect of nuclear weapons and hence strengthened their argument that nuclear deterrence had reduced the likelihood of major war. There was a question of whether there was a paradox between the goals of nuclear stability, i.e. a low perceived risk of nuclear use might then contribute to greater chance of conventional warfare breaking out hence instability. The Kargil war and ensuing conflicts in South Asia, it would appear from S. Paul Kapur's research, were not the result of this stability/instability paradox against expectations based upon European Cold war thinking (Kapur 2009). Instead he determined that it was a greater level of strategic instability in South Asia which in fact promoted a greater degree of tactical instability.

India had to adjust her nuclear policy to reflect differences anticipated by previous Cold War models. Paul S. Kapur refers to comments by a senior Ministry of Foreign Affairs (MFA) official that once Pakistan had acquired a nuclear weapon capability it "felt much less threatened" by and "more confident" in existing with Indian conventional capabilities (Kapur 2009, 184-218).[3] He viewed this new found confidence as enabling the Pakistani government to limit Indian aspirations. Instead of raising the nuclear ante as would be anticipated in a western environment to meet a conventional challenge from Pakistan, Delhi should instead conduct arms control and confidence building measures to increase nuclear stability and undercut Islamabad's freedom to conduct conventional attacks. Some Indians continue to press for a more aggressive nuclear policy in the light of Pakistan's unwillingness to disavow first response.

Islamabad took note from its failures to achieve a decisive victory in a conventional setting at Kargil and thus was seen to increase its irregular

3 Kapur quotes Jalil Jilani, director general for South Asia in Pakistan's MFA.

force contribution. In many ways, Pakistan has always made great use of irregulars, freedom fighters or mujahideen since the earliest days of the NWFP tribesmen's incursion into Kashmir in support of the Poonch rebels. The start of the 1989 insurgency campaign in Kashmir was very much blamed on Islamabad's support for 'Kashmiri freedom fighters'. In fact it was due to a combination of local uprisings against a draconian Indian security regime and a rejection of the failed democratic process of the disputed State Legislative Assembly in 1987 (Wolpert 2010, 64). India's contention that the insurgency was a nefarious Pakistani scheme to divert under-employed Afghan mujahideen forces from its home territory has some credibility although this is not to deny a groundswell of popular opinion against the Indian authorities (Ghosh 2003, 89).

The response from Islamabad to accusations of supporting terrorists has generally been that it was merely assisting 'both the Afghan mujahideen and Pakistani volunteers [who] decided to help the Kashmiris.' By 1994 the native Kashmiri separatist groups were not always been supportive of the supposed help from Pakistan (Wolpert 2010, 66). Increasingly the non-native insurgent groupings stood out from the population with their desire for Jammu and Kashmir to be ruled according to Shari'a marking a change from the more common secular character of the Kashmiri population (Ataöv 2001, 145). The disorder in Kashmir has continued at a lower level and caused thousands of deaths; it increased in violence in 2009-10 although it appears to have become less deadly in recent years (South Asia Terrorism Portal 2013).

India has frequently accused Pakistan of conducting proxy war against it, notably in Kargil when it is also alleged that regular Pakistani soldiers in garbs of 'Kashmir Freedom Fighters' infiltrated and seized territory in Kashmir. Indian threats to conduct hot pursuit across the LoC led to a sharp rise in tensions leading to an unprecedented mobilization of each side's forces. For the next six months India's mobilised forces confronted Pakistani troops in a tense nuclear stand-off across not just across the LoC but along the international border. Movement and testing of nuclear capable ballistic missiles in the region raised political and diplomatic temperatures higher as did Musharraf's interview comments to Der Spiegel that Pakistan would be prepared to use its nuclear weapons (Lavoy 2002, 31).

Pakistan's linkages with mujahideen and freedom fighters meant it was sitting in the wrong camp when the events of September 2001 unfolded. Things were meant to have changed as of late 2001 under increasing US pressure, marking Musharraf's cessation of support to the Islamists, and the simultaneous termination of the links between the army and paramilitary Islamists in Afghanistan and Kashmir (Jaffrelot 2002, 264). The direct links between Pakistan and many high profile terrorist attacks including the carnage in New York and Washington to London bombings of July 2005 made it an uncomfortable time for the Pakistani leadership (Ganguly and Kapur 2010, 47). From a Pakistani military point of view they attempted, following the 2002 stand - off with India, to "take stern action" to halt the flow of paramilitary organisations operating against the Indians from within Pakistan's territory. Musharraf imposed controls on suspected extremist madrassas (religious schools); restricted assets belonging to terror suspects; claimed the closure of Inter - Services Intelligence (ISI) offices in Pakistan - controlled Kashmir; started police reform; and brought in a range of antiterrorist laws (Lavoy 2002, 30). Pakistan complained that it was doing all that it could but that the Indian government had not halted its rhetoric on cross border terrorism. This claim was made to look hollow by the complex three day assault on Mumbai in November 2008, again tied to the Pakistan (Ganguly and Kapur 2010, 51). Given the battering India's pride had taken, Delhi showed great restraint despite calls for cross border military attacks on extremist training camps in Pakistan administered Kashmir. The Pakistani authorities failed to prove to the Indians that there was a serious attempt to disrupt the Lashkar - e - Taiba (LeT) group blamed for the outrage. Instead it blamed Indian intransigence in not providing it enough proof of Pakistani links. The peace process, known as the Composite Dialogue, launched between and India was derailed and stalled indefinitely following the Mumbai attacks.

Pakistan's dalliance with militancy and extremist groupings now appears to be coming home to roost with unprecedented terrorist activity within Pakistan against the state. This 'sorcerer's apprentice' problem shows no sign of resolution, despite lengthy military operations in both the heartlands of the Tehrik - e Talibab Pakistan (TTP) in the Federally Administered Tribal Areas, attacks within the regions and even in the heart of Islamabad have continued (Ganguly and Kapur 2010, 48). The Pakistani military continues to maintain the national Kashmir narrative referring to its lack of resolution as a probable cause for some jihadi inspiration.

As outlined above the major concern for the western powers regarding Pakistan and its dalliance with extremist groups is simple: the breeding ground of violent extremist actors who act against the west both at home and on deployed operations such as Afghanistan. This is demonstrated most acutely by US Operation Neptune Spear in Pakistan in 2011. That unilateral operation unknown to Pakistan concluded with the killing of Osama Bin Laden, The US's most wanted terrorist fighter and leader of al - Qaeda, who had been held up in a complex in Pakistan. For Pakistan it now has the problem of how to gain control of the terrorist/freedom fighters without causing a major fracture within its weak civil society.

9. EXTERNAL ACTORS

As the 'great game' played out in the mid nineteenth century, a pattern of interests in the Indian sub - continent emerged for several key actors. By the early days of the Cold War in the late 1940s, this has developed into a three way challenge from the former war - time allies of the Western Powers versus the Soviet Union and then the newly emergent Communist China. T.V. Paul and others recognise that alliance politics is a critical factor that influenced and continues to influence the power mismatch between India and Pakistan (Paul 2006, 622).

During the Cold War international relations in this Himalayan - South Asian region could be viewed as a series of strategic triangles at the regional level between India, Pakistan and China and the interlinked international strategic triangles between the US, Russia and each of the regional actors (Kapur 2011, 6).[4] For Pakistan, following the 1962 Indo-Chinese war, China neatly fitted a criterion of "my enemies' enemy" and China has remained generally supportive of Pakistan even as the US drew closer to Islamabad (Chapman 2000, 264).

Following the gradual withdrawal of UK influence in the region post-Independence, the US had stepped in as the major western Cold War superpower originally trying hard to treat India and Pakistan in an even handed and balanced way, favouring neither one nor the other. This was an impossible approach to maintain and was seen to swing more towards the weaker state as India moved closer to an impartial foreign policy that was designed avoid linkages with its colonial past and western association. The 1954 mutual defence agreement between the US and Pakistan was enhanced by US support for enabling Pakistan's membership in the Southeast Asian Treaty Organisation and the Central Treaty Organisation.

Pakistan's location was instrumental in its next key role supporting US foreign policy; that of supporting and enabling the Afghan Mujahideen fight against the Soviet invaders from 1979. The length of this campaign, as well as its perceived geostrategic importance, saw massive inflows of economic and military aid to Pakistan (Paul 2006, 623). There was a hiatus in the relationship from the early 1990s following the withdrawal and subsequent breakup of the Soviet Union. It was during this period that Pakistan found it could not rely on unequivocal US support, as with the Kargil dispute where Pakistan miscalculated the level of support it could rely upon and lost out to India.

Pakistan's relationship with China is probably more consistent than that of the west. From the end of the 1962 Sino-Indian war, Pakistani willingness to accede part of Kashmir to its northern neighbour the relation flourished. The third state in the triangle, the Soviet Union, was at this point drawing closer to the non-aligned India and providing weaponry. At the time of the 1965 war, China chose not to actively intervene against India with a second front but still remained a

4 Quoting original concept by Martin Wight in Ashok Kapur.

supporter against Russian and India linkages. Throughout the following decades it continued to provide Pakistan with highly capable weapon systems including major support to the development of nuclear weapons and missile technology (Paul 2006).

The position of China between these two states deserves special consideration for its role in encouraging, willingly or otherwise, the perpetual nature of the challenged relationship. The timing of the emergence of China as a global power has coincided with the development of the Indo - Pakistan conflict. China's general support of Pakistan has bolstered the strength of Pakistan geo - politically and shielded it at the international institution level. The enduring rivalry model that focuses on many of the actions of Pakistan as being closely related to the conflict's persistence therefore sees continued Chinese support as indirectly contributing to the endurance. This maybe differentiated from the Indian position where Indian relations with the US among others have been more dynamic with greater peaks and troughs in relations that create possibilities for change.

On occasion Pakistan has seen the need to act alone without international supporting actors and instead chosen to engage India directly. In the 1970s the then Pakistani President Zulfikar Ali Bhutto defended bilateralism as being 'our best interest of Pakistan to have a foreign policy based on bilateralism and that we must give bilateralism a chance as far as relations between India and Pakistan are concerned... With all due respect to the United Nations, I should say that it has yet been able to deal with Kashmir problem effectively (Samaddar 2004, 86).'

America's view of Pakistan has often swung from seeing it as a close ally, in either the Cold War against the former USSR or from 2001 in the 'Global War on Terror,' to other extreme seeing it as the greatest threat to regional stability. The Clinton - era US Secretary of State Madeleine Albright (1997 - 2001) has referred to Pakistan as an "international migraine" given its combustible mix of nuclear weapons, terrorism, political instability and poverty (Rashid 2009).

Following the 2001 attacks on the US mainland and subsequent Global War on Terror South Asia became the foremost area of interest for U.S. foreign and defence policy. A rapid change in alliances was needed to achieve combat operations over Afghanistan and despite huge offers of support from India it was to Pakistan that the US once again turned. This was for entirely logical reasons, for although the India offer was generous and timely US aircraft operating from India would not have gained Pakistani over flight permissions. It did mean a reappraisal of the US and India relationship with Prime Minister Atal Bihari Vajpayee referring to the two countries as 'natural allies (Lavoy 2002, 27 - 28).' This resulted in their defence ministers signing a bilateral U.S. - India Defence Relationship in 2005. Of greater concern to Pakistan was the US - India nuclear deal in 2008 which exceptionally allowed the sale of nuclear energy with a non - signatory of the Nuclear Non - Proliferation Treaty (NPT).

At this point Pakistan was beginning to feel surrounded with India encroaching on Pakistan's western border of Afghanistan. Pakistan has not been shy about regarding it as within its sphere of influence and enhanced by its close links with Taleban which had developed as that organization rose to power in Afghanistan. Pakistan's main aim has been to limit India's inroads into Afghanistan via the Northern Alliance (Chaudhuri 2010, 52).

The most significant change to the US relationship with Pakistan since the Clinton - Sharif interactions of 1999 is that the US is now actively conducting operations on Pakistani soil. Initially Islamabad is believed to have given covert support for drone strikes but has over the years increasing civilian casualties has led to its criticisms becoming more vocal. In the face of mounting public hostility, the Pakistani authorities, including COAS, made clear their formal opposition to these strikes as counter - productive and a violation of sovereignty. Similarly, American disbelief of official Pakistani declarations that they had no knowledge of Bin Laden's whereabouts was to colour the relationship over time. A former US State Department spokesman, PJ Crowley, told of Hilary Clinton while on a formal visit to Islamabad musing out loud that 'it was hard for her to conceive that no - one in the Pakistani government knew where Bin Laden was (BBC News n.d.).' This Pakistani narrative became more incredulous at the time of his death in a compound close to retired military officers and garrison town.

10. CAUSES FOR OPTIMISM

Despite a range of potential crisis points arising in the recent past, stretching back from the terrorist attacks on Mumbai to the fatal cross-border incidents involving Indian and Pakistan military forces in early January 2013, the two nations remain in a wary peace. Although there were casualties on both sides, including the alleged decapitation of an Indian soldier and mutilation of another, these events were not enough of a trigger to change the status quo. It had been thought that on-going Kashmir violence had brought the two countries back to the worst crisis in relations since the 2008 Mumbai attacks (BBC News 2013a). Yet, by late 2015 Indian and Pakistani Foreign Secretaries and Security Advisors met to discuss the relationship. Moreover, current Indian Prime Minister Narenda Modia visited Pakistan in the same year, becoming the first Indian Prime Minister to do so since 2004.

Flashpoints arose in May 2013 with the deaths in Pakistani custody of an Indian prisoner on death row, Sarabjit Singh, and the resultant death of a Pakistani prisoner, Sanaullah Ranjay, in Jammu and Kashmir (Indian administered Kashmir). Singh had been seen by human rights activists and lawyers on both sides of the border as a high profile prisoner whose release could have acted as an important confidence-building measure between the two nations. Despite loud official protests from either side including the Pakistani High Commissioner's accusation that the Sanaullah's death was tantamount to extrajudicial killing, the incident has now subsided from public consciousness.

Events within Pakistan's political and security arenas show the potential for improving relations with India. In January 2013 the Pakistani Army went public on the need to switch its traditional focus from the eastern border and the notion of India as its primary enemy. Pakistan media referred to "a paradigm shift in its decades-old policy [where the] Pakistan Army has described home - grown militancy as the "biggest threat" to national security (The Express Tribune 2013)." It noted that this was needed to deal both with the on - going guerrilla war in the tribal areas with Afghanistan as well as cross border incidents with foreign forces on its western border.

Nawaz Sharif's victory at the May 2013 polls is likely to have been welcomed by its neighbours hoping for a more stable Pakistan but the stance of the Pakistani army remains the key determinant. Pakistan has little room for manoeuvre and Sharif, despite his significant majority, has even less options given the reducing opportunities to strengthen the economy. It remains likely that the military will not completely withdraw from being able influence politics mainly to protect itself. Some commentators saw the eviction of the New York Times correspondent from Pakistan on Election Day as a military inspired act which the interim government knew nothing about, due mainly to reporting viewed as hostile to the Pakistan Army (Rashid 2009).[5]

Sharif has been seen to demonstrate a 'willingness to engage India and increase trade, a key to constructing a stable if not normal relationship (BBC News 2013b).' A strong confident elected leader will be a useful counterbalance to a military that has traditionally been obsessed with India. A promising indication has been the willingness of previous Indian Prime Minister Manmohan Singh to engage early with Mr Sharif. Moreover, this engagement has been maintained by standing President Modi since 2014. Pakistani officials have responded in kind promising a fresh start both sides to 'work peacefully to resolve all outstanding issues, including Kashmir, and it is time to shed the old way of thinking and using of stereotypes (The Economic Times 2013).'

The recently ailing US - Pakistani relationship will take time to re - develop but remains critical despite the changing requirements post the Afghanistan draw down in 2014 and the oft heard hostile public

5 NY Times Islamabad chief Declan Walsh was expelled in May 13 for apparently annoying the Pakistani military with his reporting of an alleged conflict between the CIA and the ISI over the use of drone missiles.

statements (BBC News 2013b)." What remains to be understood if Sharif can square his electoral tone that sought to dovetail with a public anti-Americanism and the need for continued support. The changes in the US-Pakistani relationship since his last time in office are considerable: greater regional conflicts, drone strikes within his borders, and a closer relationship between the US and India.

Sharif's return to governance is judged to have many positive consequences for the United States given its primary interest in Pakistan, which are to ensure the country's political and economic stability and to receive assistance for in regional security challenges. A second factor in his favour is Sharif's support and backing of the Saudi royal family, this again ensures stability of the Pakistani government and particularly the economy. This may remove some financial liability from the hard pressed US government as it makes plans to scale down its own aid to Pakistan while limiting any expansion in Chinese influence but it will add to the complexities of influencing Pakistan given another backer. Another factor is Sharif's free market approach to business which will be necessary to give the almost moribund economy an opportunity to develop in the same positive way as its relatively affluent rival India.

US policy reflects that while it is seeking to drawdown its forces from the region in 2014, it recognises the value of retaining alliances. It could be viewed that the Obama regime has a more humble or realistic global outlook, tempered in part by the recent global economic downturn, it still sees the US as continuing "to underwrite global security through our commitments to allies, partners, and institutions; our focus on defeating Al Qaeda and its affiliates in Afghanistan, Pakistan, and around the globe; and our determination to deter aggression and prevent the proliferation of the world's most dangerous weapons (Government of the USA 2010)." The critical need to maintain important alliances is shown in the admission that 'we must recognize that no one nation – no matter how powerful – can meet global challenges alone (Government of the USA 2010).' As Obama's term in office draws to a close, there will be new opportunities for Pakistan to reform the US relationship, however the challenge is in doing this positively with limited domestic support.

The complication for American interaction with the Pakistani government is its current policy of "defeating Al Qaeda and its affiliates in Afghanistan, Pakistan (Government of the USA 2010)." The continued use of the drone attack programme against Al Qaeda and Pakistan Taliban targets in sovereign Pakistani territory is seen as acting as a recruiting sergeant for the Islamic extremist groups and alienates sections of the Pakistani population. Two - thirds of Pakistanis polled in a May 2013 Pew Research Center poll opposed the drone strikes (McKelvey 2013). Whilst in opposition the incoming Prime Minister Nawaz Sharif used heated rhetoric in his condemnation of US drone strikes, this may restrict Obama's ability to influence the new government (BBC News 2013b).' Conversely this may improve the relationship, as despite the regional drawdown in Afghanistan, the Pakistani government will retain some limited leverage with its 'ally'.

In late May 2013, President Obama launched a campaign to temper the world's view and particularly that of Pakistan on the criteria for the use of drone strikes as a 'just war' that was merely a war of self-defence against militants. Given that evidence suggests he was six times more likely to authorise such attacks he has much to do to reassure the incoming Pakistani government (McKelvey 2013). Whilst a renewed campaign to justify drones to the US public may work, by promising near certainty that no civilians would die in such strikes, it will be a far more arduous task to sell to the Pakistani nation. A 29 May 2013 attack on the senior leadership of the Pakistan Taleban in the tribal regions was thought to be a demonstration of these new rules and attempt to adjust popular perceptions (Guerin 2013). It would appear to remain Pakistani government policy to condemn the attacks even when it benefits the state and the foreign ministry was quick to condemn that 'strike as a breach of sovereignty (Guerin 2013).' 'Any drone strike is against the territorial integrity and sovereignty of Pakistan (Guerin 2013),' is expected to be official line that will continue to be delivered publically despite removing a thorn in the side of the Islamabad regime.

11. CONCLUSION

Looking at India and Pakistan's recent and violent past shows just how easy it is for them to descend from their current wary peace to conflict. This paper has made clear how the events from partition onwards including four wars have contributed to the long - term antagonistic nature of their opposition, chiefly expressed over finding a solution for Kashmir. The paper supports an 'enduring rivalry' model as the most suitable in understanding the important factors of this long term confrontational relationship between India and Pakistan. The broader international relations theories of realism and liberalism were briefly referred to whilst developing an understanding of the model but it was clear they were not entirely sufficient in embracing the multilevel challenges at play.

This approach suggests how some dominant factors have caused the issue to endure with limited progress towards resolution. An enduring rivalry model leaves a focuses more on the side of the aggressor in this case as issues to be resolved within the Pakistani political system among other have been covered by a focus on heightening perceptions of an India threat. Pakistan's poorly developed civil society and political system will need to find a way to build a national identity that does not just rely upon having a neighbour as the enemy to focus upon. Currently, it is clear that there is incompatibility in the differing types of society, both politically and religiously driven, in Pakistan, and that may lead to further conflict. Furthermore, the threat of Pakistan's failure as a state, which has remained present through cycles of military and civilian governments, is as critical as ever. This consideration needs to be well appreciated by all other international actors seeking to stabilise the region, not least because of the nuclear threats that may be associated with internal instability and/or external opportunism.

Despite these significant hurdles, there are reasons for hope with the current political system in Pakistan compared to when it last decided to go to war over Kargil in 1999. Interestingly this is down to the importance of leadership and its ability to create a significant change in previous direction. Nawaz Sharif was the prime minister then and was again inaugurated June 2013. Much of Pakistan's future direction will be shaped by what he has learnt from his experiences not only from the risk of the army stepping in again but also how he can deal with US and Chinese partners. Most importantly, it is in both his political interests and the interests of the nation that more economic linkages are developed with India. This will be a critical step in the path to breaking the recurring cycle of the enduring rivalry. And, the first step to the necessary trust building process that can facilitate future resolutions for Kashimir.

REFERENCES

Ataöv, Türkkaya. 2001. *Kashmir and Neighbours Tale, Terror and truce.* Aldershot: Ashgate Publishing Ltd.

Aziz, K. K. 2005. *The Making of Pakistan: A Study in Nationalism.* Lahore: Sang-e-Meel Publications.

BBC News. 1997. "Protesters Halt Pakistani PM Court Case." *BBC News*, November 28, 1997. http://news.bbc.co.uk/2/hi/south_asia/34866.stm.

———. 2013a. "Kashmir Crisis: Pakistan Offers India Talks." *BBC News*, January 17, 2013. http://www.bbc.com/news/world-asia-india-21054897.

———. 2013b. "Viewpoints: The Impact of Elections in Pakistan." *BBC News*, May 13, 2013. http://www.bbc.com/news/world-us-canada-22476174.

———. n.d. "Monday: As It Happened." *BBC News.* Accessed June 18, 2016. http://news.bbc.co.uk/2/hi/south_asia/9473496.stm.

Brecher, Michael. 1968. *India and World Politics: Krishna Menon's View of the World.* London: Oxford University Press.

Chander, Sunil. 1987. "Congress-Raj Conflict and the Rise of the Muslim League in the Ministry Period, 1937-39." *Modern Asian Studies*, 21 (2): 303-28.

Chapman, Graham P. 2000. *The Geopolitics of South Asia: From Early Empires to the Nuclear Age.* Burlington: Ashgate.

Chaudhuri, Rudra. 2010. "The Proxy Calculus: Kabul, Not Kashmir, Holds the Key to the Indo-Pakistani Relationship." *The RUSI Journal*, 155 (6): 52-59.

Collins, Larry, and Dominique Lapierre. 1997. *Freedom at Midnight.* New York: HarperCollins.

Ganguly, Sumit, and S. Paul Kapur. 2010. "The Sorcerer's Apprentice: Islamist Militancy in South Asia." *The Washington Quarterly*, 33, no. 1 (January): 47-59.

Ghosh, Ajoy. 2003. *Indo-Pak Conflict: Threat to South-Asian Security.* New Delho: Reference Press.

Goertz, Gary, and Paul F. Diehl. 1993. "Enduring Rivalries: Theoretical

Constructs and Empirical Patterns." *International Studies Quarterly*, 37, no. 2 (June): 147 - 71.

Government of the United States of America. 2010. "US National Security Strategy." May 28, 2010. Washington, D.C.: The White House.

Guerin, Orla. 2013. "Pakistan Taliban: Senior Leader 'Killed in US Drone Strike." *BBC News*, May 29, 2013. http://www.bbc.com/news/world - asia - 22698363.

Jaffrelot, Christophe. 2002. *A History of Pakistan and Its Origins.* London: Anthem Press.

Jalal, Ayesha. 1994. *The Sole Spokesman: Jinnah, the Muslim League and the Demand for Pakistan.* Cambridge: Cambridge University Press.

Kapur, Ashok. 2011. *India and the South Asian Strategic Triangle.* London: Routledge.

Kapur, S. Paul. 2009. "Revisionist Ambitions, Conventional Capabilities and Nuclear Instability: Why Nuclear South Asia is Not Like Cold War Europe." In *Inside Nuclear South Asia*, edited by Scott D. Sagan, 184 - 218. Stanford: Stanford University Press.

Lamb, Alastair. 1997. *Incomplete Partition: The Genesis of the Kashmir Dispute 1947 - 1948.* Hertfordshire: Roxford Books.

Lavoy, P. R. 2002. "Fighting Terrorism, Avoiding War: The Indo - Pakistani Situation." *Joint Forces Quarterly* (Autumn): 27 - 34.

McKelvey, Tara. 2013. "Obama Shows a Strong Commitment to the Drone Programme." *BBC News*, May 24, 2013. http://www.bbc.com/news/world - us - canada - 22646446.

Musharraf, Pervez. 2006. *In the Line of Fire: A Memoir.* London: Simon & Schuster.

Narang, Vipin. 2009. "Pride and Prejudice and Prithvis: Strategic Weapons Behaviour in South Asia." In *Inside Nuclear South Asia*, edited by Scott D. Sagan, 137 - 83. Stanford: Stanford University Press.

Nye, J. S., and D. A. Welch. 2011. *Understanding Global Conflict and Cooperation: An Introduction to Theory and History*, 8th Edition. Boston: Pearson.

Paul, T. V. 2006. "Why Has the India - Pakistan Rivalry Been So Enduring? Power Asymmetry and an Intractable Conflict." Security

Studies, 15 (4): 600 - 30.

– – –, ed. 2005. *The India - Pakistan Conflict: An Enduring Rivalry.* Cambridge: Cambridge University Press.

Qureshi, Abdul Saleem., ed. 1998. *Jinnah, the Founder of Pakistan.* Karachi: Oxford University Press.

Racine, Jean - Luc. 2002. "Living With India: Relations between Pakistan and India." In *A History of Pakistan and Its Origins*, edited by C. Jaffrelot, 112 - 33. London: Anthem Press.

Rashid, Ahmed. 2009. "Obama's Huge South Asia Headache." *BBC News*, January 2, 2009. http://news.bbc.co.uk/2/hi/south_asia/7788321.stm.

Samaddar, R. 2004. *The Politics of Dialogue: Living Under the Geopolitical Histories of War and Peace.* Aldershot: Ashgate.

Schofield, Victoria. 2010. *Kashmir in Conflict: India, Pakistan and the Unending War.* London: I.B. Taurus.

Sen, Gautam. 2002. "Evaluating Strategic Parity and Balance: India - China - Pakistan." In *India's Security in 21st Century: Challenges and Responses*, edited by Rajendra Prasad. New Delhi: Dominant Publishers & Distributors.

Smith, Rupert. 2006. *The Utility of Force: the Art of War in the Modern World.* London: Penguin Books.

South Asia Terrorism Portal. 2013. "Jammu and Kashmir Assessment: Year 2013." Accessed June 18, 2016. http://www.satp.org/satporgtp/countries/india/states/jandk/index.html.

Talbot, Ian, and Gurharpal Singh. 2009. *The Partition of India.* Cambridge: Cambridge University Press.

The Economic Times. 2013. "Pakistan Welcomes Manmohan Singh's Positive Response to Nawaz Sharif's Initiatives." *The Economic Times*, June 1, 2013. https://economictimes.indiatimes.com/news/politics-and-nation/pakistan-welcomes-manmohan-singhs-positive-response-to-nawaz-sharifs-initiatives/articleshow/20386655.cms.

The Economist. 2011. "The World's Most Dangerous Border." *The Economist*, May 19, 2011. https://www.economist.com/node/18712525.

The Express Tribune. 2013. "New Doctrine: Army Identifies 'Homegrown Militancy' as Biggest Threat." *The Express Tribune*, January 3,

2013. https://tribune.com.pk/story/488362/new-doctrine-army-identifies-homegrown-militancy-as-biggest-threat/.

Tremblay, Rita Chowdhari, and Julian Schofield. 2005. "Institutional Causes of the India-Pakistan Rivalry." In *The India-Pakistan Conflict: An Enduring Rivalry*, edited by T. V. Paul, 225-50. Cambridge: Cambridge University Press.

Wilkinson, Isambard. 2008. "Pakistan Army Chief Ends Role in Politics." *The Telegraph*, February 18, 2008. https://www.telegraph.co.uk/news/worldnews/1579075/Pakistan-army-chief-ends-role-in-politics.html.

Wolpert, Stanley. 2010. *India and Pakistan: Continued Conflict or Cooperation?* Berkeley, C.A.: University of California Press.

Published by
Chonbuk National University Press
32, Eojin-gil, Wansan-gu, Jeonju-si, Jeollabuk-do, Korea

www.jbnupress.com

The Library of Congress has cataloged the printed edition as follows :
Chun, Kwang Ho.
NUCLEAR ARMED REGIONAL CONFLICTS : South Asia in Transition / by Kwang Ho CHUN

ISBN 979-11-6372-007-2 93340

국립중앙도서관 출판시도서목록(CIP)

Chun, Kwang Ho

NUCLEAR ARMED REGIONAL CONFLICTS : South Asia in transition / [written by] Kwang Ho CHUN. -- Jeonju : Chonbuk National University Press, 2018
p. ; cm

Includes bibliographical references
ISBN 979-11-6372-007-2 93340 : KRW22000

349.82-KDC6
327.1747-DDC23 CIP2018036669